They Felt the Fire . . . and Tasted the Ashes of Defeat . . . at Firebase Mary Ann

Lt. Col. William P. Doyle—A red-faced Irishman with a stocky, powerful build, he was a basic, down-to-earth soldier who wanted muddy boots, not a desk at the Pentagon. As battalion commander of the 1-46th Infantry at FSB Mary Ann, he molded his unit into one of the top battalions in the 23rd Division, but the surprise sapper attack, the heavy American casualties, and the subsequent recriminations ultimately ruined his career.

Pfc. Larry "Doc" Vogelsang—A conscientious objector turned medic, he ran bareheaded and unarmed through the smoke and flames, his medical gear in one hand and gas mask in the other, to treat the wounded in Charlie Company CP. His extraordinary actions that night earned him a Silver Star.

"Mary Ann has become a deep emptiness in my life. What I did I did not out of valor, professional competence, etc., but out of what I hope was love. This Silver Star is one thing I will probably never wear and certainly never display on a wall. When I send it home to you, just put it in a drawer and leave it there."

—Capt. Paul S. Spilberg

Capt. Richard V. Knight—A slim, bespectacled officer, commander of Charlie Company, he had an impish grin and one hell of a wild streak. His aggressiveness and skill in the field inspired confidence in his men—a confidence that crossed the line into cockiness. Charlie Company's contempt for the enemy may have contributed to the lax security at FSB Mary Ann on the night of March 27.

Pfc. Thomas R. Schneider—Blown out of his hammock by a mortar round that landed outside his door, fragments burning in his left knee, he still managed to take up a back-to-back position outside his bunker with his buddy "Shorty" Rivero. Communicating by hand signals, the two killed four sappers.

"To put the matter of the attack on FSB Mary Ann into the proper perspective, consideration should be given to the fact that this incident could very well have happened to other . . . like combat units in Vietnam. . . . The reduced level of combat activity and the increasing publicity by the news media focusing upon the ending of the war tend to create complacency among both the troops and their commanders."

> —From the confidential report into the sapper attack prepared by the Deputy Inspector General, U.S. Military Assistance Command, Vietnam

Maj. Gen. James L. Baldwin—Commanding general of the 23d Infantry Division, he was an undemonstrative, even-tempered officer who was unwilling to judge the grunts and NCOs on the ground too harshly. His reasoning: they had suffered enough in the battle itself. But his reluctance to pass judgment would contribute to the harsh judgment finally passed upon him.

General Creighton W. Abrams—Commander of the U.S. Military Assistance Command, Vietnam, he was a legendary, highly decorated, table-pounding military leader of unyielding standards. Furious at what had become an epidemic of unnecessary casualties as the war wound down, he was determined to give his unit commanders a wake-up call. There was no more effective, ruthless, and straightforward way to get their attention than to make public examples of those judged responsible for the debacle at FSB Mary Ann.

Books by Keith William Nolan

Operation Buffalo
Battle for Hue
The Magnificent Bastards
Death Valley
Into Cambodia
Into Laos
Sappers in the Wire*
The Battle for Saigon*

*Published by POCKET BOOKS

SAPPERS
★ IN THE ★
WIRE

KEITH WILLIAM NOLAN

POCKET BOOKS
New York   London   Toronto   Sydney   Tokyo   Singapore

POCKET BOOKS, a division of Simon & Schuster Inc.
1230 Avenue of the Americas, New York, NY 10020

Copyright © 1995 by Keith William Nolan

Published by arrangement with Texas A & M University Press

All rights reserved, including the right to reproduce
this book or portions thereof in any form whatsoever.
For information address Texas A & M University Press,
Drawer C, College Station, TX 77843

ISBN: 0-671-00254-6

First Pocket Books printing November 1996

10 9 8 7 6 5 4 3 2 1

POCKET and colophon are registered trademarks of
Simon & Schuster Inc.

Cover photo courtesy of U.S. Army

Printed in the U.S.A.

For Kelly

Contents

CONTENTS

Preface

Almost everyone who writes about the ground war in Vietnam has something to say about Fire Support Base (FSB) Mary Ann. The position was penetrated by sappers on a dark, foggy night, and the resulting action was so confusing and destructive, the casualties so lopsided in favor of the enemy, that it has taken on a mythic quality. "It was a clear case of dereliction of duty—of soldiers becoming lax in their defense and officers failing to take corrective action," wrote Gen. William C. Westmoreland in his memoirs. In fact, of all the U.S.'s less-than-glorious moments in Vietnam, Mary Ann and the My Lai massacre were the only ones he cited in his memoirs. I used the Mary Ann incident in one of my own books as a metaphor for the state of disrepair of the U.S. Army during its slow, torturous withdrawal from Vietnam. "The fact that the intensity of the Vietnam ground war was waning by 1970 and 1971 also contributed to poor morale in the field," I wrote. "Too much combat can drain a unit but no action can, contrariwise, turn an infantry unit into a mob. For example, in March of '71, the 1st Battalion, 46th Infantry, Americal Division saw little of the NVA around their basecamp, FSB Mary Ann. The men became bored and sloppy and the officers decided recon patrols weren't even worth the effort anymore—until the night the [Viet Cong] sappers hit. . . ."

PREFACE

Geoffrey Perret, a historian with a compassionate and intelligent understanding of soldiers, wrote that the defenders of Firebase Mary Ann were "too drunk, too stoned, too lazy and too undisciplined to mount a proper perimeter defense. The enemy simply walked in and took the fire base."

And there is this from a military historian:

> The unfortunate Americal Division was folded down in Vietnam at the end of November [1971], still in disgrace over its latest fiasco, the Fire Support Base Mary Ann incident, with its commanding general and several other officers being recommended for punitive action. . . . [The] 1st Battalion of the 46th Infantry failed to safeguard the perimeter, enabling fifty [VC] to overrun the outpost. They roamed through the fire base, destroying one 155mm howitzer and damaging another, throwing satchel charges in the command bunker, knifing Americans in their sleeping bags, and wrecking the communications equipment. They killed and wounded nearly half the 250 soldiers there, who got only ten in exchange because they were cringing in their bunkers.

Unfortunately, we historians got it wrong. I do not mean to whitewash what happened at Firebase Mary Ann with such a remark, for the incident was a tragic disaster with much to teach today's soldiers about vigilance. What I do mean to say is that commentary which tars the 1-46th Infantry as a "mob," as I put it at first glance, is grossly exaggerated. Most of the draftees on Mary Ann had already proven themselves in combat. My comment about "waning" action was far off the mark when it came to this particular area of operations.

While some men may have been "cringing in their bunkers" during the sapper attack, much of the inaction was typical of any surprise attack in which a unit's officers are almost instantly killed or wounded. Leaderless troops were reluctant to start blasting away at shadows in the dark, unable to distinguish friend from foe. I found no evidence of sappers "knifing Americans in their sleeping bags." There was panic and confusion that night, but there were also men like "Doc" Vogelsang, a conscientious objector turned medic, who ran unarmed through the smoke and flames to treat the wounded ... and Lieutenant McGee, who went down in hand-to-hand combat ... and Tom Schneider, who although wounded three times, took up a back-to-back position outside his bunker with his buddy, "Shorty" Rivero, and helped kill four sappers ... and Bill Meek, who got two more despite his own injuries ... and David Tarnay, who stayed on the radio in the command bunker despite the fact that it was blowing up and burning down around his head. The actions of these men and others have never been recorded in any book, and it is my purpose to finally describe in minute-by-minute detail exactly what happened that infamous night. The men who were killed or maimed for life on that hill deserve as much.

The operations of the 1-46th Infantry are also recounted here—from the original building of Firebase Mary Ann in the raw earth of a jungled hill to its evacuation after the sapper attack. My purpose here is to fill another historical gap, namely providing a day-to-day description of life in a "grunt" battalion during the waning days of the Vietnam War.

The U.S. ground war in Vietnam began in March, 1965, when the first American combat units landed, and much has been written about the battles they fought at places like the Ia Drang, Dak To, Khe Sanh, and Hue.

The U.S. withdrawal from Vietnam began in July, 1969, and the last infantry battalion packed up in August, 1972. Little has been written about the ground war during this slow retreat. For one thing, there were few big battles to focus on—the Mary Ann attack turned out to be the last high-casualty U.S. action of the war. In addition, what mattered to the press were not the continuing (but now meaningless) combat operations, but the breakdown of the U.S. Army as it disengaged from an unpopular war. It was a time of combat refusals and search-and-avoid tactics; of firebase bunkers filled with marijuana smoke, and hollow-eyed, scabby-armed heroin addicts in the rear; of intraunit conflicts pitting blacks against whites and draftees against their NCOs and officers. The troops used tear gas and

...des to intimidate their superiors, and fragmen-
...enades and claymore mines to blow them away—
...ly over supposed racial grievances or because a captain
...r sergeant tried to clean up the drug mess in his unit.

And yet, however reluctantly, there were still soldiers like those in the 1-46th Infantry out fighting the war. Their hardships should be recognized. Perret got it right when he wrote that these troops who "had faith in nothing much, least of all in men like Johnson and Nixon," still "served their country a lot better than it served them. . . ."

Part I

The Disaster

What happened on the night of March 27–28, 1971, at a remote hilltop fire support base named Mary Ann was the U.S. Army's most blatant and humiliating defeat in Vietnam. What happened, precisely, was that an enemy sapper company slipped and snipped its way through the defensive wire around FSB Mary Ann without alerting a single guard on a single perimeter bunker. The sappers tripped not one of the claymore mines in the wire, nor did they ignite any trip flares. Moving with catlike nimbleness, they caught the defenders of FSB Mary Ann asleep at the switch. In the ensuing chaos, thirty U.S. soldiers were killed and eighty-two wounded. The sappers left behind only fifteen of their own dead as they disappeared back into the night. What happened at FSB Mary Ann was as demoralizing as it was unexpected. The war was all but over. The troops were coming home from Vietnam, and the ones who soldiered on knew there were no more reasons to die.

1

Sappers in the Wire

Four days before the sapper attack, Capt. Paul S. Spilberg helicoptered to FSB Mary Ann with a three-man training team from brigade headquarters. He had previously been a company commander on the firebase. "I would do just about anything to have a command again," Spilberg wrote in a letter home from the hill. He took his new assignment seriously, though, because "the companies badly need training. I intend that these kids get the best training possible."

Captain Spilberg added that the months were going to be long and dull before "this tour is over." There was "not much new to write about. The war is going very slowly for us. . . ."

Spilberg had commanded a company in the 1st Battalion, 46th Infantry, for five months and had only recently been reassigned to the staff of the battalion's parent command, the 196th Light Infantry Brigade (LIB) of the 23d Infantry Division (Americal). Two days after Spilberg returned to FSB Mary Ann, Company C was lifted onto the hill per normal rotation, relieving the company then on the bunker line. The next day was spent policing the position and preparing for a brigade-level inspection of the perimeter defenses. Company C GIs also zeroed their weapons at the crude firing range on the southwest slope, after which Spilberg's training team worked with a squad at a time to

3

improve the troops' combat reflexes. Relatively inexperienced, they tended to fire from the hip when something popped up. They almost always missed. The training team instructed them in Quick Kill, a method of firing which called for a trooper to instantly shoulder his rifle, point it in the direction of the enemy, and open fire in one reflexive motion. The troops practiced on sandbag targets.

Toward dusk, Spilberg and Capt. Richard V. Knight, the Company C commander, opened a few beers atop the company command post (CP). The battalion commander, Lt. Col. William P. Doyle, joined them on the bunker. They were a good team. All were on their second tours in Vietnam and, despite the prevailing crisis in morale, Doyle had, through sheer force of personal example, molded the unit into one of the top battalions in the 23d Division. Knight was Doyle's best company commander. Their draftee troops might have been reluctant, forgotten grunts at the butt end of a bad war, but they still humped an infantryman's rucksack for good leaders and they still took care of each other. All of their combat actions under Doyle had been small, usually involving an enemy squad or less, and since there had been few incidents in the immediate vicinity of Mary Ann, the troops regarded the hill more as a rear area than as the division's most forward firebase.

Passing the time, the trio tested their marksmanship on various rocks or stumps at the base of the hill. Doyle had a grease-gun–style Swedish K automatic, Knight a CAR15. Spilberg made a little noise with his M16, and they all plinked away with their .45-caliber pistols. Doyle and Knight finally headed for the mess hall. Spilberg remained behind for a moment. As he stood looking out over the wire, the dog on the bunker with him suddenly alerted on something down the hill. The mongrel braced his feet, barking and snarling. His ears were up. The hair on his back bristled. Spilberg had never seen their friendly mascot behave so violently, and he squatted beside the dog, petting him and looking where he was looking. Seeing nothing, he finally decided that the dog must have spotted some rats or a snake.

That night, after staff call in the battalion tactical operations center (B-TOC), Lieutenant Colonel Doyle produced some more beer and sat up for hours in the bunker with Knight and Spilberg, talking. Spilberg recalled that Doyle was fond of Dick Knight, a slim, bespectacled officer with an "impish grin and a hell of a wild streak." Like the colonel, Knight was something of an authority on the opposite sex, and Doyle tried to convince him that when he finished his combat tour and reported to the Infantry Officers' Advanced Course at Fort Benning, he should date only the young widows of officers killed in Vietnam. The logic was that should Knight later marry, such women were not only accustomed to army life but they had their mortgages paid off thanks to their husbands' death benefits. Laughing, Knight agreed that it was a great idea.

It was getting late. Captain Knight returned to his CP, and Doyle hit the cot in his private quarters in one corner of the B-TOC. "I never said anything to Doyle about that dog being on alert," recalled Captain Spilberg, who slept in a spare room in the B-TOC that night. "But I should have known. It bothered me for years and years. I used to have nightmares about it. It was my second tour. I should have known."

Three hours later, in the dark of a moonless night, the impossible happened. Captain Spilberg woke to the sound of explosions, one right after the other. The sounds were muffled. The B-TOC was a solid, half-submerged bunker. It did not shake. Spilberg, who had been sleeping in his trousers, quickly pulled on his jungle boots and shirt, then picked up the .45 that he had stowed under the pillow on his cot. Spilberg's quarters were opposite the radio room, and he could hear the radios begin to crackle with urgent voices. He hustled down the hallway toward the bunker's east exit, intent on getting to the bunker line to help organize the troops. He was not thinking of a ground attack. He assumed that the firebase was simply under mortar fire, albeit heavy mortar fire.

Captain Spilberg reached the door to the colonel's quarters beside the east exit—and suddenly took in a lungful of tear gas. Blinded and unable to breathe, Spilberg charged back down the gas-filled hallway in a panic, threw himself onto the stairs of the north exit, and crawled out of the bunker into the fresh air. Unbelievably, he could hear enemy automatic weapons and rocket-propelled grenades (RPGs) being fired from inside the perimeter. As Spilberg's eyes began to focus, he could see figures moving in the light of various fires. They darted specterlike through the smoke of burning bunkers and living quarters. They seemed to be everywhere at once. Everything seemed to be exploding at the same time.

Inside the B-TOC, Lieutenant Colonel Doyle's quarters had filled with tear gas. Before he could get out, a satchel charge exploded in the hallway, blowing away his plywood door and knocking him down. Scrambling to his feet, he yanked his .45 from where his web gear and holster hung from a hook on the wall—just as a sapper appeared in the doorway. The sapper, naked except for a pair of shorts, was camouflaged with charcoal from head to toe. He was holding a satchel charge. Doyle shot him before he could throw it, but the charge exploded as the sapper fell backward. Doyle survived the blast, just as he survived the next three grenades and satchel charges thrown into his bunker by other sappers, but by the time he kicked his way through the debris to get out and fight he was already bleeding from the ears and had fragment wounds in one leg and both arms. His ears were ringing, his eyes were red and burning.

The sapper attack lasted approximately forty-five minutes. As it drew to a close, the B-TOC was a bonfire and Captain Spilberg had caught three grenade fragments in his lower back and buttocks. He had found the M16 he carried on the ground. Its front hand guard had been blown off, and he doubted that the weapon would work. Separated from everyone but Doyle, Spilberg took up a fighting position near Knight's CP, which was also ablaze and caving in, the ammunition inside cooking off in the heat. Spilberg darted to the collapsed entrance to see if Knight was still alive. He looked in quickly, hoping to avoid being hit by the exploding ammo, but saw only flames.

Captain Knight was dead.

Like the B-TOC, Knight's CP had been a primary target of the sappers. Altogether, thirty soldiers had been killed, most from Company C, 1-46th Infantry—and many while still in their bunkers. The sapper attack had been more a massacre than a battle.

Medevacked from FSB Mary Ann, Captain Spilberg returned to duty the next day at the 196th Brigade TOC on Hawk Hill. Two days later, he had just entered the TOC when a radioman said, "Mary Ann's getting hit again, sir. They're being mortared." Spilberg muttered an expletive. He was listening to the situation reports when the brigade operations officer suddenly wheeled to face him. "Get out of my TOC," the major barked. Spilberg was stunned. The major repeated his order, and when Spilberg started to object he screamed violently, "Get the fuck out of my TOC right now!" Spilberg did not move. The major pulled him into his office and took a seat behind his desk. Spilberg stood before him, hands thrust insolently into his pockets, and the major started up again. "Mister, get your hands out of your pockets!"

"Wait a minute, Major, I'm not a mister. You don't call anybody mister past the rank of warrant officer in this army. I'm not a fucking cadet—"

The major cut him off. "You bastards," he spat, finally getting to the point. "You bastards from the First of the Forty-sixth have ruined my career!"

Spilberg turned on his heel and stalked out of the office. He was not in good shape. "I am still pretty depressed and am having trouble sleeping," he wrote home. After his encounter with the major, he arranged for rest and recreation (R&R) in Hawaii with his wife. "All I want to do is lay in the sun, sleep and drink and forget all about Mary Ann," his letter continued. "I don't even want to be around anyone."

Except for Lieutenant Colonel Doyle, who was an outpatient at Tripler Army Hospital in Hawaii. Over drinks in Doyle's quarters during Spilberg's R&R, Spilberg said, "You know what I regret the most, sir?"

Doyle looked at him and said, "Yeah, I know—the colors."

"Yeah. . . ."

The battalion colors and battle streamers had stood to

one side of the wall map in the B-TOC conference room on FSB Mary Ann. They and the American flag on the other side of the map had been destroyed.

Lieutenant Colonel Doyle spoke to Spilberg about the friends they had lost on the hill. He did not seem to sense scandal. The major at brigade had been right, though. The destruction of FSB Mary Ann eventually resulted in a command shake-up that extended purgelike through battalion, brigade, and division. In the middle of the career-smashing, Captain Spilberg somehow ended up with a Silver Star for his actions during the sapper attack. "No one seemed very interested in an awards ceremony for me," Spilberg wrote to his wife, "and to be truthful I didn't really want one. Mary Ann has become a deep emptiness in my life. What I did I did not out of valor, professional competence, etc., but out of what I hope was love. This Silver Star is one thing I will probably never wear and certainly never display on a wall. When I send it home to you, just put it in a drawer and leave it there."

Part II

Kill
Professionally

Before Lieutenant Colonel Doyle's career self-destructed in the ashes of FSB Mary Ann, the 1-46th Infantry had operated with as much of an aggressive spirit as could be expected during the wind-down phase of Vietnamization—the Nixon policy of withdrawing U.S. units while upgrading the quality of the Army of the Republic of Vietnam (ARVN). "Bill Doyle was the division's shining star," recalled one of his captains. The Professionals, as the battalion was known, had battled North Vietnamese Army (NVA) regulars up and down the jungled mountains around FSB Mary Ann, and had uncovered numerous logistical facilities under the rain forest canopy where the enemy cached the weapons and ammunition brought down the Ho Chi Minh Trail and across the Laotian border. The Professionals had also conducted a prolonged campaign against a Viet Cong (VC) guerilla battalion in the vicinity of FSB Young. Firebase Young was in a lowland area of hamlets and rice paddies, and there Doyle's battalion, with minimal friendly casualties, had taken prisoners, unearthed supplies, and maintained a body count by way of constant patrol and ambush. "We gave them no rest," said a captain. "We kept that guerrilla battalion on the move, and bit by bit we drove them into the ground."

2

Rain, Rain, and More Rain

Captain Spilberg began his second Vietnam tour on September 26, 1970, three weeks in advance of Bill Doyle. He was enthused to be back in the game. He was not, however, happy about his assignment to the 23d Division. "The division does not have a very good record," Spilberg wrote his wife from the replacement center at Bien Hoa. "It was the division that had the My Lai massacre."

Two and a half years had passed since My Lai, but no hard charger wanted to be associated with damaged goods. "I really raised hell about it," Spilberg wrote. The 23d was originally known as the Americal Division. With the division's own 1st Lt. William L. Calley, Jr., presently on trial for the butchery at My Lai, division headquarters had recently reverted to using the unit's numerical designation in an unsuccessful attempt to blur the link with its infamous past.

Expecting the worst, Spilberg began to reevaluate the unit's reputation when he met Lt. Col. Richard F. Carvell, then the commanding officer (CO) of the 1-46th Infantry, upon helicoptering to FSB Mary Ann on October 4. The colonel, a colorful, up-from-the-ranks Korean War hero, had served earlier in Vietnam with the Special Forces and a regular line battalion of the 4th Infantry Division. He had been nicknamed "Crash" Carvell for his exploits in a light observation helicopter (LOH) when Company A stumbled into an NVA base camp south of Mary Ann in August, 1970. Carvell had his pilot, CWO Carlos Quintero, land under fire in a dry rice paddy to evacuate the wounded. The LOH dropped the casualties off at Mary Ann where a conventional medevac could safely pick them up. During the LOH's third approach, the NVA attacked Company A's positions around the landing zone. Quintero hovered over the NVA while Carvell fired an M79 grenade launcher at them. The door gunner also blazed away. Most of the NVA broke and ran, but one diehard standing beside a tree shouldered his AK-47 assault rifle and emptied the magazine at the helicopter. The LOH, hit in the underside, lost power and slammed into a nearby hillside. As it rolled down through the brush, the colonel hung on and the pilot remained strapped in, though knocked unconscious. The door gunner was thrown out and badly injured.

Lieutenant Colonel Carvell was medevacked with a bruised ribcage, raw knees, and a skinned head. That had been the Professionals' last major contact. "In the past few months the most Viets they have seen at one time was six," Spilberg wrote after his briefing with Carvell. The battalion continued to patrol the area "to disrupt and close off a main infiltration route to the large population centers along the coast," including Chu Lai, the division base camp on the South China Sea.

Carvell gave Spilberg command of Company A. Since the company's heavy contact in the enemy base camp, it had acquired a new captain, a dour career man whom Carvell reassigned as battalion supply officer. "The rumor was he was yellow," recalled Capt. John A. Strand III, who had commanded Company A in the base camp battle and was then serving as the battalion operations officer. "During missions, he stayed so far behind the lead element he never knew what was going on." Upon joining the company, Spilberg heard stories that his predecessor refused even to go outside the perimeter to relieve himself. "He didn't take any risks. When he got to a location, he put everybody around him and hunkered in. He just wasn't aggressive. The troops weren't particularly unhappy. It was slack. It was real slack, and they were complacent."

Captain Spilberg intended to change that. After an orientation period with Company D, he took over Alpha Company on FSB Mary Ann on October 9, 1970. Their first mission together, a helicopter combat assault (CA) south of the firebase, was supposed to commence on the twelfth, but the cold drizzle and low, leaden clouds of the approaching monsoon caused the lift to be canceled. The helicopters were still grounded on the thirteenth, so Alpha Company started out on foot. The southern slope of the hill was long and gradual, the terrain they descended into thickly forested. "We set up our night defensive position (NDP) and had an uneventful night," Spilberg wrote home. On the fourteenth, the three platoons moved along separate patrol routes, and Spilberg, trying to make an impression, accompanied one of the point teams. The grunts who followed talked and bunched up as they crashed noisily through the vegetation. The platoon found three empty thatch hootches and tore them down. "The weather then turned good and we were ordered to a clear area for a possible combat assault. We cleared out a good pick-up zone and after about 4 hours of backbreaking work we were told we would not be able to get choppers until tomorrow."

The next morning, October 15, Alpha Company CA'd into a valley six kilometers southwest of FSB Mary Ann where the Nam Nim River met the Tranh River. Again making a point, Captain Spilberg rode aboard the lead UH-1 Huey. After landing east of the north-south meandering Nam Nim, Alpha humped up to the high ground along the river to establish an NDP. "The jungle is brutal," Spilberg wrote. "Once you leave a trail you have to cut your way through it and it takes 2 or 3 hours to go a couple of hundred meters. Leeches cover the ground by the thousands. When they sense us they stand up on one end and try to catch on our boots. They are really horrid. . . ."

Spilberg accompanied one of his lieutenants on a squad-sized patrol that moved back down into the river valley the next day. They discovered a large hootch and several bunkers—plus several empty ammunition boxes with Soviet markings, and two 57-mm recoilless rifle rounds that appeared to have been booby-trapped. "I think the hooch is used as a way station for rest and feeding of NVA/VC troops as they infiltrate towards the coast," Spilberg wrote. "We left the hooch and found a large well-used trail along the river and there were many indications of enemy & enemy supply caches along the trail . . . a squad would not be large enough to handle things so we moved back to the patrol base."

Spilberg alerted Lieutenant Colonel Carvell, then worked up a plan for a three-prong sweep of the enemy camp that kicked off at daybreak on October 17. "I felt that 3 platoons (92 men) could handle anything in the area," Spilberg wrote home. "About half way there I got a call from Battalion . . . to cancel the attack and move east for about 4 kilometers, completely away from where the enemy was—no reason was given." After Company A completed its unexplained march and set up its NDP on a ridge overlooking the south shore of the Tranh River, Captain Strand, the ops officer, radioed Spilberg and "gave me the reason for the attack being canceled—the Brigade commander felt that it would be too 'dangerous' to go into that area and he could not get us the proper support such as artillery and Med Evac." Spilberg disagreed with the new, supercautious approach. The brigade commander "saw only what is on the map which is not the same as what is on the ground," he wrote. "In fact I could have cut a good LZ without any problems. Well, that is that. We are now in an area that is pretty free of the enemy. I am pissed off and my troops are pissed off, and it looks like we wasted quite a bit of time and energy."

Things gradually went from bad to worse. The nineteenth was resupply day, and Hueys landed in Alpha Company's NDP with mail and rations. By the twenty-second, Alpha had worked its way a klick (kilometer) to the northwest and established a new NDP atop another knob of the ridgeline. "We have yet to run into any Viets," Captain Spilberg wrote, adding that "it has been raining hard and we are all very wet." Moving two klicks southeast into lower ground,

Alpha set up on a hillock for another resupply on the twenty-fourth. "We were supposed to be taken out of the field today but the monsoon really socked in and it looks like we might be stuck out here a few more days," Spilberg wrote the next day.

The Alpha Company GIs, at the end of their normal thirteen-day cycle in the bush and expecting to spend the next three at ease on the firebase, were weathered in atop their hillock from October 25 to November 2. During Alpha's ordeal, Lieutenant Colonel Carvell finished his six-month command tour and was replaced by Bill Doyle. The new battalion commander was a deep, professional voice on the radio net assuring Spilberg that, "We're doing everything we can to get you guys out of there. Everybody's worried about you all the way up the line. . . ."

Alpha Company eventually ran out of rations. Unfortunately, when a slight break in the weather developed, Lieutenant Colonel Doyle had to report to Spilberg that the chopper inbound with his company's resupply was being diverted to conduct an emergency medevac on Mary Ann. It was a sign of the times. Several troopers on the hill had eaten C-4 plastic explosives in a crazy attempt to get high. Instead, they'd become deathly ill.

"Sorry 'bout that," Doyle said, "but we're going to have to use your resupply chopper to get these guys back to Chu Lai."

"What?" Spilberg shouted, knowing that his men were listening and expecting him to stand up for them. "Those motherfuckers are up there eating C-4 while we're out here starving? Let 'em die!"

"Shut your mouth," Doyle barked back on the radio.

The weather turned dark again and the monsoon resumed its lashing of hungry, miserable, hunkered-down Alpha Company. "I don't understand why they send companies out on extended operations during the monsoon when the weather is so poor and air support practically nonexistent," wrote a furious Captain Spilberg as the rain beat down on his poncho shelter. "This damn Americal Division is so sorry. I'm seriously considering checking with the 101st Airborne Division or the 1st Cav to see if I can get a company with them. When we do get back in I'll have a few strong things to say to our staff and our new battalion commander about the way we conduct operations here."

Firebase Mary Ann had been built eight months earlier when the weather was clear and helicopter support unrestricted. "The firebase was planned only to be a temporary one," wrote Lt. Col. Peter J. Foss, the battalion commander who originally opened the position to support a limited foray against the K-7 Corridor and the Dak Rose Trail—two branches of the Ho Chi Minh Trail the NVA used to shuttle men and material toward the coast from Laos.

"I was surprised when I found out the battalion later operated permanently from that position," Foss wrote.

Lieutenant Colonel Foss commanded the 1-46th Infantry from November, 1969, until April, 1970, at FSB Professional in Tien Phuoc District, Quang Tin Province. Tasked with carving out a firebase twenty kilometers southwest in Hau Duc District, Foss, a West Pointer, selected a 600-foot-high hilltop called Thon Mot (8) after the abandoned, weathered-away hamlet on its slope—a position fifty-seven kilometers inland from Chu Lai and fifty klicks short of the Laotian border. Foss would name it Mary Ann after his oldest sister, a former army nurse. After establishing a forward CP in the hamlet of New Hau Duc, seven kilometers southeast of Thon Mot (8), Foss was joined by infantry and artillery units from the ARVN. Following an artillery preparation by the ARVN, Foss airlifted Delta Company onto the hilltop on February 19, 1970. The Hueys had to hover ten feet off the ground because of the brush and small trees covering the hill. The grunts jumped down from the skids. Combat engineers were flown in next with chain saws, demolitions, and a small dozer to level the trees and clear fields of fire. The mountains and valleys around the new firebase were uninhabited except for a scattering of nomadic Montagnard tribes—and enemy soldiers moving down the trails and manning the way stations along them, invisible under the jungle canopy.

By the twentieth, the men of Company D had sandbagged their holes and positioned felled trees as protective berms and overhead cover. The next day, two 105-mm howitzers from Battery B, 3d Battalion, 82d Field Artillery (FA), were slingloaded up to FSB Mary Ann under CH-47 Chinook helicopters. Meanwhile, the NVA mortared the dusty, scorching hot hill. "Surprisingly, the NVA mixed tear gas shells with the high explosive," noted Foss, who had several men killed and wounded by the shellings. "I went up there to show the company commander how to put rocks on top of the bunkers to cause the shells to burst before they penetrated the log cover. I had learned this trick in Korea."

The mortar fire ceased when Foss lifted his other three line companies into the area after getting the arty set up on Mary Ann to support them. The Professionals spent two weeks in the FSB Mary Ann area of operations (AO). The firebase was well located in that it sat astride the K-7 Corridor, which followed the Tranh River past the eastern side of the hill, and between the two east-west branches of the Dak Rose Trail. "We had many small firefights in the area," wrote Foss. Two members of the battalion's reconnaissance platoon were killed, along with numerous NVA. In addition, a handful of prisoners were taken, including two female medics, and several base camps were uncovered with "ten to twelve tons of rice. We couldn't evacuate it, so we poured gas on it and put tear gas crystals in it. We also shot several water buffalos who had pack marks on their backs, indicating they had been used to haul supplies. Water buffalos are hard to kill. . . ."

"We filled in the bunkers on the hill when we left," noted Foss, who passed the battalion colors to Lieutenant Colonel Carvell less than two months later back on FSB Professional.

The battalion's next foray began on June 7, when it was shifted north to the Hiep Duc Valley to reinforce other 196th Brigade elements engaged in a pitched battle with the 31st NVA Regiment. This campaign, initiated by the enemy, had as its prize a showcase resettlement village. The division commander, Maj. Gen. A. E. "Ernie" Milloy, put Carvell in control of the action—which was then an uncoordinated mess—and the Professionals' sweep commenced as soon as they landed on the valley floor. The fighting was at close quarters, and in the first contact even Captain Strand, the Alpha Company CO, dropped an NVA with his

M16 as his company assaulted and seized Hill 245. Strand eliminated another NVA with a hand grenade, but ended the day aboard a medevac with mortar fragment wounds. The Huey took numerous hits on its way out.

The Professionals broke the NVA on day six when Company B, pinned down near the NVA command post, desperately closed with the enemy bunkers in squad rushes to kill the occupants with grenades. The Professionals claimed a body count of 112 NVA, with another 300 to 400 probable kills from all the firepower that had shredded the enemy's tree-line and hillock positions. The enemy survivors straggled back into the mountains to regroup. The resettlement village had been secured.

Nine Professionals were killed in the Hiep Duc, and another sixty-nine wounded. The shock of these casualties resulted in a company-sized combat refusal during the battle. It was another sign of the times. "Nobody remembered why we were there in the first place," reflected Pfc. Dennis A. Ziems of Company C. The U.S. ground war in Vietnam had been conducted with much vigor from 1965 to 1968. But motivation began to dryrot when the withdrawals began in 1969. "The war didn't make any sense anymore," said Pfc. Edward W. Voros, who pulled a 1970–71 tour with Company A. "We all thought it was bullshit. We weren't solving anything, we weren't helping to win the war. We were just there, and it basically came down to staying alive and keeping your buddies alive."

Private First Class James P. Creaven of Company C said:

We weren't stupid. We knew we were pulling out, and we knew the ARVN weren't willing to fight their own war. Why risk your life for people who didn't even appreciate your being there? The only ones who wanted to be there were career officers. Grunts did a year in the bush. Officers were only out there for a few months, just long enough to get some body counts and some medals so they could pop up in rank. Anybody who was gung ho and wanted to "kill gooks" was incredibly suspect to most of us grunts. If we went out on an ambush and had NVA coming down, if there was a good chance that they wouldn't see us or hassle us, the general consensus was to let them go. Life's too short, and these people never did a darn thing to me—and the war was winding down anyway. Why kill people just to kill them?

The Professionals returned to FSB Mary Ann on June 27. Before the lift ships went in, Carvell's LOH buzzed the adjacent ridgelines—"no apparent activity," the battalion commander wrote in his journal—then hovered around the barren firebase, spotting only "some old wire, no booby-traps." The NVA, thinking troops had landed, lobbed six to eight 82-mm mortar rounds from a camouflaged position to the west. Some fell short, and the rest went over the hill and landed in the river. Carvell could not spot the mortar from his LOH, but within two days the battalion killed five NVA in the area, including a forward observer. The hilltop was not shelled again until the night of the sapper attack—which was actually surprising because Mary Ann did not occupy the area's commanding terrain. "It was a terrible place for a firebase," said Carvell, noting the steep cliffs on the east side of the hill which fell away to the deep and swift Tranh River. "It was a poor position to defend. The firebase was on a hill, but in a saddle with hills around it on three sides. To the west, and east across the river, there were hills that were higher, and the ridgeline on which the firebase was built extended to higher elevations towards the north."

The NVA could study FSB Mary Ann in intimate detail with binoculars from the surrounding high ground. "On the other hand, the firebase was in a great location because we were interdicting the enemy in their own backyard," said Carvell, whose campaign to reduce the NVA in the K-7/Dak Rose AO was more prolonged than Foss's initial foray and included total evacuation of the Montagnards. Had Mary Ann been built on the high ground to the north or east, its artillery fan would not have extended south and west as it did to cover the most active stretches of the enemy infiltration routes. Had the high ground to the west been chosen, Mary Ann—which was already at the extreme range of the division's heaviest artillery—would have been completely out of range of supporting fires, and even more isolated from its helicopter lifeline. The firebase could be reached only by chopper, and the flight from Chu Lai to FSB Mary

Ann took forty-five minutes in a Huey. For these reasons, the NVA had come to enjoy sanctuary in the area. Once the Professionals became familiar with the NVA trail networks, however, they covered them with mechanical ambushes—claymore mines rigged with trip wires—and left behind sniper teams after a line company was lifted out so as to catch enemy soldiers moving in to scavenge the site for discarded rations and ammunition.

"We had fantastic contact," said Carvell. "We could just scarf up NVA every day, and do it our way—and not have to suffer booby-trap casualties like the battalions fighting the guerrillas along the coast. We were getting as many kills and prisoners as the other three battalions in the brigade combined."

The NVA probed FSB Mary Ann four times during July and August, and several enemy recon soldiers were killed in the wire. One was captured. "Says his unit planning to attack us," Carvell wrote in his journal. "It was hard to maintain alertness on the line at all times, but it had to be done," Carvell later wrote, noting that he "reminded the troops regularly that the guerrilla is patient, he lulls the opposition into a complacent routine—and then he strikes."

Meanwhile, Carvell faced another type of problem:

We had a fragging incident on FSB Mary Ann at 0115 on July 30, 1970. At the time, I'd just made my rounds along the bunker line. I was standing outside the B-TOC, gazing at the skyline, getting ready to sack out—and all of a sudden I heard an explosion in the mortar platoon area. A fragmentation grenade had been thrown into the bunker used by the senior members of the mortar platoon [which was part of Company E, 1-46th Infantry].

I immediately ran toward the bunker. I was the first guy on the scene, and I saw a black trooper jump behind another bunker almost like he was hiding. His eyes were glassy and he appeared very nervous. He said, "It was an incoming mortar round!"

I said, "No, it was a grenade!" The B-TOC security guard, a real nice black kid, had run up with me, and he said, "I think he did it, sir, I think he did it."

It turned out that the grenade had killed a sergeant first class, and wounded another ranking NCO. There was no way to prove who threw the grenade, and I have no idea why the sergeant who was murdered would have been fingered for a fragging. I suspect he was an innocent bystander because he was just such an even-tempered, well-liked NCO. Maybe the other NCO in the bunker, or maybe the platoon leader or even the company commander may have been the real target. The whole battalion was in a state of shock over the incident.

When four Professionals were killed in an ambush south of FSB Mary Ann across the Tranh River, Captain Strand and Company A helicoptered in. On August 4, while working uphill out of the valley, they too were ambushed by NVA hidden somewhere above them in camouflaged positions. The point man took a round in the forehead and in a matter of moments, Strand, a West Pointer, had dead and wounded all over the place. "Strand had a lot of courage and good sense," remarked a fellow captain. "His attitude was, 'Let's take the fucking hill—but let's do it smart.'" In this case, though, Strand—unable to take the hill—couldn't even break contact to evacuate his casualties. He blasted the crest with artillery and air strikes without visible effect on the enemy. "I couldn't believe we couldn't get them to back off," Strand recalled. One trooper had a shattered ankle and was shrieking. Two other men were wounded trying to get to a gut-shot sergeant who eventually died in the killing zone. "Another company CA'd onto the ridgeline five hundred meters away," Strand later said. "We hunkered down for a very traumatic night, and in the morning the other company linked up with us. We moved back down to the valley floor and medevacked our three dead and ten wounded. We had to get them out one at a time on a jungle penetrater lowered by a helicopter hovering right above the treetops."

Heavy contact continued, with six more Professionals being killed, until August 13—the day Lieutenant Colonel Carvell's LOH was shot down during Company A's fight in what was probably the NVA command post for the area. That was the end of organized enemy resistance. "By the time I left, we were in complete control of that AO," noted

Carvell, who was relieved by Bill Doyle at the battalion's rear area in Chu Lai on October 25. During the last two months of Carvell's watch he'd had only two more combat fatalities—both caused by booby traps. Carvell had other worries, however. The rapid turnover of battalion commanders and other officers tended to degrade institutional memory. Carvell wrote that "except for Strand, my best leaders have or are ready to depart." After the ceremonial passing of the colors, he warned the brigade commander, who was also new, that the battalion was "getting cocky—the 'newbies' are awfully complacent. . . ."

Upon helicoptering out to FSB Mary Ann on October 26, 1970, Lieutenant Colonel Doyle requested that division commander Milloy relocate the Professionals toward the coast. "I was rather appalled [that] we were going to stay out that far during the monsoon season," said Doyle, who knew from his first tour how risky resupply and medevac missions were in those fog-shrouded mountains. He was of the opinion that "a firebase could not be supported during the monsoon that far out toward the border."

Milloy denied Doyle's request on the grounds that if FSB Mary Ann were shut down, the enemy—presently wasting time hacking out new infiltration routes outside the position's artillery fan—"would merely pick up and take the easier route back along the Dak Rose Trail," as Doyle paraphrased the general's reply.

The answer was more complicated than that, however. General Milloy, an infantry veteran of three wars—including two command tours in Vietnam—basically agreed with Doyle. On November 7, Doyle's battalion would be airlifted to FSB Young, located to the northeast in Tien Phuoc District where the mountains ebbed into foothills and the effect of the monsoon was not so severe. At the same time, Milloy, wanting to keep the NVA as far from the populated coast as possible, upgraded Mary Ann from a temporary to a permanent firebase. Milloy ordered Doyle to leave one line company and a half-battery of artillery behind so as not to totally abandon the area.

When the monsoon ended, the Professionals would return in force to FSB Mary Ann. Meanwhile Doyle, believing he was stuck, stocked up on supplies whenever the weather allowed. Because Mary Ann had been a temporary firebase, no planning had gone into making the position monsoon-proof. "The bunkers were primitive, usually just a hole with log cover and sandbags over it," stated Doyle. "The floor, if any, consisted of C-ration boxes. [The troops] get just as wet on the firebase [as in the field] and have all sorts of immersion foot problems. I kept asking for somebody to tell me whether it would or would not remain there, and if it would remain I wanted some permanent construction."

Captain Strand wrote that when Lieutenant Colonel Carvell originally reopened the firebase "the battalion was to occupy Mary Ann for only six weeks [but] the operation was extended for another six weeks, and then again extended." Carvell's requests for the "material needed for permanent fire base defense" were "denied by Division. . . . The Division staff procrastinated in its decision as to make Mary Ann a permanent Fire Support Base. By the time the decision was made, monsoon weather prevented the build-up of Mary Ann."

When Lieutenant Colonel Doyle got to FSB Mary Ann, the perimeter defenses were manned by Company B, which was replaced on October 27 by Capt. Donald M. Sampson's Company D, 1-46th Infantry. Before moving to the firebase, Delta Company's last mission under Carvell had been successful in that the unit claimed several unconfirmed kills and captured a tired, hungry NVA deserter. The mission was most memorable, though, for an incident that began when Delta Company GIs spotted movement among several hootches on the forested slope across the river they were following. The distance was too great to make out faces, so the company command group radioed battalion, noted the location of the unidentified personnel, and asked if there were any friendly forces in that area. The response from battalion was negative, so the grunts stretched out along the brushy riverbank proceeded to rake the hootch area with rifle and machine-gun fire.

Immediately, someone up there shouted, "Friendlies!"

The bellowing from the shot-up hillside included obscenities in plain English. Someone popped a smoke grenade, but a staff sergeant from Delta Company shouted, "It's a trick—keep shooting!"

"Jesus Christ, shut up!" a Delta grunt hollered back. "It ain't no trick. We need to find out who the hell's over there!"

Delta Company had, in fact, just fired up the Reconnaissance Platoon of Company E, 1-46th Infantry. Apparently, the Recon Platoon leader, 1st Lt. C. Barry McGee—a West Pointer who was destined to play a major role in the sapper attack—had deviated from his assigned patrol route, as often happened in that torturous terrain. Several Recon troopers had been wounded by the friendly fire. "I was deathly afraid of Echo Recon baggin' us when we got to the rear," recalled a squad leader in Company D. Meanwhile, on October 20, Echo Recon found an enemy bivouac that showed signs of recent use on a jungled hillside three klicks west of FSB Mary Ann. After establishing a position there, McGee sent out several local patrols. Circling back as instructed, one of the patrols—unaware that it was lost—approached the platoon position from the wrong side. Recon troopers fired on the unexpected movement, hitting one of their own men, who died after being loaded aboard a LOH.

Lieutenant McGee was relieved of command.

"After that, there was never any word to us from Echo Recon about firing them up," remembered the worried Delta Company squad leader. "They understood then that accidents happen."

Two nights after Doyle met Captain Sampson on FSB Mary Ann, four of his Company D GIs were carried sick and delirious into the battalion aid station across the camp road from the B-TOC. They had pried the back off a claymore mine and eaten the white, claylike C-4 plastic explosive inside. They had heard a rumor that C-4 would make them high, but the actual results were disastrous. The soldier who had eaten the most ground his teeth as he writhed and convulsed on a cot in the aid station. At one point he jerked the intravenous line (IV) out of his arm and splattered a jet of blood against the wall. It appeared he was going to die.

Because of the monsoon, all of the division's aircraft had

been grounded by General Milloy. When informed of the medevac request, the fighting general refused to make an exception. "I am not about to risk the lives of a good aircrew for people who have done something this stupid," he said. "I hope they make it. God willing, we'll get them out in the morning if the weather's better."

But the weather did not clear the next day, and at midnight the troop who'd eaten the most C-4—a replacement with five weeks in country—died in FSB Mary Ann's aid station. The three survivors were medevacked during the third afternoon of the crisis, October 31, when a Huey was finally able to make it up from Chu Lai. The dead man was loaded aboard in a body bag. His three buddies and two grunts with jungle rot also got on board. "Do you want to ride out on it, too?" Doyle asked Captain Strand, the ops officer. "Do you want to risk it for R&R?" The weather was still rotten. Strand, unsure of what to do, hesitated before finally swinging aboard the crowded Huey with his weapon and rucksack. He sat in the only space available—right on the dead guy's chest. Strand grinned broadly at everyone on the pad as the helo lifted off. The pilot then took them out the way he'd come in—ten feet off the river and directly underneath the fog that filled the valley and erased the mountains.

Meanwhile, Captain Spilberg and Alpha Company had to weather it out on the south side of the raging Tranh River during nine straight days of unflyable downpour. "We were in the watery equivalent of a blizzard, and the war stopped," wrote Spilberg. "We just hunkered down. We could not get warm. We could not get dry. We could not pull out—and the constant pounding of rain on our helmets and ponchos was damn near driving us crazy!"

The Alpha Company GIs set up poncho shelters on a jungled hillock and planted claymores and trip flares around them. It seemed an unnecessary precaution. "The enemy wasn't going anyplace either," Spilberg said. It was cold and windy, and the hail-like rain was constant, day and night. They never saw the sun, and their hands and feet turned a sickly and wrinkly white. Those who had hammocks used them to stay away from the leeches. Troops without hammocks woke up covered with the leathery bloodsuckers. To prevent immersion foot, Spilberg made sure his men changed their socks daily, drying the wet ones against their skin inside their shirts. They slept with their boots off and built C-4 fires when possible in an attempt to dry out their footgear. They wrote piles of letters, read and reread the ones they still had from home, and passed around the paperback books they carried in their rucksacks. After smoking all their cigarettes, they rolled their own using toilet paper and the inferior pipe tobacco from their C-ration sundry packs.

Some of the troops ran out of food on day three, and all were out by day six. The acting 1st Platoon leader, Sgt. Francisco Concepcion of Guam, had several fellow islanders in his platoon—these Guamanians were great, cheerful soldiers—and he got permission from Spilberg to check out an abandoned hootch the company had passed on the way to the hill. Concepcion didn't find any bananas or rice as he'd hoped, but his islanders did pluck all they could carry from a nearby manioc field. Everyone got a share, and they ate the jungle tubers raw or semiboiled in canteen cups. The manioc filled their stomachs with starch but did not relieve their hunger.

When there was a break in the rain during the late afternoon of day eight, November 1, two 196th Brigade LOHs landed with a load of rations. "You never saw so much yelling and cheering," wrote Captain Spilberg, who secured the LZ with one platoon. The grunts cheered not only the food, but the flying skills of the two pilots who brought it in from Hawk Hill. The rain may have stopped, but the cloud cover was still heavy. The two pilots, flying without door gunners to save space and carrying dehydrated long-range recon patrol (LRRP) rations to conserve weight, had no sense of direction because there was no sun. They made it only because they were intimately familiar with what they could see of the landscape. It was an exceptionally hairy trip as they tried not to fly into "cumulous granite"—the side of a mountain. The LOHs were buzzing down the river valley at seventy knots, one behind the other, when they'd hit a scud cloud hanging in the trees and suddenly have to drop into a five-knot hover to assess the situation. The lead LOH would blow a path through the fog, and then they'd continue on, their skids just above the raging river.

The lead pilot was short, gruff, cannonball-shaped CW2 Joseph Kane. Captain Spilberg ran to his window. "You guys look like a bunch of kids," Kane said, gesturing at the excited grunts ducking under the blades to unload the rations. The LOHs contained a day's worth of food. Spilberg asked if they were going to bring in more. Kane said no, it was too dangerous. Spilberg pressed him: "I've got guys who've gone five days without chow."

Kane hesitated, then said, "Fuck it, I'll be right back." The two LOHs found their way to FSB Mary Ann, where they loaded up with enough C rations to give Company A a four-day reserve. "After the resupply I called the Colonel on the radio and told him I wanted to put the pilots in for a medal," Spilberg wrote home. "Morale has just skyrocketed now that we have food."

The clouds lifted the next afternoon, and several Hueys shuttled Alpha Company back to FSB Mary Ann. There Spilberg met Bill Doyle for the first time. He expected to be chewed out for the flap they'd had on the radio over the C-4 casualties. Instead, the new colonel congratulated Spilberg for the "outstanding" job he'd done, especially by preventing immersion foot during the soggy ordeal. Spilberg wrote home that he was "so proud of my men I could bust. When we were without food and it was cold & pouring down rain . . . there was good humor and the highest degree of cooperativeness."

3

The Children's Crusade

Four days into the FSB young mission, 1st Lt. Hugh W. Harrell and his platoon, Delta Two, laagered on a brushy finger leading off a ridgeline. The NDP overlooked a rice paddy that was carved like a shelf on the narrow spine of the finger. In the morning on November 12, one of Harrell's machine gunners, Pfc. Zeddie T. Bell, having cleaned his M60 because of recent malfunctions, passed the word that he was going to test fire the weapon into the muddy paddy. Bell stood up so he could see over the brush—and found himself looking at three NVA approaching through the high grass. The enemy soldiers, their AK-47s held ready, wore pith helmets, green fatigues, and packs. They stopped fifteen feet in front of Bell to get their bearings before continuing uphill from the paddy. Unseen, Bell sighted his M60 on the lead soldier—and dropped him with a short burst. The weapon then misfired. Bell manually recocked it, brought down the second NVA with another burst, and continued firing as the third man disappeared into the high grass, leaving a blood trail.

The enemy patrol had been taken completely by surprise. FSB Young was an ARVN position and, given the ARVN's capabilities, the enemy in the area—the 72d VC Local Force Battalion—had enjoyed relatively safe passage between their ridgeline hideaways and the farming hamlets that dotted the valleys. Intelligence indicated that the 72d, which had been filled with NVA replacements, was going to cut the road between Tam Ky and the Tien Phuoc District headquarters twenty kilometers to the west—then launch attacks on FSB Young, which was on a hillock immediately south of the road, on two other outposts along the road, and on the district headquarters itself.

Thus, the arrival of the Professionals. The enemy was caught off guard, and on November 15 Lieutenant Harrell's Delta Two got three more kills when it caught a VC/NVA platoon crossing an open rice paddy. These incidents were great for morale, for under Captain Sampson Company D had not earned much of a reputation. "Sampson was competent enough," said a fellow captain, "but he wasn't somebody that we had a lot of confidence in. He wasn't a hard charger. He wasn't one of the crazy ones."

Lieutenant Colonel Doyle eventually reassigned the amiable, balding Sampson to Company E, the battalion's support company. "Sampson wasn't a gung ho, pursue-the-mission-at-all-costs commander," said Lieutenant Harrell. Sampson had served a previous combat tour with the 1st Cavalry Division, but "understood the new era in which we fought. We weren't going out and 'Killing a Commie for Christ' anymore. The guys didn't want to be there. They were pissed off about being there, and we had to find a happy medium between their welfare and the mission so they could trust that we wouldn't waste their lives, and still develop them into a cohesive enough unit that could do what we had to do."

The problem with having a personable, easygoing company commander was that there were few taskmaster-type NCOs left to take up the slack. "This company is really a mess," wrote Captain Spilberg when he was working with Sampson atop a resupply hill in the FSB Mary Ann AO. "The security around the perimeter is weak. The troops sit around reading newspapers, playing cards . . . most of the time they don't even carry their weapons. . . ." No one had dug in. Instead, they'd inflated air mattresses or strung hammocks. Spilberg noted in his letter that "they do not dig pits to throw their garbage and they do not destroy their C-Ration cans, which the Viets could police up and use for boobytraps. At night there is talking and yelling and men light their cigarettes in the open instead of getting under their ponchos. They feel secure. There are few Viets in the area, but if they ever go into a hot area they will get wiped out because their habits are poor."

The temperature turned up in the FSB Young AO. On November 15, seven days before Captain Sampson was replaced, Delta Three's platoon sergeant, S.Sgt. Council D. Vaughan—who was Regular Army—was killed by a booby-trapped 60mm mortar round when the platoon was walking on a trail. He was Bill Doyle's first combat fatality. Lieutenant Harrell almost became the next while Delta Two was working another section of the trail network. The area was studded with booby traps—better known as BTs or bravo tangos—and at one point Harrell saw three rocks arranged as a warning to guerrilla groups. He passed the word to be extra cautious, but only fifty feet farther down the trail the slack man behind the point accidentally kicked over a stone. A U.S.-issue grenade was concealed underneath—its pin removed, the safety spoon held in place by the stone. Harrell saw the spoon pop off when the stone moved and, screaming a warning, dove into the brush. The point and slack men caught fragments in the backs of their legs.

Lieutenant Harrell, who always moved with the point team, had been decorated once for leading an impromptu assault into an NVA bivouac and killing three enemy soldiers. "We had a lot of dumb-ass lieutenants, but I would have followed Harrell anywhere," said Sp4 Jeffery E. Parks. "He was the best."

Harrell was not a career man, but a citizen-soldier who meant to do his best while he did his time. When Harrell first joined Delta Two in August, 1970,[1] he pumped his predecessor for information about the platoon. "We're laid back," the outgoing lieutenant said, adding that the men called him by his first name and that he blew grass with them at night. Harrell was shocked. When he introduced himself to the Delta Two GIs he immediately set a new tone: "My first name is Lieutenant—and, hey, we don't smoke in the field. What you do in the rear is your business. When I get back, I'm going to buy the biggest bottle of Scotch I can get. Back there, you guys do whatever the hell you want—but not in the bush!"

All of Lieutenant Harrell's grunts were short-timers, regardless of how long they had been in the bush. None wanted to be The Last Man Killed in Vietnam. Most were just going through the motions, and a few were playing turtle. "We can't depend on this guy," a squad leader would tell Harrell. "He's not covering our ass, he's covering his." Such troops were reassigned to the rear. More often than not, according to Harrell, they were black. It was another sign of the times—and an overwhelming, division-wide problem that reflected the militancy of many of the soul brothers, who saw no reason to be cannon fodder in the "White Man's War." "We had street-tough black guys," remembered Specialist Parks, "and the first time they took fire, they were lyin' on the ground, crying. They got what they wanted. They got shipped to the rear."

Lieutenant Harrell came to depend on a hard-core few like uncomplaining, unassuming Sgt. Andrew H. Olints, and Jeff Parks, a draftee from rural Ohio who hated the army but who walked point on most patrols because he meant to do right by Olints and the lieutenant. "It shook itself out," said Harrell. "I could count on the three who usually walked in front of me, and the next two behind me. That was the group. We all trusted each other. We could almost read each other's movements before anyone said anything."

Captain Sampson was replaced by 1st Lt. Thomas F. Schmitz, formerly the battalion intelligence officer and Recon Platoon leader, and on the drizzly, overcast afternoon of November 27, Company D moved off FSB Young and through the ARVN-occupied village at the foot of the hill. Passing the guard position at the break in the perimeter wire, point-man Parks had just started off into the tall grass when he unknowingly snagged a trip wire attached to a U.S.-made frag secured to a stake. Parks had a claymore bag containing a mine, two hand frags, and a smoke grenade secured to the top of his rucksack. The BT explosion ignited the latter and, with purple smoke hissing out everywhere, Parks threw off his ruck and dropped into the grass, prepared to return fire. At the same time he realized what had happened, he also discovered that he had been wounded in the buttocks. It could have been worse. The frag's five-second delay had allowed him to walk past it, and his rucksack had taken the brunt of the explosion. He later pulled forty fragments from the shredded, purple-stained pack. His bush hat also had a couple holes in it. The frags and claymore in his claymore bag were too hot to touch, but somehow only the harmless smoke had gone off.

Lieutenant Harrell was knocked down by the blast. When he started to get up, there was a sharp pain where a metal fragment had punched through the ammunition bandolier around his waist. It was a bad, intestine-piercing wound, but there was only a speck of blood to show for it. Harrell's immediate concern was the inside of his right elbow, where a chunk of muscle was missing.

Five grunts had been wounded. Lieutenant Schmitz, rushing forward with his radio-telephone operators (RTOs), told Sergeant Olints to secure a team of medics coming down from FSB Young. "On the way out, we talked about how we were going out to the jungle to fight the ARVN's war while they just sat there," recalled Olints. "When I was heading back to get the medics, they were laughing at us. I came so close to shooting 'em."

Meanwhile, Specialist Parks had furiously swung his M16 on the grinning ARVN at the guard post after discovering more BTs in the tall grass. They were part of the ARVN perimeter defenses. "Them fucking ARVNs let us walk right into it," said Parks. "It was my fault. I wasn't looking because I thought if the ARVN had set something out there I thought they would have told us! The ARVNs and I locked and loaded. I told 'em to shut the fuck up, or I was going to waste 'em. I was ready, and I had every right in the world, buddy."

Several of Parks's buddies got ahold of his weapon and calmed him down. Lieutenant Harrell was helicoptered to the 91st Evacuation Hospital in Chu Lai, where he awoke the next day in great pain after surgery. The doctor told Harrell that his war was over—he would soon be evacuated to Japan. Harrell said that he couldn't go, and the surprised doctor asked him why not.

"Because I can't leave my guys," he answered, near tears.

Lieutenant Harrell made it back, but seven months after hitting that first BT—when he was only weeks away from rotation—he tripped a bigger one while setting up an NDP on a grassy foothill under a gray, rainy sky outside Da Nang.

Hugh Harrell went home without his left leg.

Meanwhile, shortly after the encounter with the ARVN BT, Sergeant Olints's squad was laagered on a brushy, tree-dotted knoll beside the main road when an ARVN patrol fired it up in a case of mistaken identity. The friendly fire included M79 grenade launcher rounds. Olints's new point man, Pfc. Sexton M. Vann, was in his hammock when a round ripped through the poncho he'd rigged overhead because of the drizzle. Olints was writing a letter home. He rolled to cover, then blindly returned fire with his M16—only to have the uncleaned weapon blow up in his hands. The ARVN quickly ceased fire, and "Doc" Ricks, a medic, rushed to Donny Carr, who'd been shot through the cheek—the bullet coming out the back of his neck. Blood poured from his mouth, but he would survive. Rex Armstrong had taken fragments in one leg. Olints bandaged his wounds and calmed him down before helping to load him onto the colonel's LOH. Olints later received a stack of thank-you cards from everyone in Armstrong's family, a gesture which touched him deeply.

When Sergeant Olints and 1st Lt. Arthur D. Schmidt, the new Delta Two platoon leader, spotted the first Vietnamese at 1340 on December 7, 1970, it was not clear if he was a villager or a guerrilla. The man, unaware that he was under observation, emerged from a hootch in what had appeared to be a deserted ville, then drew a bucket from a well to wash. Schmidt's men—teamed with an ARVN squad—watched from the crest of a ridgeline. The picturesque ville below consisted of only three hootches; it was a palmy green island in a sodden expanse of rice paddies. Olints glanced at the dike running into the left side of the ville and was stunned to see a VC/NVA with bush hat and pack coming down it, toting an AK-47. As soon as the enemy soldier reached the ville, a second one trotted down the dike. The man was followed by another, then another, and another—all of them moving smartly across the open paddy, making sure there were never two in view at the same time. Olints counted fourteen all together.

Lieutenant Schmidt, who had been in the bush only two days after spending two months as the company executive officer, radioed the company commander, Lieutenant Schmitz, to work up a call for artillery fire on the ville. The ARVN district headquarters, however, refused to clear the mission on the grounds that the VC/NVA-occupied hamlet was a "friendly ville." Schmidt tried instead to get gunships through U.S. channels. That request was denied because of the overcast. Despite the lack of fire support, Schmitz, who came up the back side of Schmidt's ridge with the U.S./ARVN patrol he'd been accompanying, considered the VC/NVA platoon too lucrative a target to pass up. Schmitz decided to assault the hamlet. He instructed Delta One and Three to break off their patrols and move in on the flanks while Delta Two launched its attack. The ARVN were to remain atop the ridge to provide suppressive fire on the ville.

Sergeant Olints, whose squad was to lead the charge, couldn't believe they were going to go in under ARVN M60 fire. But it was either that or no fire support at all. Feeling totally out of control, Olints and Lieutenant Schmidt used the brush as cover to get the squad downhill. They spread out at the edge of the long, muddy paddy, then fired two M72 Light Antitank Weapon (LAW) rockets, the signal for their supporting machine gunners to commence firing. Schmidt and Olints's squad took off across the paddy, firing bursts of their own into the hootches as they splashed toward them. They thought they were taking enemy fire but couldn't be sure because of all the racket. Within moments they were in the ville, but to everyone's amazement the place was empty—despite being completely surrounded by open paddies that offered no concealed avenue of retreat. The enemy apparently had tunnels.

Upon reaching the rear of the ville, Olints saw another hamlet about fifty meters away. There was movement among the hootches. "Where's the other platoons?" Olints shouted.

"Everybody's back behind us!" Schmidt answered.

"Well, who the hell's over there?"

It was the enemy, and the firefight was back on. Sergeant Olints lined up his M16 sights on two VC/NVA who flickered into view among some windblown banana leaves. He thought he dropped them.

"Andy Olints was the best guy around," remembered Parks. Olints, then twenty-five, had been a tool and die maker in civilian life, but had enlisted because he was curious about Vietnam. "He was the old man. If it wasn't for him, a lot of us guys would have went nuts. He kept us in line, and he was a friend."

Enemy fire plunked into the paddy behind the ville where Lieutenant Schmitz—who, like Olints, won a Bronze Star Medal for valor (BSMv) that day—was moving across with his CP and M60 teams. One of the gunners, Sp4 Dennis L. Rouska, ignored the fire as he sauntered down the dike leading into the ville. He had his M60 balanced over one shoulder, his fatigue shirt open, and his web gear unbuckled and hanging loose from his shoulders. The M60 was known as the pig because it ate ammo like one.

"Rouska, get the hell off that paddy dike!"

"I'm not getting down in that shit, LT!"

Lieutenant Schmitz, fire splashing around him, roared, "They're shootin' at *you*—but they're gonna get *me* instead!"

Gunships finally arrived. While the sleek, shark-nosed Cobras tore the second ville apart with rockets and miniguns, Lieutenant Colonel Doyle had his LOH drop him off so he could meet with Lieutenant Schmitz in the first ville. When the Cobras broke station to refuel and rearm, the VC/NVA opened fire again. It was unbelievable. Doyle started blasting back with his short-barreled CAR15—then launched an impetuous one-man assault on the ville. Schmitz sprinted out into the paddies with him. Although Olints thought the colonel was crazy, he had to join the charge when his platoon leader, Lieutenant Schmidt, ran past and grabbed him by the shoulder. They ended up single file on a dike, firing as they ran. The enemy, apparently stunned, ceased fire, but Olints kept his eyes open for a spot to dive when the enemy recovered from the shock of the spectacle. All he could think was that an enemy private was going to kill a colonel, two lieutenants, and a sergeant all in one burst.

The VC/NVA force did not fire, it simply disappeared out the back door again. There were no bodies, no blood trails. The ville's only remaining occupants were five stoic children and two old women, one of whom emerged from a bunker with a concussion and bleeding ears. Before the detainees were lifted out by Huey, an ARVN lieutenant took the oldest boy around the side of a hootch and whacked him around a bit. The boy talked. He said that the enemy used the villes to bivouac when they passed through the area. He said fifty VC/NVA had been there the night before.

Lieutenant Colonel Doyle intended to catch them. He instructed Schmitz to laager around the second ville, then had a Huey dispatched with an ammo resupply for Delta Company. The LZ was the flooded paddy between the two villes. Olints deployed his squad along a dike to provide security, but when the Huey departed an enemy soldier about ten feet to the sergeant's right fired a burst from his AK-47, shocking everyone. Olints had been looking back over his shoulder at the Huey—they were always fun to watch—and never saw the sniper, who was apparently in a tunnel with a camouflaged cover. The sniper didn't fire a second burst, and vanished before the squad could sweep the area. It was like fighting ghosts.

Although most battalion commanders fought the war from a helicopter seat, Lieutenant Colonel Doyle still believed that the only way to command was to lead by personal example. "Doyle was a warrior," said 1st Lt. R. Scott Bell, a platoon leader in Company A. "The army has plenty of good soldiers, but when you get into combat you want warriors—and that's what Doyle was. He would do anything for his people."

Bill Doyle was a red-faced Irishman with a tight, whitish-blond crewcut, a stocky, powerful build, and ham-sized forearms. He was from Pittsburgh, where his father had been a steel mill foreman, and graduated from the Reserve Officers' Training Corps (ROTC) program at Duquesne University in 1954. Married the same year, he had four children by the time he and his wife divorced after his second Vietnam tour. Originally commissioned in the artillery, Doyle commanded two firing batteries before transferring to the infantry, where he commanded a rifle company and a headquarters company. His staff assignments were mostly in operations. He was a basic, down-to-earth soldier who wanted muddy boots, not a desk at the Pentagon. He loved soldiers and soldiering.

During his first Vietnam tour, Doyle, then a major, compiled flawless, glowing efficiency reports while serving with the 3d Brigade, 4th Division: ". . . the finest operations officer I have known in three wars . . . has almost limitless potential . . . is general officer material at an early age. . . ."

At thirty-nine during his second combat tour, Lieutenant Colonel Doyle was considered one of the best battalion commanders in the American Division. His radio call sign, picked by his company commanders, was "Big Brother"—after the all-knowing, all-seeing presence in George Orwell's *1984*. Doyle humped with his grunts on patrol. On occasion, he laagered with them in the bush at night, and if a contact lasted long enough he was always there. "During my first firefight, we were laying in rice paddies up to our noses in water," remembered one company commander. "I turned around to say something to my radioman, and there was Doyle and the brigade commander laying in the muck. I didn't even know they were coming in I was so busy. I asked them what they were doing, and Doyle said, 'Well, we're just takin' a walk in the park.'"

Chief Warrant Officer Kane, the 196th Brigade LOH pilot, stated:

We were flying north of FSB Mary Ann with Doyle in the backseat when an NVA took a few shots at us. Either his weapon jammed or he was out of ammo because he took a running dive under a rock ledge in a stream. We didn't have a door gunner, so I pushed my CAR15 into Doyle's hands, and he started firing—but he ripped off the whole thirty-round magazine in four or five seconds. We had brass casings spraying all over the cockpit, even down into the controls. I handed him another clip, but shouted at him to aim and fire single shots—and in about four shots Doyle had this guy. The NVA was in a still area of water near a waterfall. We saw him jerk, and then a big puddle of blood formed around him, and when it hit the waterfall the whole thing turned red. It was a very vivid picture.

Doyle expected much from his officers, and was not chary about offering "career guidance," as Lieutenant Schmitz put it—that is "a good old-fashioned chewing out." Captain Spilberg noted that when Doyle was angry he had "the palest, most penetrating blue eyes you've ever seen." Captain Strand said that the colonel was "really easy to read. There was no BS. He told you what he expected, and you knew that this wasn't a guy you were going to fool with. He just looked harder than nails. He was not a screamer, but he could raise his voice and very pointedly tell you where you messed up."

Doyle had a sign outside his B-TOC that read:

FT. COURAGE
KILL PROFESSIONALLY

The sign was topped with a water buffalo skull that had curved horns—and a bra fastened over the eye sockets. Doyle, who had the battalion emblem—a blue star—drawn on his helmet, was big on symbols and slogans. His favorite rhyme was, "This army's all right—hard but fair—God bless the infantry."

"When units would be on the helipad getting ready for missions, Doyle would be down there with them," said Captain Strand. "Doyle would say, 'Tell me what's going on, soldier,' and they'd sit in groups, carrying on a conversation with the battalion commander. Doyle could talk their language. He had a rapport from the soldier on up."

Lieutenant Schmitz stated that

> Lieutenant Colonel Doyle was quite proud of his prowess with a .45-caliber pistol. He would often load it with tracers and fire at trees around the base of FSB Mary Ann, and challenge us to hit other targets like rocks. He always won. When I asked him about it once, he told me his secret: the .45 rises up when it discharges, so most misses are vertical—long or short—not to the right or left; so when he chose vertical targets like a tree while we were given horizontal targets like rocks or logs to try to hit, he always won.

Doyle definitely had a gregarious side. Schmitz recalled one boozed-up night in Chu Lai when Doyle and several junior officers in his quarters "tried to see who could shoot the rabbit ear antennas off his TV with the colonel's .45—at least until the 23d MPs showed up to suggest some other indoor sport."

Doyle fought hard and partied hard. "The colonel was a little cocky, and a little crazy," said Lieutenant Harrell. "He was a hard-drinking hard charger once we got off the choppers. It seemed like he had a short man's syndrome."

Rather than get caught up in Doyle's macho antics, Harrell tended to shy away from the colonel in the rear. Most of Doyle's junior officers did not. "Doyle was a kick," said Strand. Once, when Doyle sent Strand to Chu Lai for a one-day R&R, he told the young captain that he "wasn't worth a shit" if he didn't come back with a Disciplinary Report (DR). Strand obliged him by tap-dancing across the lacquered bar at the division officers' club. Meanwhile, the recon platoon leader, who the colonel had also sent back for a break, mounted the stage where they showed movies in the club, shouted that the officers there were "a bunch of chickenshit, rear-echelon motherfuckers," and challenged any of them to try and take him off the stage. "Doyle wanted a DR," remembered Strand. "Well, instead he got a call from the division chief of staff who told him he didn't want to see anyone from our battalion in the division officers' club again. We had a reputation. We weren't political. We didn't go back and behave."

After Company D's resupply Huey took fire in the late afternoon of December 7, Lieutenant Schmitz had Delta One secure the high ground from which the assault on the first ville had been launched. Schmitz's command group set up in the second ville with Delta Two and Three and the attached ARVN. "Half of these ARVN, we don't even know if they're on our side," Schmitz told his platoon leaders that evening. "You're going to have to be able to fall back and regroup in case something happens tonight and these guys just disappear."

If the ARVN were as bad as ever, the Americans weren't what they used to be. "Morale was okay, but the level of expertise in the field was incredibly low," Schmitz later recalled. "It was like a Children's Crusade." Schmitz wondered if he was part of the problem. "I was proud to be selected to be a company commander, but now I think it was damn near criminal. I had no experience. I had never even been in a rifle company before."

"So, what do you think?" Doyle had asked a few days earlier.

"You're going to get my ass killed," Schmitz answered. "Recon was a cakewalk compared to Delta Company. This is a three-ring circus out here!"

"Just take it easy and use your NCOs."

"I don't have any to use!"

Schmitz had three career NCOs in Company D. The rest were NCO Candidate School (NCOCS) graduates—the aptly named "shake 'n' bake" sergeants shipped to Vietnam as squad and fire team leaders. "All the old lifer NCOs were hiding in the rear," noted Schmitz. Most were on their second or third combat tours and had no intention of getting killed or wounded this late in the game. They were sorely missed. "It was ridiculous," said Schmitz. "The grunts were all kids, and the sergeants and platoon leaders were about two hours older than the troops they were in charge of. They were really well meaning, but very unmotivated, unaggressive, and inexperienced."

Lieutenant Schmitz was exhausted from the running firefight, and his temper snapped as he checked the lines that night. "For Christ's sake, you gotta dig in," he barked at his platoon leaders and sergeants. "Listen, goddamnit, you guys know what you're supposed to be doing. Get out there and get your people dug in. Get some security out. This is bullshit!"

Delta Company's grunts did not dig in, given that the company had not been mortared in six months. That night, however, the unexpected happened. They were hit. The action actually began before the shelling, at 2015, when an enemy soldier was detected on the ARVN side of the perimeter. The guerrilla and an ARVN were killed in the ensuing brief firefight. Less than two hours later, the ARVN and Delta Company GIs heard a clanging sound echoing across the paddies from a ville about three thousand meters away. It was the sound of a mortar base plate being pounded firmly into place, which they realized when they heard the first round launch into the night sky with a hollow *thunk*.

The first round was followed quickly by another. Lieutenant Schmidt of Delta Two—who won a Silver Star for this day and night of action—was sitting beside his black platoon sergeant, S.Sgt. Freddie Walker, who was using a large banana leaf to get out of the rain. Walker sprang up, shouting, "Incoming!"—then the rounds exploded inside the laager and grunts began screaming in pain and confusion. Schmidt was stumbling toward his lines as quickly as he could in the dark when another round burst directly in front of him and a fragment nicked his nose. He didn't feel a thing, didn't know he'd been hit.

Walker went down, wounded. Schmidt reached the men he had positioned at the edge of the raised hamlet. His machine gunner, Specialist Rouska, was sprawled across Pfc. Leroy W. Bruch, the trooper to his left. Bruch had a finger blown off, and his arms and legs were peppered with shrapnel. Schmidt rolled Rouska off the screaming man. Rouska was dead. Apparently the first round had hit Bruch, and the second—which they could hear coming and which had exploded in a tree like thunder—had killed Rouska instantly as he covered Bruch with his body, riddling him with the metal fragments meant for his buddy.[2]

To Rouska's right, Private Vann was in such pain that he wasn't even aware anyone else had been hit. When the first shell had exploded to their front, Vann—stretched flat, hands on his helmet—took a fragment across his left cheek amid numerous stinging hits by rocks and debris. The earsplitting tree burst then splattered his lower back. Buckshot-sized fragments from the third round hit him in the face, and he was backing up in a desperate effort to get out of there when the fourth blast peppered his right leg, tore open the back of his left leg, and crushed his left foot. His helmet blown off and his fatigues hanging in shreds, Vann crawled rearward and slid into a shallow hole he had not seen in the dark. The pain was unreal. The toes on his left foot were twisted around, and bone was showing on his leg.

"So much muscle was gone, I thought if I didn't hold onto that leg it would literally fall off," remembered Vann, who would spend five years recovering from his wounds.

Nearby, Sergeant Olints and Pfc. Robert H. "Cowboy" Stainton, having rushed to the cover of a stone wall, huddled there in terror during the first four explosions. My God, don't let any more go off, Olints recalls thinking—then they heard the enemy hang the next salvo. Olints curled into a fetal position with his back against the stone wall, keeping one arm across his chest to protect his heart. The concussion of the explosions was terrific. Olints hurt all over, and realized that warm blood was dripping down his face. He had not been wearing a helmet, and had been hit in the top of his head by rock fragments from the wall. His left side also started burning from a single piece of hot metal that was small but had gone in deep.

Stainton had been hit, too.

Lieutenant Schmitz, who had been inspecting the company's perimeter when the shelling began, had also sought cover against the stone wall. "It was like Dante's Inferno," he wrote, "pitch-black, mortar rounds screaming in, men screaming and crying in the darkness—'Oh God, oh God, no more, no more, please stop!'—hearing the rounds leave the tube and waiting, waiting, waiting for them to impact—mortar rounds exploding in the treetops, raining white-hot shrapnel down on cowering soldiers who hadn't dug in. I was pretty fucking rattled. I felt that I had totally failed."

The casualties were dragged to the company CP when the shelling stopped. After sprinting back there himself, Schmitz secured tourniquets to one bloody GI who screamed hysterically, "I can't breathe, I can't breathe—don't let me die, LT!"

Lieutenant Schmitz's radioman, Pfc. Peter Detlef, had been seriously wounded. His artillery spotter, 2d Lt. Dan Vollmar, had been hit in the back, as had his own RTO. Schmitz shouted at Vollmar to fire their preplotted defensive targets. The mission was refused, and Schmitz grabbed the radio handset. "You gotta fire the delta tangos!" he screamed. "We're getting hit here and you're talking about 'friendly villes!' There ain't no friendly people out here!"

The mission was being refused by the operations officer of the direct support artillery battalion at Hawk Hill. "He wasn't really technically competent as an artilleryman," said Capt. Ed W. Conatser, commander of Battery B, 1-14th FA, which was under the operational control of the 3-82d FA. Conatser had four 105-mm howitzers on FSB Young. The major at Hawk Hill reported that the ARVN would not clear the mission. Captain Strand, who was monitoring the transmissions, cursed the major as a stiff-necked idiot more concerned with the rulebook than with saving lives. Acting on his own, Conatser finally ordered his gun crews to fire with a fed-up, "Shoot the fucking guns." They did, and in the morning Conatser became the subject of an official investigation. "When I gave my battery permission to fire, the mike was keyed on the artillery battalion net, and that's how they found out we were firing. They got a little pissed. The major got on the phone and threatened me with deprivation of my nuts, and said he was going to have me court-martialed."

Strand later called Conatser "one of the best guys ever to

get screwed by the army," and noted that after this incident "Conatser just signed off from his own battalion. He said, 'You need fire—I'll fire it.'"

Meanwhile, a medevac from Chu Lai and gunships from 3 Hawk Hill rendezvoused over FSB Young. Lieutenant Colonel Doyle had the medevac land near his B-TOC so he could get aboard. "I can help you find the ville because I was out there today," Doyle explained to the pilot. Doyle also wanted to get on the ground to lend some moral support to Schmitz, who was sounding shaky and tentative on the radio after this rough baptism of fire as a company commander. The Huey that landed was marked with a red cross on a white square. Medevacs had noncombatant status, and the pilot objected when Doyle ordered ammo loaded aboard.

"Don't give me any shit," Doyle snapped. "You're flying me *and* this ammo out to the company."

The wounded platoon leader, Lieutenant Schmidt, used C-4 plastic explosives and a cardboard ration box to start a fire on the dike between the two villes. Schmidt instructed the pilot to "set down right on top of this light." The C-4 burned with terrific intensity, and the Huey swung into a hover above the shimmering paddy. The propwash whipped the calf-deep water, and there was much splashing as Doyle jumped out and the wounded were loaded aboard. The Huey, too overloaded to lift directly up, regained altitude in a shallow, plane-like ascent right over the enemy ville. It drew no fire. "The next morning, it just scared the hell out of me," recalled Schmidt, "because within twenty feet of where I had lit the fire was a huge boulder that a chopper blade could have easily hit. It would have killed everybody on the chopper, plus us. I don't know how we brought that medevac in without hitting it. It was just meant to be, I guess."

Notes

1. Lieutenant Colonel Carvell had just relieved the Delta Company CO after learning that a sign had been posted in the enlisted latrine at FSB Mary Ann offering a $300 bounty for his head.

2. Rouska was recommended for the Medal of Honor. The award was downgraded to the Distinguished Service Cross because it was impossible to determine conclusively whether Rouska had meant to shield Bruch—or if the first explosion had killed him and simply rolled him lifelessly across Bruch.

4

Many Wars

"Captain Spilberg was a war fanatic," said one of his grunts. Many company commanders never fired a shot in anger. That was not their role. In contrast, Spilberg was such an active participant in his unit's firefights that he eventually started wearing a leather gauntlet on his left hand to protect his forearm from the hot metal barrel of his CAR15. "He had a Captain Ahab obsession about killing dinks, but we followed him because he knew his way around the jungle—and he wasn't afraid to do anything he asked us to do," the soldier recalled.

Captain Spilberg was lean and high-strung, with black hair, intense eyes, and a hawk-nosed profile. His call sign while commanding Company A, 1-46th Infantry, was "Odd Job" because he was "kind of nutso," as one officer put it, and specifically because of an odd job request he had made of Doyle for piano wire. Spilberg wanted to make garrotes with the wire, and train his men in hand-to-hand combat. It was another way he thought of to impress upon his troops that the war wasn't over yet. No piano wire could be found, however.

Another sign of Spilberg's attitude was the human skull he proudly displayed. He originally picked it up during two rainy days Alpha Company spent dismantling an enemy supply base containing enough demolitions to make a thousand grenades and booby traps. Enemy dead were buried at the site and Spilberg offered a three-day Chu Lai R&R to the first man to unearth a perfect skull. He ended up with several to choose from, and christened his macabre buddy "Morton" in honor of the massive amount of salt also discovered in the supply base. He had photos taken of himself kissing the skull, and one hard-drinking night with Doyle at the division officers' club, he set the skull on the bar, stuck a cigar between its teeth, and had the battalion chaplain baptize it with a can of beer. The doctors and nurses there were seriously offended, and in the morning the brigade commander read Doyle the riot act. Fearing that he would be brought up on charges, Spilberg immediately traded the skull to some rear-echelon troops for a case of steaks.

Spilberg was a long way from home. The son of a Jewish Chicago businessman, he had dropped out of college, gotten married, and joined the army at nineteen in search of adventure. He earned his sergeant stripes with the 101st Airborne Division. Following Officer Candidate School (OCS), Spilberg served a 1967–68 Vietnam tour, during which he won the BSMv and Purple Heart on a raid into Laos with the 5th Special Forces Group.

When Captain Spilberg, then almost twenty-six, assumed command of Company A, he was appalled by the bead-wearing, foot-dragging grunts in its ranks. In his own hardnosed, high-pitched way, he tightened the screws. Spilberg was accompanying a night ambush when a new man got caught up in a tangle of vines while moving into position at dusk. The soldier was on his knees, cursing out loud and giving away their position as he yanked at the vines. Spilberg came back down the column, located the source of the commotion, and pressed the muzzle of his CAR15 against the GI's mouth, whispering in a hard voice, "If I hear another word from you, you're a dead mother-fucker."

"Spilberg was a real asshole," said Lieutenant Bell, "but when I was in combat I wanted him right there—he had guts."

Captain Strand considered Spilberg suicidally aggressive.

"I didn't like Spilberg, but Doyle told me, 'Back off, he's good,'" Strand recalled. During a meeting at FSB Young, Spilberg proposed to saturate an area with multiple small patrols, to include roving three-man ambushes. Doyle agreed, but when Spilberg left, Strand exploded. "How in the hell are we going to maintain command and control with the company broken down into those teams? We don't even have enough radios!"

"You think Custer had any radios?" Lieutenant Colonel Doyle asked with a grin.

Captain Spilberg validated Doyle's faith in him on December 19, 1970, when one of his small patrols captured Senior Capt. Ne Ngoc Noi, a high-ranking member of the communist shadow government in Quang Tin Province. Noi had been a guerrilla fighter for twenty-five years. "This was one of Ho Chi Minh's originals," recalled Spilberg. He was captured by 1st Lt. James Redmond and S.Sgt. Max Braithwaite of Alpha Two when their patrol happened upon a half-dozen enemy soldiers in a hootch conducting a meeting. Redmond shouted at the guerrillas to surrender, but in response one of them whirled around the side of the building with his AK-47. He was instantly cut down. The other guerrillas got away—except for Noi, who ran out the rear door only to catch a round in the chest. Disarmed before he could use his pistol, he refused to say anything to his captors except, "Go home, Americans!"

Captain Spilberg moved to the contact area, and Noi was medevacked along with documents from the shot-up hootch that would identify him when translated. ARVN troops at FSB Young roughed Noi up. Doyle pulled them away from the prisoner's stretcher, then said through an interpreter, "Look, you've got to tell us something or I can't protect you."

Grimacing in pain, Senior Captain Noi replied only, "This is not your country; this is not your war."

On Christmas Eve, Spilberg was visiting a number of his men who were in the 91st Evac Hospital with jungle rot when he spotted Noi in a bed surrounded by intelligence officers. "Ask him if he remembers me," Spilberg said to an interpreter. Spilberg, however, had just showered, shaved, and donned a fresh set of fatigues. Noi did not recognize him. "Tell him I'm the sonofabitch that captured him," Spilberg replied. Noi pulled himself up on the bar over his bed to take a better look—then snapped off a salute and said through the interpreter, "You're a very good commander. You have very good troops. I've never been captured before."

Most of Captain Spilberg's troops would have agreed with what Noi said to Doyle. It was not their war. "Doyle and Spilberg wanted body counts, but the grunts just wanted to go home with their body parts," reflected 1st Lt. Robert J. Noonan of Alpha One. "Being a platoon leader caught in the middle was really rough."

Having followed an enemy trail to the top of a jungle-covered hill during one mission, Lieutenant Noonan's GIs spotted eight guerrillas bathing in the stream below. Noonan brought in the arty while Spilberg, apprised of the situation by radio, ordered an assault. Muttering that it was crazy, the grunts reluctantly moved down to the stream. Noonan instructed his platoon sergeant to secure the crossing site with a machine-gun team, but the Regular Army sergeant first class objected, saying that he did not want to stay behind with such a small group. Noonan made it an order, then proceeded across the stream with the rest of the platoon. "We did look for the bad guys," said Noonan, "but quite frankly we didn't look too hard because my people were scared shitless. When we came back, the platoon sergeant's group was gone. They'd already taken off back up the hill!"

The problem of motivation was insolvable. The game was too old. "You had to convince people to put their lives on the line when they knew everybody back home hated the war," recalled Lieutenant Bell, another Alpha Company platoon leader. "Spilberg used to get on us lieutenants for being good guys with the troops, but if I had gone in with the attitude that I was the lieutenant and you're going to do what I say, I may have gotten fragged."

During a patrol in December, 1970, Lieutenant Noonan was fourth in their column when the point man crested a rise and caught four enemy soldiers coming out of the tree line below. He opened up on automatic—the range was about fifty meters—but fired high in his excitement. Noonan brought his M16 down on one of the guerrillas as they turned back for the trees, hitting him in the chest. The man kept crawling and an M60 gunner raked him, blowing part of his head away. The platoon moved out in pursuit, but Noonan, being new, stopped the sweep so he could search the dead man for intelligence material. The guerrilla turned out to be an exceptionally young-looking medic.

"LT," a grunt shouted, "this ain't a good place to be stopping—we're all out in the open here!"

Noonan was too busy on the radio to listen. "LT," the grunt finally barked in a menacing tone, "you'd better get us out of here right now—or something's going to happen!"

The sweep continued. Lieutenant Noonan was still new to the platoon when he broke up its best point team, making point man Sp4 Carl E. Cleek an acting squad leader, and assigning his slack man to another squad so as to spread their experience around. Angered, Cleek handed Noonan a 40-mm grenade launcher round on which he had written the lieutenant's name. Noonan made the best of it, laughing that he would carry it as a good luck charm.

During a patrol shortly thereafter, Cleek sat down on his rucksack, angry and exhausted. They were lost. "This piss-poor lieutenant," he muttered when they passed the same paddy dike for the second time. Noonan was actually a decent, conscientious leader—the well-respected Sergeant Concepcion considered him a "great guy"—but to an aggressive, immature country boy like Cleek the LT was simply green, green, green. Noonan had once called in a marking round, only to have it explode fifty meters away instead of five hundred as planned. "Enough of this shit," spat Cleek. He passed the word for the LT to come back to his position, then unholstered his .38-caliber Smith and Wesson. "I cocked it, and when the lieutenant came around the bend I was just going to shoot him," he later said. "I wasn't going to kill him, but I was going to wound him enough to get him out. I knew I was going to get it, but I felt it was better to go ahead and maybe pull a year in the Long Binh Jail than for this lieutenant to get my platoon killed."

Luckily, it was Sergeant First Class Reed, the platoon sergeant, who came back to see what Cleek wanted. Reed took one look at the snub-nosed revolver and said, "What're you doin', Cleek?"

"I'm going to shoot that damn LT!"

"You can't do that."

"Yes, I can! I'm going to send him home!"

"Well, no," said Sergeant Reed, who was a tall, black career NCO. "But let me ask you this: if we put you back on point, do you think you can get us to where we're supposed to be going?"

"Without a doubt," said Cleek, putting his revolver away.

Captain Spilberg remembered Cleek as a "tough little soldier"—not for the lieutenant he almost shot, but for the guerrilla he did shoot. Moving down a trail that was suspiciously well traveled, Cleek halted his squad and set off alone to recon the area. He packed a 12-gauge shotgun. Reaching a hootch, he stepped off into the brush just as a bareheaded guerrilla came around it with an AK-47. The man started down the trail, thinking he was alone. Cleek's heart was pounding, and when the enemy soldier was six feet away he cut loose with his shotgun from where he stood unseen in the bushes, hitting the man in the chest. He emptied the shotgun, then—because he was scared to death—yanked his revolver out and shot the dead man six more times.

Elite in comparison to the line platoons, 1st Lt. Carl D. Hewitt's Reconnaissance Platoon, Company E, 1-46th Infantry, made its heaviest contact during a search for a VC/NVA base camp on a jungled hill mass ten kilometers southwest of FSB Young. The mission began on January 7, 1971, after Hewitt reconned the target from a LOH. Deciding on an indirect approach that involved swinging wide and then moving in from the west, Hewitt's fifteen-man platoon left the firebase, marched west on the muddy main road, then turned south and disappeared into the jungle. Moving silently through this cover, Echo Recon broke out late the next day. The platoon was regrouping among some banana trees that skirted an abandoned rice paddy when two of the men approached Hewitt.

"LT, we just saw a dink across those paddies," one said, pointing to a tree line three hundred meters north. "He was wearing a white shirt. He saw us—and then he disappeared."

Hewitt decided not to pursue. If the man was a guerrilla and not just a villager, he wouldn't have worn white unless he wanted to be seen. Perhaps he was the lure for an ambush. Fearing the platoon might have been compromised, several Recon GIs wanted to press on and hit the base camp before the enemy could get organized. The camp was three hundred meters east of the platoon's present position. Hewitt disagreed. The men were exhausted from humping all day through the thick stuff, and it was already dusk—a bad time to start a fight. In addition, he wasn't convinced that it hadn't been just a farmer out there. They set up for the night amid the banana trees, deploying claymores and flares, then slinging hammocks with ponchos overhead to keep them dry. It was a common practice, but an unprofessional one, for the sound of rain on a poncho was distinct, and moonlight reflected off the wet surface.

Lieutenant Hewitt, a twenty-one-year-old Tennessean who had dropped out of college to get to the war, later regarded his decision not to press on as a terrible tactical error, although most of Recon had agreed with him—and respected him. Sergeant Michael Norris, walking point the next morning, had just started down the trail to the enemy camp—it was January 9, and the tension was as thick as the mist hanging over the paddies—when he spotted the footprints of someone who had approached their NDP during the night. Advancing cautiously with his M16 on semiautomatic, Norris watched the front and right while Sp4 Robert J. Downey, the slack man, covered the left side of the trail. Hewitt was third in the column, followed by the rest of the platoon, which maintained a good interval between each man. Recon usually avoided trails, but the brush to either side of this one was too thick to pass through with a rucksack. Chopping through would only give them away, forcing Hewitt to choose between the trails or the paddies to the north and south, which were even more exposed. Once they reached the hill mass, though, they could disappear into the jungle that covered it.

Sergeant Norris had seen heavy combat with the 4th Division in 1967–68, and again in 1970 before the unit was withdrawn and he was transferred to the American. A country boy from Kentucky, he took fifteen minutes to cover the hundred meters to a left turn in the trail, beyond which it ran straight toward the enemy hill. Norris was shocked at how exposed he was when he turned the corner. The VC/NVA, stripping to their shorts to get through the brush, had positioned an RPD light machine gun beyond the curve so as to fire straight down that part of the trail. Norris saw the barrel move when he was only thirty paces from it and fired his M16 as he jumped to the left. The machine gun opened up at the same time. Norris, firing from the prone, saw his rounds shaking the big bush that shielded the RPD, but when he went to change magazines he realized he'd been hit. The thumb on his left hand was hanging by a thread of skin, flapping around as he slapped the fresh magazine in and snapped the bolt back. He had also been shot in the right leg, just above the ankle. His jungle boot was torn open, and blood was pumping out.

More guerrillas had wormed themselves into the tangle on the left side of the trail, and they opened fire with AK-47s. "They were right on top of us," remembered Lieutenant Hewitt. Private Lloyd, a black machine gunner, wheeled around with his M60 to return fire but dropped with two rounds in his chest. One of the medics—"Doc" Johnson, who was also black—caught a round in his elbow as he tried to scramble forward. Somehow unscathed, Hewitt fell backward, his head and shoulders propped up by his rucksack. Unable to twist out of it, and feeling insanely exposed, he threw his four grenades over his head and into the bushes, dirt clods and debris pelting him from the explosions.

Out of grenades, Hewitt, who won the Silver Star for this action, flipped his M16 on automatic and while still on his back blasted away until there was a lull in the enemy fire. The lieutenant thought he was the sole survivor—no one else was firing—and expected to die on the spot. Up ahead, slack-man Downey, a shy, quiet kid on his second tour with the American, looked back during the lull to see the platoon's rucksacks sitting in a row on the trail. It looked to him as though everyone had pulled back. Then he spotted an enemy soldier stepping out of the tall elephant grass to grab one of the packs. He could see the silhouette of a second guerrilla behind the first. Winning a BSMv, Downey—in a prone firing position with his M16—squeezed off a single shot, dropping the first VC/NVA. The second one spun around, AK-47 blazing. One of the rounds grazed the top of Downey's left hand on his rifle stock, punching down at an angle through his chest right below the hollow in his throat—breaking his clavicle, puncturing and collapsing his right lung, and exiting under his right arm. He dropped his head to the ground, trying to get his bearings. Still gripping his rifle, he looked back up and saw that the second guerrilla had stepped from the brush to drag his dead comrade back into cover. Downey shot him, too.

Subsequently awarded the Silver Star for continuing to fight despite a maimed hand, Sergeant Norris pumped off several magazines at the RPD before his M16 jammed on blood and gristle in the chamber. Crawling back to Downey, who had passed out, Norris recovered his slack-man's M16. The lull suddenly ended with the sharp blast of a whistle, the enemy's signal to rush the trail. "We all held our fire for a couple of seconds when they opened up," wrote Pfc. Brad L. Brown in a letter to his wife. The second to last man in line, Brown—a soft-spoken soldier from Montana—had gone down with green tracers zipping all around him. He sought cover by squeezing behind his rucksack. "Everyone thought at first they were the only one alive. Perhaps by holding our fire, it drew them out of their positions. After the first fusillade they rushed us, and then we opened fire."

Norris, meanwhile, saw a U.S.-made frag bouncing his way, safety spoon flying off. Knowing he had five seconds, he reached for it to fling it away but couldn't bring himself to pick it up. He tried to get up to run, but his leg wouldn't support him, so Norris began crawling as fast as he could. The grenade exploded before he could get clear, shredding his left buttocks.

The guerrillas screamed and fired as they came on, and Brown blasted one who stood up just a few feet in front of his barrel. The man was lunging forward as Brown fired, and his movement carried him into Brown even though he was dead. "It was very chaotic," Brown wrote. "We had to sometimes hold our fire because they were in between some of our men. I remember opening fire then looked up the trail and saw our M60 gunner standing up and shooting into the grass and brush and dinks running all over."

The platoon's back-up machine gunner, S.Sgt. Frank S. Ferguson, a black veteran of two earlier combat tours with the 25th Infantry Division, won the BSMv for gaining fire superiority with his M60. Brown received the Army Commendation Medal for valor (ARCOMv). The enemy to the left of the trail were devastated—a seriously wounded VC would be captured in the shredded vegetation—but the RPD around the bend was still firing. The platoon sergeant, Sgt. Jack R. "Mad Jack" Farmer, rushed toward the machine gun, pausing momentarily beside Sgt. Ervin E. Powell, who was up near the point team. Powell had been hit in the opening burst—a round had grazed the side of his neck, leaving an angry red welt. While Powell had been firing from the paddy to the right, a guerrilla had suddenly appeared in front of him, throwing down his empty AK-47. Panicked and looking for cover, the man jumped over the berm between the trail and the paddy—right onto Powell, who shoved him away. Powell held his fire as the guerrilla, a teenager, simply sat there shaking.

"We gotta knock out that machine gun up there and get the wounded off the road!" Farmer shouted to Powell.

"Well, let's go."

"Whaddya gonna do with this dink?"

Powell swung his M16 toward the unarmed, shell-shocked guerrilla. "I should never have done it, but I blew him away. I wasn't going to leave him behind us. That's the way it was. The burst just cartwheeled him out of the way." Farmer and Powell ran up to Norris and Downey. Norris was still firing. Farmer had an XM203 rifle/grenade launcher, and after thumping a few shells at the RPD position, he advanced on the left side of the trail with Powell on the right. The RPD was concealed by a large bush. "We shot the hell out of it," remembered Powell. "I just held my M16 at waist level and kept walking and firing on automatic—and when we got up there, there's three guys lying there with little holes all over them, smokin'. I was kind of in shock by then."

Sergeant Powell won the Silver Star.

* * *

At approximately 2200 on January 13, Alpha Company was shelled by U.S. mortars. Lieutenant Bell had the company at the time—Spilberg was in the rear, checking on a resupply problem—and it was securing the artillery on FSB Mary Ann. The incident began when the grunts on an Alpha One guard bunker spotted an enemy recon team in the trash dump outside the wire at the north end of the perimeter. In response, the 81-mm mortar section on the hill put six rounds in the air. Unfortunately, a computation error caused the salvo to land on the bunker line, setting off several high explosive (HE) and white phosphorus shells in an artillery gun pit.

The fire threatened to spread to the artillery ammo bunker, but Bell, along with Sgts. Kenneth J. Fair and John F. Cannon, a black squad leader on his third tour, put out the roaring blaze with fire extinguishers. All three were awarded the ARCOMv.

Meanwhile, the Alpha One GIs, thinking they were under attack, hastily manned the trench line linking the bunkers and commenced firing into the wire. Lieutenant Noonan, winning a BSMv for his efforts, ran to a demolished bunker and found one of his sergeants crawling away in shock, the back of his head a bloody mess. The ammo fire was still being fought at that point, and Noonan ordered everyone under cover in case the bunker blew. When the others were safe, he and a select few used stretchers to carry the injured to the aid station.

Five infantrymen and three artillerymen had been wounded, and Pfc. Harold E. Carr, a black Alpha One GI, had been killed by a single metal sliver that pierced his skull inside the wrecked bunker.

Illumination burst over FSB Mary Ann to guide the medevac in through the damp overcast, and as the Huey landed on the resupply pad the entire perimeter erupted with small-arms fire to suppress possible enemy action. Spilberg helicoptered back in the morning and conducted a memorial service with the battalion chaplain. Spilberg wrote home that Carr—a devout Baptist from Nashville—had been "very well liked" and that he "always did his job well." During the ceremony, Spilberg stood behind the traditional upturned rifle, a helmet on the butt and a pair of jungle boots at attention in front. "I spoke a few words, but there is really not much to say. For a man that dies on the field of battle you can speak of the honor of laying down one's life for one's country. But how does one speak of a man who died in his sleep because of a stupid error on the part of a fellow soldier. It's sad, very sad. . . ."

"Coming to the rear was like getting off a spaceship on a strange planet," Captain Spilberg wrote after Company A stood down in Chu Lai, January 22–24, 1971. "The grunts were clean in the jungle—no drugs—and in the jungle, we did not have the time or inclination to judge each other by race. You could either depend on a man or you could not. Color had nothing to do with it." In Chu Lai, everything changed. "Without the shared risk and mutual dependence of combat there was no brotherhood, and the rear was out of control with drug and racial problems," Spilberg wrote.

Half the grunts drank during stand-down, the rest smoked marijuana. "There was almost total pandemonium after being straight in the bush," said Pfc. Edward C. Gittens of Alpha One.

One grenadier in the Professionals later stated:

Drugs were readily available, and incredibly cheap. For three bucks you got what looked like a regular carton of Kents—but every cigarette in every pack had been replaced with machine-rolled, opium-dipped joints. Each package was then resealed, and so was the carton.

Heroin was two bucks a gram—and you could buy the stuff off a five-year-old kid. The kids used to wear army OD hats with little green cloth strips sewed inside them, tacked down every half-inch—just enough to slip a vial of heroin in. When a kid took off his hat, there would be rows and rows of heroin vials inside.

The heroin, better known as "smack," was so pure it could be either snorted or smoked in a menthol cigarette. Marijuana was strong, but heroin had no smell. "You could be talking to the captain and smoking smack, getting blowed plumb away, and he'd never know," said Specialist Cleek, the Alpha One point man.

Marijuana was not really a problem compared to alcohol. Heroin was. It was too easy to get strung out. "I never smoked pot in the bush, and I never smoked smack until I was reassigned to the rear," said Private Gittens, who transferred to the 196th Brigade headquarters after picking up a Purple Heart in February, 1971.

I was overloaded, and the heroin was self-medication. It mellowed you out, it helped you sleep. Finally, it was taking more and more to do less and less, and I decided I had to wean myself off the junk. I was smoking a pack a day, and I started smoking one less cigarette a day, and I loaded them more lightly than usual. It was hard at the end, but I couldn't go home a junkie.

"You're in a firefight and some asshole high on shit could shoot you in the back," said Sgt. James L. Salmen of Company C. He said he had three "soul brothers" in his squad who were hooked on smack:

They'd fall asleep on guard because they were on drugs, or plain didn't give a shit. When I confronted them, they told me to fuck off, it wasn't none of my business. I'm a pretty big farm boy, and I hit one up alongside his head with my rifle butt. I had to look over my shoulder a lot because they threatened my life. I had people backing me up, and we finally told the company commander that these guys were going to get somebody killed. They shipped their asses back to the rear.

According to white officers and enlisted men, most of the battalion GIs awaiting court-martial for drug use or for refusing orders to go to the field or who were shamming with bogus medical problems, were black. They occupied a barracks in the 1-46th Infantry rear. "They basically terrorized the rear," said one NCO. "The officers accommodated them because if you tried to do anything you would just create more commotion," said another sergeant.

Black Power militants throughout the 23d Division, believing their war was at home, not in Vietnam, expressed their outrage with organized protests—and with grenades, usually the tear-gas type for shock effect, but sometimes fragmentation grenades.

Drug dealers also used grenades to intimidate—or to kill or wound—officers and NCOs who tried to maintain discipline.

Chu Lai pulsed with violence. During the first night of Alpha Company's stand-down, Gittens left the partying with his buddy "Peachy," and crashed, stoned, on a pile of duffel bags in the company supply room. There was a racket outside, and they found two Chicano buddies in a drunken, cursing, bare-knuckle brawl in the pouring rain. Gittens and Peachy pulled them apart, and the two stumbled off arm in arm. One of the Chicanos felt himself to have been challenged, however, and Gittens and Peachy were sleeping again among the duffel bags when the door suddenly flew open, the light went on, and there the guy was with a .45-caliber automatic pointed at them. "So, you fuckers want to fight!" he screamed. Peachy, a big, boisterous GI, jumped up, thrust his finger at the madman, and walked right at him shouting, "You sonofabitch, you better not be pointin' that thing at me and not be plannin' on usin' it!" Peachy jerked the .45 out of the Chicano's hand, ejected the magazine, and hit him in the head with the butt. He then returned the unloaded weapon and screamed at the guy to get the hell out. Before Gittens and Peachy went back to sleep they stacked duffel bags against the door. The next day they told the sobered-up Chicano about the incident, but he could hardly remember it.

Lieutenant Noonan was moving with a squad down a jungled finger sticking out into a paddy, when the point team opened fire on a VC/NVA ville at the tip. The guerrillas sprinted away across the water-filled paddies toward a nearby hill. Sergeant Concepcion was moving down a fingerlike ridge on Noonan's right flank with another squad. Because it jutted out all the way to the hill, they were able to put flanking fire on the retreating enemy. Concepcion's machine gunner thought he dropped two of the guerrillas. The rest disappeared into the brush at the base of the hill and Noonan's squad moved out in pursuit. He and his men had just started sloshing across the paddy when they came under heavy fire.

Lieutenant Noonan pulled back to the ville at the tip of the finger and radioed a request for arty support. Captain Spilberg denied it, unwilling to give the enemy time to continue their retreat while Noonan worked up a call for fire. "You don't need artillery," Spilberg told Noonan. "You've got your machine guns and grenade launchers—get across there, lieutenant!"

Noonan passed the order to assault. "Fuck you, sir!" Private Gittens shouted over the din as he manned his M60 from behind a stone wall in the ville, bullet-clipped leaves dropping past his helmet. "The other pig's jammed, and mine ain't enough to suppress the dinks' fire!" Others felt the same way, so Noonan, improvising, kept his squad's fire going while Concepcion worked toward the enemy's flank hill along his narrow ridge. Concepcion's squad then halted and laid down a base of fire for Noonan, who finally got his element going. Noonan, in the lead as they hit the hill, kept waiting for a guerrilla to pop up and blow him away, but the enemy soldiers were gone by then, leaving only a blood trail. Afterward, Noonan asked his radioman what would have happened had he insisted on an unsupported assault across the paddy. The trooper said, "LT, you would have been the only one going."

It was a difficult time to be a leader. "We did our jobs halfway," recalled Sergeant Concepcion, who had volunteered for duty in Vietnam. The grunts knew they were not fighting to win, "and we kind of compromised with them. We could have done a better job, but it wasn't that kind of war."

Captain Spilberg wrote home that he had to "chew out" his lieutenants because they "want to be nice guys and be buddies with their men. First names, *asking* their men to do things instead of *telling* them, and all sorts of other small things that affect discipline. There are certain rules of the Infantry that cannot be broken and if you do break them men die. . . ."

Captain Spilberg violated one of his own cardinal rules on January 26, when he laagered Alpha Company atop the same grassy knoll he had used as a patrol base two months earlier. "That was my biggest mistake," he later said, noting that the guerrillas were known to booby-trap old NDPs. As the grunts set up on the hill, Noonan tied his flank in with S.Sgt. George L. Robertson, the Alpha Three platoon sergeant. Noonan liked Robertson; previously, back on the firebase, this sharp black career NCO had handed him a couple beers and said, "Look, LT, you're doin' a pretty good job, don't let the captain get you down."

After Noonan and Robertson had set their machine guns in overlooking the likeliest avenues of enemy approach, et cetera, Noonan said, "Well, let's take another walk around the perimeter to make sure."

"After you," said Robertson.

"No, after you," said Noonan, joking back.

The hilltop was covered with GI garbage. Sergeant Robertson took two or three steps away from Noonan, grabbed a pole that had supported a poncho hootch the last time they'd been there—and disappeared in a roar of black smoke.

The pole had been booby-trapped. Lieutenant Noonan, blown off his feet by the explosion, realized that he was speckled with blood. He thought he'd been wounded, but he had not. The gore was from Robertson, who had been killed instantly—emasculated, an arm blown off, a leg blown off—his body thrown about thirty feet down the side of the hill, where it got caught up in some rocks. Noonan made his way down to the body, which was still smoking, then called for "Doc" Riley, his medic, to bring a poncho. Unable to find Robertson's missing limbs, they trussed his body up in the poncho. Noonan vomited, then he and Riley started back up with the body, moving a careful step at a time.

Sergeant Robertson was twenty-four years old at the time. "They spelled out his name phonetically when they radioed in the casualty report, and when I heard it I just about died," remembered Lieutenant Bell, then serving as the company executive officer in Chu Lai. He had been in the rear only four days—after spending six months in the bush with Alpha Three. "I'm from Arkansas and I had never been around black people, but I go to Vietnam and here's this black man as my platoon sergeant. Robertson and I became really close friends." After one contact, Bell was on point as they followed a blood trail down a path. When they rounded a corner, Robertson, in the slack position, saw a guerrilla pop out of a hootch ahead of them. The enemy soldier leveled his AK-47 at Bell, who didn't see him because he had his head down, looking for trip wires. Robertson jumped on Bell's back, pushed him down, and covered the lieutenant's body with his own as the guerrilla emptied his magazine all around them. "Then the dink disappeared and we realized we were still alive. Of course, we didn't say anything, but after the war I named my son after George Robertson."

Captain Spilberg had just opened his canteen when the BT exploded. He was spun around and dropped flat on his face by a rock that hit his left shoulder and two fragments that caught his left hand, whipping his arm behind him with such force that he initially thought it had been blown off. Getting back to his feet, Spilberg saw seven or eight men sprawled about with concussions and minor wounds. Dust and smoke hung in the air.

"Nobody move!" Spilberg shouted. "We're getting out the way we came up. Okay, everybody stand up—turn around—take one step at a time, and look where you're walking. . . ."

Captain Spilberg won a BSMv for getting Company A off the booby-trapped hill without further injury. Lieutenant Bell took over after Spilberg was medevacked. The company made heavy contact on January 28 when Lieutenant Noonan and Alpha One skirted the left flank of a hill mass, then came upon a manioc field at the base of the hill, divided by a low stone wall. The point man stepped through an entranceway in the wall and hit a buried bear trap. He was quickly freed from its jaws without injury, but Noonan and Concepcion, the acting platoon sergeant, smelled trouble. They immediately put the men under cover and got their machine guns set up. Their mission was to link up with Bell in the valley they had entered by coming around the hill. The ridge at the end of the valley had campfire smoke of unknown origin rising from it, so Noonan and Concepcion squatted behind some bushes and studied their map for a covered approach to the area. They determined that their best option was to move into the foothills to their left. Noonan glanced at a little ville, apparently deserted, at the edge of the foothills about a hundred meters to their left front. He saw an old papasan. When he looked again the papasan was gone—and shots suddenly rang out from the ville. Concepcion went down with a bullet through the neck. Noonan, turning toward him, took a round in the muscle of his left shoulder. He saw the spray of blood, but couldn't believe it. Feeling no pain, he grabbed his platoon sergeant's collar and dragged him behind a boulder as shots cracked all around them.

Sp4 Michael P. Riley rushed to the boulder, pulling his rucksack over his head for some meager protection. Concepcion wasn't breathing. Riley was scuttling back toward the stone wall like a crab when he saw Concepcion move a hand. The medic screamed for help, and Sergeant Fair, a squad leader, responded, helping Riley to drag Concepcion back behind the wall. Riley had just started working on Concepcion when a round kicked up dirt between the sergeant's sprawled legs, and he hurriedly dragged him to a safer spot along the wall.

"Doc, how do you think he'll do?" Noonan asked.

"I don't think he'll make it." said Riley.

Sergeant Concepcion was paralyzed. The round, which had entered the right side of his neck and exited on the left—where it drilled through his shoulder—had concussed three vertebrae, numbing him from the neck down and collapsing his lungs.

While the platoon returned fire, Noonan, Fair, and Riley took turns giving Concepcion mouth-to-mouth resuscitation. The sergeant sputtered back to life—but he didn't want to spend the rest of his life a paralyzed shell. "Please, just let me die," Concepcion mumbled as Riley wrapped battle dressings around his neck.

"Fuck no!" Doc Riley replied. While Noonan and Fair kept up the mouth-to-mouth, the medic never stopped encouraging Concepcion. "Hey, you're on your way home, buddy . . . you're going to make it, man . . . you're going to make it. . . ."

As it turned out, the round had passed just in front of

Concepcion's spine, missing the major arteries in his throat. He would recover. He would walk again.

Meanwhile, Lieutenant Noonan had a bandage slapped on his shoulder while he worked two radios—one to the medevac and one to Bell who was moving up with the rest of Company A. Arty started shaking the hillside where the snipers were ensconced. Noonan told the medevac pilot arriving on station that the LZ was not secure, but the pilot was willing to land as gunships rocketed the ville to cover the medevac's approach. Concepcion was loaded aboard in a hastily constructed litter, a poncho secured between bamboo poles. Noonan jumped on, too. The Huey was just lifting off, taking hits, when Noonan saw one of his squad leaders drop while rushing back to cover after helping load Concepcion. The Huey swung back around, landed again, and the wounded squad leader scrambled aboard. He had been shot in the hand.

Captain Spilberg helicoptered back out to FSB Young when he saw the medevac land at the 91st Evac Hospital. Resuming command of Alpha Company, he wrote home that ARVN intelligence, which would prove inaccurate in this particular, had predicted a ground assault on the base. "I hope this is true," he added, "because we have taken quite a few casualties without killing any Viets and it would do the men good to see some dead ones."

Part III

Blindman's Buff

Lieutenant Colonel Doyle's first operation was highly successful. During the three-month mission, he lost three men killed in action, plus one by friendly fire, while accounting for 150 kills from the guerrilla battalion in the FSB Young AO. "We annihilated that battalion, at least as far as effectiveness goes," stated Doyle. His next operation, which began in late January, 1971, when the monsoon petered out and the Professionals returned to FSB Mary Ann, and which continued through February, was against those elements of the 37th NVA Transportation Group securing the caches and infiltration routes southwest of the firebase. It was a frustrating affair. The NVA, intimately familiar with the terrain, operated in two- and three-man teams known as "trail watchers," and they inflicted multiple casualties in ambushes that usually lasted less than sixty seconds. "We were running razorback ridgelines in triple-canopy jungle where you couldn't see anything," observed Lieutenant Schmitz. Fire support was a mess because the artillery shells tended to detonate in the top of the thick jungle cover. "There was no room to maneuver, and you couldn't hack your way through at more than a hundred meters per hour," said the lieutenant. "We'd totally lost the element of surprise. You were just going to walk up there until somebody punched you square in the nose again. I don't know who the genius was that thought of this operation, but it wasn't going anywhere."

5

Chargin' Charlie

When Captain Knight and Company C combat assaulted into the mountains eight kilometers southwest of FSB Mary Ann on January 24, 1971, the troops were glad to be getting back to what they remembered as a quiet area. "You're going to like this place," a squad leader told one of his replacements before they boarded the Hueys that picked the company up in the FSB Young AO. That area had been hot. The sense of security around FSB Mary Ann, however, was such that after Company C humped up a steep slope to establish a hilltop NDP, the company potheads lit up as the sun went down. "Actually, I had a lot of fun over there," recalled one of the marijuana smokers, a grenadier. He and several buddies snapped their ponchos together to make a little shelter in the space they had hacked out of the brush. They had a small portable tape player turned low as they passed the weed. "We were just trying to make the best of it. You had to be pretty cool about it. There were guys totally against it, but you knew who was who and you weren't obvious about it. You just wanted to sit back and take the edge off."

Captain Knight separated his platoons the next day, intent on locating those branches of the Dak Rose Trail winding through the jungle where the Tranh and Nam Nim Rivers met. The NVA, dormant during the monsoon, were running the trails again. Towards dusk on the fifth day of the mission, January 28, Knight radioed 1st Lt. Peter K. Doyle of Charlie One, whose platoon had just set up atop a sharp incline overlooking a tributary running west from where the Tranh curved south into the Nam Nim. Knight instructed him to recon the blueline for a crossing site so the company could cross in the morning. Doyle moved down with a five-man patrol, carrying the platoon's empty canteens with them. Three men deployed to provide security while the other two knelt in the open, filling canteens. When they were done, Doyle started across on some boulders that were mostly underwater. Halfway to the other side, he ran out of stepping-stones, so he turned around, only to realize that one of his troops had been following him step for step.

"Jesus, we *both* don't need to get killed out here!" Doyle blurted before they doubled back to their starting point.

Lieutenant Doyle told Sergeant Dutcher to cover him while he climbed a twelve-foot-high boulder that was snug against the hillside at the waterline. Doyle figured he could spot a crossing site from there, and he was one handclasp from the top when an AK-47 suddenly opened fire right over his head. There was an NVA in a crevice atop the boulder. "I'm not sure he was an honest-to-God sniper," Doyle later reflected about this, his first time under fire. He noted that the NVA had held his fire when the patrol had been in the open filling canteens. "I think he was some poor bastard heading east who'd just stopped there when he heard GIs coming down. He probably wanted us to get our water and go back up, but then here comes this asshole climbing up his rock." Doyle froze, expecting the next burst in his head, but Dutcher was already returning fire, hitting the AK's ammo magazine, it was later determined, and disabling the weapon. Doyle, who was flush against the boulder bracing himself with both feet and one arm, swung his M16 over his head with his free hand and started blasting away, too. His magazine emptied, he went limp and slid down the boulder into the water. "All I had to do was take three steps to my left around this rock, out into the tributary, and I'd probably have had this guy dead in my sights as he headed back to Hanoi—but after getting down in the water there was a period of time before I could even make my mouth work."

In the confusion, Pfc. William G. Cahill, a great, gung ho soldier who humped an XM203—an M16 with a tubelike 40-mm grenade launcher under the barrel—was spraying the trees across the tributary, the likeliest place for a sniper.

"Cahill, grenades, grenades!" Doyle shouted, unsure if the NVA on the boulder had really taken off. "He's behind you!"

Cahill fired two grenades over the boulder, then the patrol moved cautiously up the incline. The NVA was gone, but there was a blood trail dotting a path along the blueline. The grunts, following it around a curve in the tributary, spotted the enemy soldier about two hundred meters farther downstream. He was in full flight and, as the patrol opened fire, Cahill lobbed another round, knocking the man down in an explosive puff of smoke.

The grunts cheered, but then the NVA got back up, dropped his weapon, and limped away into the brush. "Fuck!" Cahill exclaimed, as he frantically reloaded and pumped off another grenade. The patrol recovered the man's AK-47, but only briefly pursued the now-heavy blood trail that led away through the bushes. It was already dusk, and the situation was ripe for ambush.

The next morning, January 29, Captain Knight reassembled Charlie Company at the tributary and, with Charlie Two in the lead, used ropes to ford the swift, chest-deep stream. Once across, the point team, moving out along a trail, had gone only fifty meters when it spotted a squad-sized NVA supply party coming in their direction. "The point team opened fire, killing two while the rest of the NVA fled back down the trail," recounted Lieutenant Doyle. The GIs in Charlie Two and Three dropped their rucks, and took off in hot pursuit; Knight ordered Doyle to move up and secure the contact area with Charlie One. "The two dead NVA on the trail were very small, and wore nothing but green gym shorts," Doyle wrote. "Someone had placed a cigarette in the mouth of one of the dead NVA. Everyone laughed at how silly he looked. I ordered the cigarette removed, and told the men to leave the bodies alone. Both of the enemy soldiers had sealed metal containers on their backs, which weighed about as much as they did. They had also been carrying two mortar rounds each, tied to either end of a rope suspended around their necks like a yoke."

Unable to regain contact with the enemy supply party, Captain Knight moved back to Charlie One, then the entire company humped up a ridge west of the Nam Nim River. "The sun was beating down as we walked slowly up this steep trail which zig-zagged up the side of the ridge," wrote Doyle. The battalion chaplain, Capt. Neal Davidson, humped along with them. Charlie Company dug in along the crest of the ridge. That night, one of Doyle's perimeter guards reported a dim light about four hundred meters to the east. When Doyle requested permission to fire the defensive target previously plotted on that area, he was joined at his position by Knight and his forward observer, plus the other platoon leaders. "We took turns calling in the fire mission," Doyle recalled. "Some of us chose high-explosive rounds which detonated on impact, while others chose proximity fuses which would result in an airburst over the suspected enemy position. The light disappeared within five minutes."

The forward observer, 1st Lt. John L. "Larry" Hogan, knew the cost of the various types of ordnance being used, and kept a running total as each round went in. The final tab was twenty thousand dollars.

In the morning, Charlie One led the company out of the NDP, heading east toward the Nam Nim. Sergeant Salmen's squad, walking point, moved parallel to a well-worn trail running down the center of the ridgeline. Within four hundred meters they spotted enemy fighting holes. "We approached cautiously with one squad on either side of the trail," Doyle later wrote. The trail was lined with punji pits, but the bamboo stakes were rotted away. "Just beyond the punji pits, a position of the type used to accommodate a .51-cal machine gun had been dug in the center of the trail," Doyle wrote. "Perhaps the light of the previous evening had been an attempt by the enemy to reoccupy these positions. It was definitely a scary scene. We continued along the ridge, and at one point we walked straight through a swinging-gate booby trap before we saw it. Fortunately, it was collapsed and overgrown."

Later in the day, Charlie One secured an LZ on the left side of the trail and Lieutenant Colonel Doyle choppered in to confer with Captain Knight. That evening, Knight issued his operations order for the following day. Company C was going to continue east into the river valley where caches were thought to be located. Enemy resistance was expected. "This was the first time I had been part of a textbook-type battle plan," Lieutenant Doyle wrote. "If even half the things described in the briefing were accurate, we were in for a hell of a day. I went to sleep that night saying Hail Mary's until I fell asleep."

Doyle's turn was coming, but on the morning of January 31 it was 1st Lt. Frank M. Brosnan's platoon, Charlie Three, that ran into trouble after working its way down to the Nam Nim. Brosnan faced the river—map in one hand, compass in the other—and an AK-47 suddenly cracked from the hillside fifty meters behind where he was standing. The round hit Brosnan in the left lower back and exited through his stomach, an excruciating wound. The grunts, who'd been leaning back on their rucks resting, scrambled for cover as the sniper emptied his magazine, then swept the jungled hillside with automatic fire. While one squad fanned out and conducted an unsuccessful search for the sniper, the other two moved Brosnan to a small clearing and whacked down enough brush so that it would accommodate a medevac. Afterwards as the platoon backed out of the area, it called artillery down on the hillside, which seemed mostly an exercise in wishful thinking.

The action along the Nam Nim was just beginning.

Destined to die ingloriously in the sapper attack, Captain Knight originally took over Company C, 1-46th Infantry, with much bravado on October 18, 1970. "The captain he replaced was just doing his time, and wanted out of the bush," said 1st Lt. Daniel J. Mack, then the Charlie Two platoon leader. Twenty-four-year-old Captain Knight—who was short, slender, and boyish-looking with his crew cut and glasses—got his first look at Charlie Company at a unit formation on one of the helipads at FSB Mary Ann.

"Most new company commanders would give long talks about their goals and what they expected from their units," recalled Mack, "but Knight's talk was only about twenty seconds long. He said he was now in charge and that his main goal was body counts. That was it!"

Captain Knight, a native of Lake Wales, Florida, where his parents owned a restaurant, dropped out of college to join the army. After earning an OCS commission and paratrooper wings, he was badly wounded while serving with the Americal Division in 1968. The joke among Knight's contemporaries when he joined Company C was that he was a two-time loser, that nobody could be so unlucky as to be assigned twice to the rotten Americal. He was, however, exactly what his draftees needed. Lieutenant Doyle observed that:

> Captain Knight was just one of those commanders who inspired a lot of confidence. He was aggressive, but he cared very deeply about his people—more so than other commanders I saw in Vietnam.
>
> When Captain Knight traveled with the individual platoons, he would often go tramping up to the point of the file with his whole CP. It used to make me nervous, but once when I called him on it and asked him to be careful, he growled, "This is my sandbox, and I'm only letting you play in it, lieutenant."

Lieutenant Mack noted that "Knight got involved with the guys. He'd walk the perimeter in the evening and sit down and talk with them. He had the respect of every man in that company."

"The whole attitude changed under Captain Knight," said Sp4 Dennis J. Murphy, a grenadier in Charlie One. "We finally had a leader we really cared about. He let you know he wasn't there to just go through the motions. He demanded perfection."

Lieutenant Mack remembered that:

> Captain Knight was so gung ho that even when the company was on the firebase between missions, he would arrange to fly in the LOH scout ships. He would also

volunteer my services. I was his favorite platoon leader, and he'd say, "C'mon, Dan, you're gonna enjoy this!"

Knight sat next to the pilot in the copilot's seat, and I'd cram myself in the little space behind them. The LOH would fly just over the treetops and Knight would have his head sticking out the window—and when he saw green tracers coming up at us, he would pop smoke and we'd kick out of there. Then the two Cobras that had been flying high above the LOH would come out of the clouds and just pepper the shit out of the hillside we had marked. Knight would have the biggest grin on his face. He loved it!

One of Captain Knight's favorite tricks was to leave an ambush behind when the company packed up and moved out of an NDP, knowing that the enemy would soon move in to scavenge the ammo, frags, and claymores his less-disciplined troops had discarded to lighten their loads. Charlie Company's most successful stay-behind ambush was on Turkey Hill, the patrol base it had used during Thanksgiving. "The NVA point man came up the hill, and when he reached the top five more appeared," recalled Sp4 Harold D. Wise, who usually served as Knight's RTO, but who'd gotten caught up in the new élan and volunteered to join the ambush. "We had one squad, a grenadier, and a machine gun team. The enemy point man didn't spot where we were dug in behind some brush, and the sergeant in charge of the ambush actually waited until the enemy soldier was about two feet from the bush—then he opened up, and we opened up. When it was all over, we had five kills out of the six. One got away."

Captain Knight was Lieutenant Colonel Doyle's favorite company commander not only because he brought home the bodies, but because "although he looked like Mr. Peepers," as Lieutenant Schmitz put it, "he was a real pisser." Knight was raucous and quick-witted, a "helluva partier in the rear." Once, Knight had his field first sergeant, S.Sgt. John C. Calhoun, pin on a pair of his captain bars so they could both get into the first-rate artillery mess hall at Chu Lai. They were sitting at their table eating when Knight said in a voice meant to be overheard, "You know what, John?"

"What's that, Captain Knight?"

"I'd rather have a sister in a whorehouse," Knight boomed, "than a brother in the damn artillery."

With Knight leading the charge, Charlie Company had some wild stand-downs. One night, several lieutenants and NCOs were getting plastered in the first sergeant's orderly room when top himself, 1st Sgt. Charles A. Gibson—a hard, hard man with a heart of gold and a Combat Infantryman's Badge (CIB) indicating that he'd fought in three wars—pulled out his .357 Magnum and cranked a few rounds into the floor and ceiling. One of the platoon sergeants, S.Sgt. Joshua E. Carney, a full-blooded Chickasaw Indian from Oklahoma on his second tour, got wobbly to his feet, held out a cup, and said, "Hey, Top, see if you can shoot this out of my hand."

First Sergeant Gibson certainly could, and when the cup went flying, a new lieutenant who'd been drinking with them got eyes as big as baseballs and blurted, "I thought he was shooting blanks!"

Another lieutenant said something then that Carney didn't like, and Carney, who was a crazy drunk, snapped, "You better shut up, LT. I'll throw you down and stand on your chest."

"You're not going to stand on my chest—"

Before the lieutenant knew it, Carney had wrestled him to the floor. The lieutenant hollered, "Get off my chest . . ."

Although Captain Knight was considered one of the best company commanders in the Americal Division, there were limits to what he could do with what he had. "We were putting in our 365 days, and that was it," said Pfc. Thomas R. Schneider, who admired Knight but who was also fully aware that the war was winding down. "Sandbagging on patrols was kind of common. On the very first patrol I went on, we went about two hundred meters down a trail from the laager—then everybody just sat down, got out a can of C rations or a magazine, and after about an hour we stood up and went back in. The captain never knew that we'd pulled the wool over his eyes."

When Echo Recon was ambushed in January, Company C was helicoptered in to pursue the scattering guerrillas. "We saw their trails, and hauled ass," recalled Lieutenant Mack of Charlie Two—the lead platoon. Knight accompanied the point with Sergeant Calhoun, a bright, good-humored black man from South Carolina who was destined to lose his leg during the sapper attack. Calhoun was a college graduate, a married draftee who had been selected for the NCO Candidate School. Shake 'n' bakes were supposedly lousy by definition, but "Calhoun was just an awesome guy," as one platoon leader put it—brave, level-headed, always in control.

During the chase, Captain Knight and Sergeant Calhoun swung their CAR15s on two guerrillas who were trying to get away down a footpath. They dropped the enemy soldiers on the spot, their tracers homing in with those of other grunts who were also firing.

Captain Knight and Charlie Two got five confirmed kills that day. During another patrol in the FSB Young AO, Knight and Calhoun were with a platoon that captured a diminutive Montagnard who was cooking rice in an open-sided hootch. The man, who stood about four feet tall and was maybe forty years old, said, "No VC"—but there were three rice bowls on the floor. In short order, three enemy soldiers appeared, coming down a paddy dike toward the hootch at sling arms. Knight set up a hasty ambush and eliminated all three. "When our machine gun stopped firing, they looked like rotten tomatoes," recalled Calhoun. Afterward, the platoon headed back with the Montagnard in tow, blindfolded, his hands tied behind his back. The paddies were divided by stone walls, and each time they got to one a couple of the grunts considered it great fun to pick up the helpless midget and heave him over, then jerk him to his feet and get him going again.

The prisoner was turned over to the ARVN. When it was determined that he was simply an old widowed farmer who had been pressed into service as a cook by the enemy, Lieutenant Colonel Doyle employed him in the mess hall. "He'd probably never had it so good," remarked a captain. The little Montagnard—who was to become the uncounted casualty of the sapper attack—was nicknamed "Pro" after the battalion logo, and he became the colonel's mascot and court jester. One night, Doyle took Pro with him to the division officers' club. Pro wore white sandals and a snappy little set of camouflage fatigues and—after he'd gotten sloppy, cross-eyed drunk—Doyle introduced him to several American nurses as "Colonel Pro," a visiting province chief. Flustered by the attention, Pro began slapping himself on the forehead. Doyle thought it was a riot. "Wherever Doyle went, Pro went with him," said one officer. "He just followed him around like a puppy. He even slept outside the door of the colonel's quarters at night."

Captain Knight lost his first man killed on February 1, 1971, during the operation along the Nam Nim. Knight's plan that morning was to work his three platoons down three parallel fingers that descended into the valley from the company's hilltop NDP. Charlie Three moved out first, but almost immediately came under sniper fire. Pulling back, the platoon blasted the area with machine guns and grenade launchers.

In the silence that followed, Knight sent Charlie Two down the same finger Charlie Three had taken. With Mack recently reassigned as the company exec, the platoon had a new lieutenant: an ex–Marine Corps sergeant who had attended army OCS. He was a serious, well-meaning man who had yet to win the respect of his troops, mostly because he tried to cover his mistakes with bluster. Charlie Two's point squad, led by Sgt. Walter Brandt, got farther than the other platoon had before also taking sniper fire. After suppressing the fire, Brandt's squad cut onto a supply trail that was wide and undetectable from above the jungle canopy. The new platoon leader left Brandt's squad to check the area out while he and the other two squads continued toward the river on their original heading. They hit another trail, a narrow one, swung onto it, then halted while the lieutenant got his bearings on his map.

They were still waiting on the trail when Sgt. Jerry Ledoux's squad, bringing up the rear, heard movement on the ridge to their left, which was somewhat lower than the one they were on. Ledoux's RTO got the lieutenant to call and check on the progress of the other platoons.

"The lieutenant says there's nobody supposed to be within a klick of us," the RTO reported to Ledoux.

Sergeant Ledoux's squad set up a hasty ambush trained across the brushy gully that separated the two fingers. The sound of movement was getting closer. "We were on pins and needles," remembered Ledoux. Suddenly, Sp4 Myron B. "Chief" Johnson—a great soldier with seven months in country—snapped off two shots at a figure that materialized in the brush. The rest of the squad opened fire in a chain reaction. "We just raked that area," recalled Pfc. James P. Creaven, who fired his XM203 from a standing position beside their machine gunner, who was blasting away from behind a fallen tree. "We couldn't see who we were shooting at, but I was shooting everything I had, popping out a grenade, then blowing off a magazine, then slapping another grenade and magazine in there, and pumping that out. . . ."

"Medic!" someone screamed in the kill zone, while someone else shouted, "Friendlies, friendlies—cease fire!"

"Medic!" the screaming continued as the fire petered out.

The Charlie Three point man was down, perhaps hit by friendly fire, perhaps not. Charlie Three's perspective was this: the other platoons had already moved out when Charlie Three stepped off in its turn with Sp4 Clyde W. "Randy" Coble, a twenty-year-old draftee from El Paso, Texas, taking the point as he often did. He was a nice, easygoing guy, rangy and mustached. Chopping through the undergrowth, Coble reached a rocky trail with a mild incline. The platoon followed it, and as the staggered column came around a curve in the trail where the underbrush was thinner, Coble was shot twice in the chest by what sounded like an AK-47. In the limb-snapping fusillade that followed the initial burst, the slack man, who had a hole blown in the canteen on his ruck, opened fire on a sniper he saw pop up from behind a boulder and take off down the ravine between the two fingers. Coble was dead.

The Charlie Three GIs thought the sniper had also fired uphill at Charlie Two, thus provoking the intramural firefight. Meanwhile, Sergeant Brandt's Charlie Two squad, which had been detached to check out the enemy supply trail, could hear someone moving quickly through the brush. The unseen figure was about to break out onto the open trail and right into the squad's rifle sights when one of their new guys panicked and squeezed off a single shot. Whoever was out there veered off in a different direction, crashing away at full speed.

"Who fired that shot?" Brandt asked, furious.

"Uh, I did," the new guy said.

"Why'd you do it?"

"To scare him off."

Whether it had been the sniper and not simply a trail watcher trying to evade the sweep was unclear—as was whether there had been an NVA involved in the firefight at all. "I wish I could believe that we didn't kill Randy Coble, but I know there wasn't any enemy sniper down there," said Private Creaven, the Charlie Two grenadier. The men in the other platoon had no doubts: they had distinctly heard the sniper's first two AK-47 shots, and the NVA had even been spotted as he made his getaway. "We were set up that whole time, waiting to open fire, and there's just no way we wouldn't have heard that AK," said Creaven, who believes that the ambushed GIs heard and saw what they had expected in the situation, and not what was really happening. "You're walking along a trail and you're nervous, and all of a sudden you take fire—and your mind sort of fills in the blanks. I've done it myself. You know you saw somebody moving through the brush, but then you look again and it was just leaves moving."

The men in Sergeant Ledoux's squad blamed the incident on their new lieutenant's incoherent map reading, and Chief Johnson—convinced he had just killed a fellow grunt—let out an angry, anguished scream and charged the lieutenant with a bayonet in his clenched fist. Johnson had fired the first shots.

"He liked to went crazy, and we had to grab him and restrain him from getting to the LT," recalled Ledoux.

Johnson was later killed in the sapper attack.

The two platoons linked up without rancor. The men of Charlie Three were sure the enemy had killed their point man, and that was how the incident was officially reported. Ledoux's squad was detailed to carry Coble's body in a poncho rigged between two sturdy branches. "I remember carrying it, and putting it down, and sitting next to it as the patrol continued in stops and starts," said Creaven. "There was hardly any talking—we were just totally freaked out." Creaven and Coble were in different platoons, but had been buddies as both were mellow, dedicated potheads. They had partied together the night before when the platoons laagered together, a situation that always increased laxness because there was security in numbers. Coble had shown Creaven photos of his girlfriend—"and to turn around the next day and kill him is about the only thing that happened over there that I can still hardly talk about."

Meanwhile, Lieutenant Doyle's Charlie One was working its way down the third finger when the point man, Sgt. W. Allen Eades—an outstanding shake 'n' bake squad leader from a small town in North Carolina—spotted a little weather-beaten hootch that seemed out of place sitting there in the middle of nowhere with no trails leading to it. The underbrush around it had been cleared away. Eades deployed his squad in a skirmish line, then he and Carney, the platoon sergeant, cautiously advanced on the hootch. They avoided the door in case it was booby trapped, and slipped around to the back, where Eades used his machete to chop a hole in the thatch. He looked inside and was stunned to see that the hootch was stacked from floor to ceiling with enemy weapons.

"Set up security around this hootch," Sergeant Eades said when he hustled back to his squad. "We got something here."

Mostly what they had was trouble. Eades was convinced that they were being watched. He was certain the NVA would never abandon a cache this big. Each grease-coated weapon was wrapped in plastic, then wrapped again in oil cloth, two rifles per bundle. Lieutenant Doyle radioed Knight that they had ten weapons ... twenty ... thirty. ... Eades and Carney kept hauling them out and stacking them on the ground like cordwood. It looked like they had a couple hundred weapons in there! Knight told Doyle that he was on the way with the rest of the company. When he got there, Doyle excitedly showed him the weapons. The captain, however, upset that one of his men had been killed, talked mostly about how they were going to get Coble's body out.

"Yeah, really, I guess that is about the most important thing," mumbled Lieutenant Doyle, who was still new.

Captain Knight quickly corrected him. "No, it's not *about* the most important thing, it is *the* most important thing."

During the hump to the cache site, S.Sgt. John N. Roeder, Charlie Three's acting platoon leader, spotted a hootch that his point team had already passed without notice. Roeder discovered a 12.7-mm machine gun under the hootch floor. The final haul from Charlie One's cache, meanwhile, was 198 SKS assault rifles, 57 AK-47s, 16 RPD light machine guns, and another 12.7-mm. Knight planned to evacuate the captured weapons from his hilltop NDP by helicopter, so while one group started clearing an LZ, the rest of the company organized security on the finger leading to the cache and started humping the enemy rifles and machine guns uphill. It was real pack-animal work, but they got everything piled up in the middle of the laager, ready to go. Coble's poncho-wrapped body was also laid out there.

There wasn't enough daylight left, however, to finish the LZ. Lieutenant Colonel Doyle called Knight on the radio, warning him that "what's going to happen is they're going to try and take it back tonight." There was still enough time, Doyle said, to land another company in a nearby clearing and have the reinforcements link up with Knight before dark. Knight declined the offer with typical bravado: "Hell, if we found it, we can keep it."

The Charlie Company GIs were digging in and digging deep, expecting to at least be mortared. The NVA began probing at about one in the morning, not firing but crackling through enough bushes on the thickly covered slope to give themselves away. Knight and Hogan, the forward observer, put the illume up, bringing the artillery in so close that the trees above the laager caught fragments. The arty fired all night, and Knight also ordered several mad minutes. As soon as the sun came up, an LOH maneuvered down through an opening in the canopy and unloaded picks, shovels, and a chainsaw. The LOH also brought in twenty or thirty cases of plastic explosives on subsequent trips. "We spent the better part of the day finishing the LZ," remembered Calhoun, the field first sergeant. "Man, we was blowin' trees down, and really having a great time—but the guy that got killed, we had him in a body bag by then, and it was depressing because I don't care where you got on that little hilltop, you could see that body bag."

6

Trail Watchers

Charlie Company finished the LZ during the afternoon of February 2, and a Huey hauled out the captured weapons. It took several trips. Meanwhile, Lieutenant Colonel Doyle was full of praise for everyone, especially Sergeant Eades, who won a three-day Chu Lai R&R for finding the cache, as well as a Bronze Star Medal for meritorious achievement (BSM). Doyle wanted to see the cache site for himself, and Eades, who thought highly of the colonel, ran a patrol with him back to the weather-beaten hootch. Where there was one cache, there were usually others, so Doyle brought in Company D from the firebase to thoroughly search the area. Charlie Company took Delta's place on the hill, the single Huey shuttling the men in and out one cabinful at a time. When Knight climbed aboard, he sat on the floor with his legs hanging out the door. The Huey pilot hovered six feet off the ground while Sergeant Calhoun took a dozen photos from the landing zone. Everyone was smiling. Compared to the bush, being on the firebase was almost as good as going on stand-down.

The division commander, Maj. Gen. James L. Baldwin, helicoptered out to FSB Mary Ann to congratulate Doyle and Knight. The general was accompanied by several staff officers and a photographer from the division newspaper. The cleaned-up AK-47s and SKSs had been laid out in rows on the sandbagged sides of the B-TOC. The machine guns were set up on top of their bipods. There were so many SKSs that Doyle was able to offer one to Baldwin and each member of his entourage—even the general's door gunners. The grunts had already picked out their souvenir SKSs. It was legal to take an SKS back to the States as a war trophy.

Captain Knight did not enjoy firebase duty. "Knight always preached that you had to go get 'em, because when you sat back they'd take advantage of you," stated Ledoux. During Company C's stay on Mary Ann, Knight called his platoons together to offer each the same warning. "He told us that if he was going to be killed in Vietnam, it wouldn't be in the bush," remembered a grenadier. "He said he would either be killed during one of his LOH missions—or on the firebase. He sensed how lax we were on the hill, and was trying to prevent exactly what happened later."

On Christmas Day 1970, shortly before Doyle gave Capt. Charles D. Kirkey command of Company D, 1-46th Infantry, he walked him through the amputee ward at the 91st Evac Hospital in Chu Lai. By the time they came out the other side, both were on the verge of tears. "I don't ever want to come here for any of your people," Doyle told Kirkey.

Captain Kirkey's platoons established separate patrol bases in the mountains after Company D replaced Company C during the cache-hunting mission along the Nam Nim. On February 4, Delta Three's point man was killed instantly by an AK-47 burst that came out of nowhere, fired by an NVA trail watcher who remained unseen as the platoon shredded the jungle in response with M16 and M60 machine-gun fire. Captain Kirkey, on the way to the contact area with the rest of the company, ran out of daylight and was not able to link up with Delta Three until the next morning, February 5. The platoon had established a hasty defensive position, and the dead point man had lain there during the long night, wrapped in a poncho. It turned out that he had been shot on the outskirts of a base camp built under the canopy amid the foliage so that its thatch hootches went almost unnoticed. The NVA who lived there had built supply boats. There were several of them in the camp, real beauties that resembled broad-bottomed whale-boats, and there were paths of flattened brush where work crews had pushed other boats down to the river—eight hundred meters away, downhill and due east of the camp.

Delta Three worked its way down the same slope, and a helicopter evacuated the dead point man from the open river bank. The platoon was still down by the river when two NVA with AK-47s were spotted several hundred meters to the north, where the Tranh hooked south and became the Nam Nim River. The NVA disappeared when one of the platoon's M60s opened fire.

Later that afternoon Captain Kirkey was talking with the battalion adjutant, who had helicoptered out to see the supply boats, when Echo Recon spotted three more NVA a thousand meters due east of Delta Company. The NVA were on the jungled slope of the mountain across the river. It would take several minutes to work up an artillery request, so Kirkey got one of his grenadiers to provide immediate fire support. The grenadier was totally against the idea, complaining that a round might simply detonate on contact with the foliage above them. Kirkey and the adjutant thought they could pull it off, however, and they tried to figure an angle that would get a round through the trees and over to the next mountain. The grenadier dutifully took aim and fired. But, just as he had predicted, the shell exploded in the canopy, snipping the adjutant in the nose with a fragment. Embarrassed, he made the other officers there swear never to tell Doyle.

When Echo Recon finally got its arty, Kirkey's FO had to cancel the mission because some of the rounds were landing west of Delta's NDP and the target was to the east. After the rattled grunts got under cover, the FO had the artillery fire one tube at a time. When the errant howitzer was identified it was relaid and the mission was fired with unknown results.

Lieutenant Colonel Doyle instructed Kirkey to cut an LZ so that the NVA boats could be lifted out. "He wanted one to put on top of his TOC," said Kirkey. Unfortunately, the weather closed in, and Delta Company spent three drizzly days, February 5–8, laagered around the boats. The LZ, carved out with plastic explosives and dull, rusty machetes, was like a mineshaft—the kind pilots hated because it made them an easy target and put enormous strain on their engines as they hovered straight down, then straight up. When the weather cleared, Doyle flew in on the first Huey. The pilots looked the boats over and rocked one to see how much it weighed, then said it couldn't be done. They were too heavy. With that, the grunts destroyed them in place with a two-man bucksaw found in the camp, then knocked the hootches down. The company moved out the next morning. "I didn't want to just sit there," recalled Kirkey. "We all wanted to find a cache. There was some professional jealousy involved. We took a bunch of heat because the other company found weapons and all we came up with was those damn boats."

Kirkey was a career man, and one of his platoon leaders considered him too concerned with pleasing his superiors. "I was back in Vietnam to get my CIB," said Kirkey, who after graduating from ROTC had pulled a 1968–69 tour advising an ARVN training center. "Kirkey was likable and friendly," said the platoon leader, "and he never put us in danger by being reckless, but he just did not instill a lot of confidence in the troops."

Intelligent and soft-spoken, Captain Kirkey was in one sense bearing the brunt for certain circumstances beyond his control. He was Company D's fifth commander in seven months, and the grunts had come to some hard conclusions about the sincerity and abilities of their officers. "I could feel their resentment," recalled Kirkey, who tried to impress upon his people that he was going to be there at least six months—that he wasn't going to get his combat ticket punched and then hightail it for the rear. He also set about making immediate changes. Delta Company, having had no real leadership for so long, was a mess. It was the poorest outfit in the battalion. "When I took over, half the guys were wearing boonie hats and some weren't wearing any headgear at all," said Kirkey. "They didn't dig in, and there wasn't an established basic load or anything else. I came up with a basic load of more ammunition than they usually carried, and I made them all wear steel pots, and I made them dig in at night."

Those changes were proper. It did not help Captain

Kirkey's case, however, when he got dysentery during his first operation with the company. Exhausted and debilitated, he finally gave Lieutenant Schmidt the most undignified of details. Schmidt, keeping his anger to himself, marched down to where his men were setting up for the night. "We need two volunteers," he said. "The captain shit his pants—somebody's got to go wash 'em out."

The announcement was greeted by a chorus of jeers, but Sp4 Frank P. Strzempka, a machine gunner, exclaimed brightly, "Yeah, I'll do it!"

Strzempka, a big, tough kid from Buffalo, New York, handled his M60 like it was a pogo stick. After volunteering to clean the captain's stained and stinking trousers, he said to his good buddy, Jeff Parks, "C'mon, go with me!"

"Man!" Parks exclaimed, shaking his head.

"Please go with me—pull security for me!"

Parks agreed, and they walked back to the captain's shelter half. Someone tossed the trousers out—"Wash 'em out, but don't get 'em too wet 'cause he has to wear 'em." As they headed for a nearby stream, Parks asked, "What in the fuck is in your mind?"

"Hey, I want to do this for the captain," replied Strzempka.

Parks laughed. "You're bullshittin' me—"

"You just pull security. I'll take care of the pants," snapped Strzempka.

Parks positioned himself atop a boulder and Strzempka went down to the stream. "What'd he say, don't get 'em too wet?" he called back.

"Yeah," Parks answered.

Strzempka threw the trousers in the stream and stomped on them. Picking them back up, he asked, "Then what'd he say?"

"He said to get the spot out of 'em."

"Sure, okay," Strzempka muttered. He pinned the trouser legs with his foot, pulled his bayonet from the sheath on his jungle boot, and cut the seat out of the pants. He held them up, grinning. "How's that look?"

They went back up the hill to the captain's shelter half. "Sir, sir," Strzempka said in mock sincerity, followed by, "Here's your fuckin' pants!" as he threw them inside.

Three weeks into Captain Kirkey's command tour, Company D went to the rear on stand-down. When they arrived, Kirkey's first sergeant walked up and said, "I don't know what the hell's going on, but I'm picking up rumbles that they're ready to get rid of you."

"What?" Kirkey blurted in surprise.

"Yeah," the first sergeant said grimly.

"Why?" asked Kirkey.

"Well, they don't like all the lifer shit you're doin' to 'em—diggin' in, makin' 'em wear steel pots, and all that stuff."

Captain Kirkey did not seriously think he was going to be fragged—the company had not yet suffered any casualties under his command—and he told the first sergeant, "Okay, let's get it out in the open. Let's find out."

The Delta Company grunts were outside, cleaning their weapons prior to securing them in the company arms room. There was a trailer there with beer on ice. "Look here, guys, I've got one goal in life," Captain Kirkey began, "and that's to get every one of you home the way you got here—and that's with a hat on your head, a bag in each hand, and walking on your own two feet. We're all going to wear steel pots and we're all going to dig in at night, and we're all going to carry as much ammunition as we can because those are safe things. I don't like digging in either. That damn entrenching tool ain't worth a shit, it breaks every time you look at it, and the steel pot gives me a headache, too. But you gotta wear it."

Captain Kirkey knew he was okay the night one of his lieutenants invited him down for steel-pot stew with the guys. That was later, after the operation in the mountains along the Nam Nim where everything was dark and gloomy under the giant trees—and after the ambush that began early in the morning on February 11 when Company D, 1-46th Infantry, was on a trail moving southeast toward the river. The company at that point was one klick out of its NDP. Delta Three, in the lead, crested a jungle rise, followed the trail down into a saddle, and then started up the next slope. The NVA were on the crest of that second rise, and when the point team was thirty feet from their camouflaged positions, they began sweeping the trail with automatic weapons fire. The surprise was total. The noise under the canopy was deafening, but the brush was too thick to even see the muzzle flashes of the ambushers.

In seconds, Delta Three had two men dead and seven wounded on the trail. The surviving grunts ceased to function as a unit. "They weren't returning any fire, and the NVA had the complete upper hand," said Lieutenant Schmidt of Delta Two, whose platoon was next in the column, back on the safe side of the first rise.

Captain Kirkey, whose command group was right behind the point platoon and under heavy fire itself in the saddle, ordered Lieutenant Schmidt to move up and get Delta Three back in action. Schmidt grabbed one of his machine gunners, Pfc. William B. Meek, a tough, blue-collar draftee, and they dropped their rucks and started up the trail. "We were flat ass runnin'," remembered Meek, who, like the lieutenant, won a BSMv. "We ran right by the company commander, and we ran right by the field first sergeant who was huddled behind his rucksack with his hands over his helmet. They were kissing their ass instead of directing fire." Schmidt and Meek, hollering, trying to find out where the Delta Three survivors were, gradually made their way to the point of contact on the hillside. Schmidt was stepping around a tree to the side of the trail—when he suddenly came face-to-face with an NVA in green fatigues coming around a tree in front of him. The NVA was ten paces away. They looked at each other and Schmidt—stunned, scared, barely able to aim—opened up with his M16 on automatic, pumping off the whole magazine. All he could see was the muzzle flash of the AK-47 as the NVA began firing at the same instant. Schmidt thumped a fresh magazine into his weapon. The NVA was gone. Schmidt hadn't seen the enemy soldier go down wounded. He hadn't seen him spring to cover. The NVA had just vanished. "Everyone was just laying there," said Schmidt. "They were laying off the trail, just completely out of it, and I screamed at them to fire, to do something. When Meek started working out with the pig, then they reacted, then they started firing because they knew they had some assistance. Meek was fantastic."

Captain Kirkey was on the trail, lying prone behind his rucksack, calling for immediate artillery support. The handset cord stretched to the radio on the back of his RTO, who had rolled off into the bushes. The RTO kept pulling his antenna down, garbling the connection, and Kirkey had to keep reaching over to pull it back into position.

"It'll draw fire!" the RTO screamed.

"No, it won't—it's gotta stay up!"

But the antenna *did* mark their position. With scythelike precision, enemy fire cut and flattened the foliage a foot above where Kirkey and his RTO lay. One burst of AK-47 fire ripped down the path right past Kirkey. Up ahead, Private Meek, who had thrown himself down on the right side of the trail, was firing his M60 continuously, unable to see anything but the smoke from his weapon and the brush shuddering as he swept it back and forth. The pig was living up to its name, and Meek began shouting, "Andy, I need some ammo!"

Sergeant Andy Olints, who had a belt of machine-gun ammo over each shoulder and another around his waist, froze when he heard Meek. Oh God, he recalls thinking, I'll pretend I didn't hear him. Olints was behind a tree, squeezing off M16 bursts as NVA maneuvered up on the flank, covering each other with fire of their own. He couldn't imagine leaving his covered position, but Meek was going crazy, leaving him no choice. You have to face this person after this action, he told himself. Olints finally dropped his ruck and took off down past the command group and began moving from tree to tree up the slope on which Delta Three was strung out. The grunts were ensconced behind the six-foot-high roots of the giant trees along the dark, smoky trail. Several men screamed at Olints when he went past, warning him to stay off the trail, but no one got up to go with him. The best they could do was to throw their machine-gun ammo to him. Scooping up each belt until he had at least ten flapping from his shoulders, Olints suddenly came upon one of the dead grunts. The body's eyes were open, its skin already pale white. It looked like the man had been hit in the legs and had died of shock and blood loss. Five feet away, a medic sat on the trail, cradling the other dead man in his arms. He had inserted a plastic trachea tube in the casualty's throat, and was still trying to breathe life into him.

It was a searing scene. "I stopped, and the medic stopped what he was doing and stared right through me," Olints remembered. "He was totally in shock at losing those guys."

Sergeant Olints made it up to Meek with his ammo, then took up a firing position beside Specialist Sutton, a black Delta Three machine gunner who was also laying down a wall of fire. The NVA above them started rolling grenades down the trail—then launched a rocket-propelled grenade with a screaming whistle that the grunts didn't recognize because they had never before seen an RPG. Lieutenant Schmidt was firing his M16 when his week-old beard suddenly felt like it was on fire. He didn't realize what had happened—that the RPG had just missed taking his head off, searing his face in its superheated wake—until he heard a shattering explosion behind him. The NVA fired a second RPG and Olints, hearing the omnious crack and shriek, frantically dove through the brush. After the explosion, he discovered his arms were bleeding. He thought he'd caught a few fragments, then realized he'd simply scratched himself going through the brush. He was disappointed; he had been hoping he'd been wounded so he could get out.

The RPGs impacted against the hardwood trees just ahead and to one side of Captain Kirkey's command group. The NVA had fired the RPGs to cover their getaway. The battalion and brigade commander flew overhead as Delta Company's lead elements swept forward a hundred meters to secure the area, and Doyle leaned out of his LOH to fire his M79 along the probable path of enemy withdrawal. Doyle brought in Cobra gunships, then ran air strikes on the river valley. The latter resulted in secondary explosions from an enemy cache hit by chance.

The jet pilots released their bombs behind Delta Company. The high-drag bombs, fins popping out to retard their descent and increase accuracy, sailed over the grunts' heads on their way downhill. "I thought we were going to get blown away by friendly fire," recalled Lieutenant Schmidt. "We really got on the horn quick to stop the air strike. By then it was sort of a wasted effort anyway." Three hours into the action, a medevac with gunship escort hovered over Delta, and lowered a jungle penetrater through the canopy. The four most seriously wounded grunts went out that way.

The two dead men were trussed up in ponchos and secured to a long heavy stick so litter teams could carry them, poles over shoulders. The bodies swung a bit under the poles as Delta slowly headed back the way it had come. In the morning, the company started downhill again, looking for a clearing that would accommodate a Huey. "The most demoralizing thing you can ever have to do is carry your dead down a mountain," reflected Kirkey. "It took us two days to get them out. We had to hump all the way down to the river. We couldn't find any clearings all the way down."

Shortly after Company D broke contact, Lieutenant Doyle and Charlie One, having loaded aboard four Hueys at FSB Mary Ann—the whole hill was buzzing—began their descent toward the sandy streambed that was to be their LZ. The blueline, in the shadow of jungled mountains to either side, was a tributary running west from the Nam Nim. The spot selected for the LZ was at the foot of the mountain where the ambush had occurred, a klick south of the contact area. NVA had been spotted by a LOH as they maneuvered across the tributary, and another air strike had plastered the area. The door gunners on Charlie One's Hueys opened fire as the helicopters came in on the north shore, sand swirling on the white slip of beach as the grunts jumped out. The Hueys pulled off with a roar. The jungle began about sixty feet off the beach, and the platoon immediately fanned out and headed for it so the landing zone could be secured and the rest of the company choppered in.

The gunships escorting the lift ships spotted more NVA in a hootch complex about a klick southeast of the LZ, on the other side of the Nam Nim. The Cobras rolled in, rocketing the twenty or thirty hootches. Smoke billowed up through the jungle canopy, a sight that chilled the blood of the grunts coming in aboard the Hueys.

After getting organized on the beach, the company moved out with Charlie One in the lead, using a trail that ran northwest up the side of the mountain. Sergeant Eades's point man hadn't gone a hundred meters when an enemy soldier opened up from behind a rotted tree stump. The point man shot the stump to pieces as he returned fire. It was all over in less than a minute. Lieutenant Doyle was breaking out his map so he could get the arty going when his platoon sergeant, Carney, came up with the rear squad. Carney went right past him and grunts popped up from the brush and followed him forward. Doyle walked the artillery down the mountainside until Carney got on the radio and told him he'd brought it in close enough.

Carney also reported that the enemy had abandoned weapons and ammunition along the trail. The stuff was packed so it could be carried—Charlie Company had apparently landed right in the path of an enemy supply party moving downhill, away from Delta Company.

Company C dug in just off the beach, its morale high.

7

Ambush

Come daylight, the attitude in Company C's laager was casual as helmetless grunts opened rations and cleaned weapons under the trees along the beach. They were simply waiting for helicopters to evacuate the captured cache—including such souvenirs as chopsticks and camouflage scarves—when five NVA with packs and weapons walked into the open to the southeast, across the tributary. Realizing their mistake, the enemy soldiers fired a few bursts to cover themselves as they rushed back into the brush. The GIs scrambled into a line at the edge of the trees and blazed away with much gusto and some excited laughter, expending several magazines apiece on automatic while grenadiers lobbed high-explosive shells.

First Lieutenant C. Barry McGee, the acting company commander—Knight was on leave in Thailand—called for arty and ordered that an effort be made to cross the tributary. It proved too deep and fast, but Charlie Two, working along the bank, did find a dead NVA lodged between some boulders. The enemy soldier had presumably been hit during Charlie One's contact the day before, when the enemy cache had been found. The haul was laid out in the laager: 16 SKSs and 33 AK-47s, 10 500-round cases of small-arms ammunition, 27 RPGs, 138 82-mm mortar rounds, and 17 land mines, plus such assorted odds and ends as primers, blasting caps, and communications wire.

There were also foodstuffs, which were destroyed. To evacuate the enemy weapons and ammunition, Lieutenant McGee planned to hold the beach LZ with Charlie Two, while Charlie One and Three secured the high ground overlooking the tributary. Charlie Three moved out to the northeast, while Lieutenant Doyle and Charlie One filed up a trail snaking northwest to a piece of commanding terrain five hundred meters away from the main laager. Doyle moved with the point team, while Carney controlled the rear. They hated trails, which were easy to ambush, but took this one because they were running out of daylight. The trail reeked with the smell of the enemy—fish and fish sauce— and it made for a hairy walk up the mountain as the column frequently stopped, watched, and waited before continuing on. They could hear faint noises to the front and on the right flank, but nothing was visible through the thick vegetation.

Moving left on a branch off the main trail, the grunts spotted an arrow constructed of fresh green wood posted twelve feet up a tree. It was an enemy directional marker. Despite all the indications of imminent contact, the platoon made it to the new laager site without incident. The men dropped their rucksacks, unfolded entrenching tools and began digging in. The soil was hard and rocky, the forested slopes around the laager almost primeval in the hot green haze of dusk that hung darkly under the canopy. The jungle was alive, humming.

Lieutenant Doyle stood with Sgt. William A. "Jack" Daniels, one of his squad leaders. Doyle wanted Daniels to organize a recon patrol to investigate the trail's route toward the jungled ridgeline and to deploy two mechanical ambushes along the trail, which was the likeliest avenue of enemy approach to the laager.

Sergeant Carney joined the huddle. "LT, this patrol ain't a real good idea," the platoon sergeant said.

"Why not?" Doyle asked.

"Well, you don't want contact this late in the day," explained Carney.

"I know it, but I want *something* out in front of us."

Blond, bespectacled Doyle was a citizen-soldier with an ROTC commission and a wife and son waiting for him in Massachusetts. He adjusted the mission somewhat because Carney was a pro, but in the end he made his own call. "Okay, at least get the Mickey Mouses in position," Doyle told Daniels, referring to the mechanical ambushes. "We also need to know which way the trail is going to go so we can get a sense of what we're going to do tomorrow. If you can get a peek, do it—but if the terrain looks dangerous just forget the recon. We don't want contact."

Sergeant Daniels saddled up, and word was passed around the laager that friendlies were going out. The jungled ridgeline was about three hundred meters to the north. Daniels's squad slipped toward it on the trail, which curved to the right as it descended into a saddle where the brush opened up on either side and the trees were thinner and less numerous. The ridgeline to the front, looking down on the dip, was thickly forested with giant hardwood trees with high, spreading roots, and layer upon layer of greenery. There were a thousand hiding places.

A fallen tree draped across the trail, hung up in the brush at one end. The point man, Sp4 Willie Gardner—a black GI with eight months in country—went over the log, then down a dozen steps into the hollow of the saddle. The jungle exploded in ambush and he was stitched across the stomach. Sp4 Duane Weinfurter, walking slack with his machine gun, had not yet traversed the log, but he also dropped in the opening sweep of fire, his leg shattered. The NVA had two RPD light machine guns, one to either side of the hollow, creating a cross fire. There was a lot of AK fire, too, and the grunts, scrambling off to either side of the trail as the vegetation was slashed above them and around them, returned it as best they could, not sure where the enemy was in the dark green blur.

It was 1645 on February 12, 1971. Lieutenant Doyle, his heart sinking at the sound of the firefight, radioed Sergeant Daniels. "We got ambushed," Daniels shouted. "I got two down!"

"Hang on, we'll be right there!"

Doyle got on the company frequency and told Lieutenant

McGee to fire the preplotted defensive target behind the enemy ridgeline. "Eades—1st Squad—let's go!" Doyle shouted, putting down the handset. "Salmen, leave a fire team to secure the laager—then get the rest of 2nd Squad down that trail!"

Sergeant Daniels had the 3rd Squad. He was a big man with a black handlebar mustache, a great soldier who had transferred up from the 25th Division. Using what cover existed on the right side of the trail, Daniels and Sgt. Craig A. Neill made it to Weinfurter. They hauled him to his feet and scrambled back toward a tree, the wounded man between them. Meanwhile, Lieutenant Doyle and Sergeant Eades were in the lead as the backup squad rushed head-long toward the ambush. Carney, the platoon sergeant, was right behind, screaming at them to get out of his way. Carney elbowed past them on the narrow trail. They couldn't see anything until they rounded the downhill curve—and then, suddenly, they were right in the middle of the fight, rounds snapping everywhere. Doyle dropped down beside Daniels. Carney dove for the old tree across the trail. Eades piled in beside him and they both opened fire over the log. The rest of the platoon came around the curve and down the hill—Salmen, running, had a round ricochet off his steel helmet—then deployed to either side of the trail, firing like mad into the ridgeline, firing blind. Gardner, pinned on his stomach in the ambush's killing zone, screamed for help, then slumped silently, apparently dead.

A moment later Gardner screamed again, and Sergeant Carney turned to Eades and said, "I gotta go get him."

Carney scrambled over the log and started crawling. Private First Class Paul G. Grooms, the platoon medic, squeezed off a burst as he hit the dirt on Carney's right, then dropped his M16 so he could crawl faster. He realized that Gardner was looking right at him.

"Doc, I don't want to die!" screamed Gardner.

"Hang on, Will!" Grooms hollered back.

"We were right in the middle of that goddamn trail, right out in the open," recalled Grooms. "I was literally touching Carney's shoulder with my shoulder when Carney took a round in the neck from the right side—meaning the bullet went over me and into Carney. He went 'Unh!', and shuddered once. I'll never forget the feel of him shuddering against me when he got hit . . ."

One of their machine gunners back up the trail fired furiously as Sergeant Eades rushed down to Grooms, and together they pulled Carney back behind the log by his feet. Eades cradled his best friend and told him everything would be all right.

"Carney didn't say anything," Eades remembered, "but he looked up at me and smiled, and that was it . . ."

Sergeant Carney, twenty-six, was the color of brick. Lean, wiry, and hawk-nosed, he had black hair and eyes. Carney had fought near Hue during Tet of '68 with the 101st Airborne Division, winning the Silver Star and Purple Heart. The story was that when he went home, his marriage went south. Carney joined the Americal in September, 1970. He was a man to be avoided in the rear. "After I drank with him one time, I never drank with him again," joked Sergeant Calhoun, "because once he got drunk he wanted to fight everybody." Carney used to march up to the front of the post exchange (PX) liquor line in his starched stand-down fatigues and polished jump boots, cut in front of the twenty rear-echelon NCOs standing there, and talk about all the people whose asses were going to get kicked if anybody said anything about it. Nobody ever challenged him. The grand old sergeant first class running the platoon when Carney began his second tour once squared off with him toe-to-toe, but both were so drunk at the time they literally could not land their punches. Carney and the platoon sergeant decided to have a duel instead, and both had their .45s out before the guys stepped in. In the bush, Carney was a different man—hard-nosed about discipline, but cheerful, almost happy-go-lucky. His troops loved him. "He was cool under fire," they said, "and he knew how the dinks thought and how they operated. He was a tough sonofabitch. He had an uncanny sense of direction. He was a super soldier and a super guy . . ."

Sergeant Carney wore four watches, including one with the USSR's trademark hammer and sickle on its face. He had taken them off dead NVA. The morning of the ambush, Carney stood the last radio watch for the platoon back in the laager by the beach. "You know what, Calhoun?" he said, joking with the field first sergeant, who had radio watch at the CP. "My family didn't like it when I came home the first time. Everybody was mad at me."

"Why's that, Josh?" Calhoun asked.

"Because they thought they was going to get that ten thousand dollar life insurance policy."

"Well, don't worry about it, Josh, it's just a long-term investment because this time they can get fifteen thousand."

"I ain't worried about that," Carney said, cracking a paratrooper's grin, " 'cause I got my shit together."

Ten hours later, Carney was dead. The next man to go after Gardner was Sp4 Dennis Murphy, a grenadier in Salmen's squad with six months in the bush. When the contact first erupted he had assumed the recon patrol was firing up some NVA. "I remember a smile going across my face, and I thought, hot damn, let's get some!" said Murphy. "My immediate reaction was to get there as quickly as I could so I could be part of the fun." Murphy, age twenty, from blue-collar Philadelphia—his people were devout Irish Catholics—was in junior college when his number came up in the draft lottery. He enlisted to get it over with. He was bright, idealistic, always ready to help—"a super little guy," as Sergeant Eades put it. Murphy, bareheaded, his sweaty green undershirt plastered against his back, dropped his entrenching tool and scooped up his XM203, and a single bandolier of ammo. He left behind his helmet and grenade launcher ammo vest. "We were so confident, we didn't even bring all our ammo," said Murphy, "but when I got down the trail there was complete chaos. Carney was down—I didn't know what his status was—and Gardner was out there yelling, and shit was hitting in the trees all over the place. Everybody was down low and firing, and we had no idea what the hell was going on. We were very undisciplined when it came to firing. We just pulled the trigger and went crazy on automatic."

Murphy opened fire, too. Up ahead, on the right side of the trail, Lieutenant Doyle was screaming on the radio about their nonexistent artillery support. Doyle, frantic, thought out loud, "We need to get this fuckin' guy out of there!"

In a moment of raw courage that would result in Murphy's being awarded the Silver Star, the young grenadier took it upon himself to make the rescue attempt he thought Doyle was calling for. He ceased fire and muttered a resigned, "Oh, fuck!" as he prepared to spring into action. Throwing down his XM203 as he got up, Murphy ran brazenly right down the middle of the trail toward Gardner without any coordination for covering fire, then veered through the brush on the left side of the log. Gardner was lying on his stomach, his eyes almost glowing in the hazy dusk. "I don't want to die, Murphy—save me!" he cried. Murphy got his hands under Gardner's arms and started to pull. But Gardner was bigger than Murphy and, weak from his wounds, he was just dead weight. Just as Murphy realized he couldn't save Gardner a round hit him in the leg, which slapped against Murphy's right leg as the bullet went through him, too. The bullet sheared the flesh of his ankle and Murphy fell in a sprawl atop Gardner. Murphy looked toward where the shot had come from—and there to the left of the trail, much closer than he had imagined, were several enemy soldiers in a vegetation-covered entrenchment. They wore pith helmets, and one was behind a light machine gun pointed directly at Murphy. "I saw his face, and I could literally see the bullet leaving the muzzle of the machine gun, I literally followed that tracer and then it hit the top of my left hand, grazing across the knuckles, and caught me in the left forehead. My head snapped back like it was going to rip off."

Murphy was pushing up to get out of there when two more rounds hit him in the lower back, thumping deep into the muscle at an angle. "That hurt—that felt as if a truck hit me. I was slammed into the ground. Oh shit! I couldn't believe it. I could not believe that I was shot to the point that this could be bad news." Gardner was still screaming, but Murphy wasn't listening. He had just started to crawl toward the log when the machine gun opened fire again. He felt a burning, excruciating pain as a round went through his right thigh, blew off his left testicle, and blasted into his left thigh. Everything was just meat and blood. He couldn't move. "If it wasn't for my religion, I'd be dead today, there's no doubt in my mind. All I did, I started saying Hail

Mary's, and I lay there for a while because I knew if I moved again, they'd get me. It was getting darker. Our guys were firing away, doing what they could . . ."

When Dennis Murphy charged down the trail, "Doc" Grooms thought that his buddy was pulling the bravest and most foolish maneuver he had ever seen. Murphy was only ten paces past Grooms when he was gunned down. But then Grooms, sickened, thinking his buddy was dead, realized that he was still alive when Murphy cried out in an astonished voice, "Doc, they shot me in the nuts!"

Private First Class Grooms was the next man to win a Silver Star. The son of a Missouri farmer, he wanted to be a teacher. He had a wife and child, but when he graduated with his education degree, he lost his student deferment. Grooms never considered himself a very good soldier. During the turkey shoot across the stream that morning, he had gotten so excited he forgot to pull out the toothbrush he used to clean his M16, which he kept jammed in a vent on top of the front hand guard. Four magazines later, the weapon was smoking, the toothbrush melted.

But now Grooms crawled down the left side of the trail, trying to get to Murphy. To his rear, their machine gunner was still firing his M60. The rounds were going directly over Grooms's right shoulder. "Get that goddamn pig off my ass!" he screamed, afraid that if he had to jump up and dodge he would run right into the friendly fire. At that moment Lieutenant Doyle shouted, "Frag!" as he flung a hand grenade toward the enemy position in the hollow. It hit a tree, bouncing back at the medic. Grooms, who had spun around into a crouch to get out of there, didn't hear the explosion or feel the fragments that peppered his buttocks and the back of his neck because as soon as he got up he was shot through the left arm just above the elbow. The bone was shattered, most of the biceps muscle was blown away, and the radial nerve and artery were severed.

The pain was unreal. Grooms ran like a crazy man back up the trail. He made it to where his assistant medic, Sp4 Timothy J. Carmichael—one of the nicest, smartest guys around—was working on Weinfurter, the wounded machine gunner. They were all behind trees in the bushes. Carmichael was actually a grunt whom Grooms had been training on the job, and he stared shocked at Grooms, whose arm hung bloody and useless.

"What the shit am I going to do?" Carmichael blurted.

"Take my Bowie knife scabbard and make a splint for me," said Grooms.

Carmichael tossed Grooms's sixteen-inch knife aside, used the scabbard as a splint, and wrapped a pressure dressing around the shattered arm. He also thumped a morphine syrette into Grooms, but it did no good. Grooms was in too much pain to even move.

Lieutenant Doyle had lost three men trying to rescue one, and he shouted that no one else was to go down that trail—"which is a friggin' bizarre command," he said later. "I mean you've got to order people to *stop* racing down into the killing zone of an ambush? I needed to say it because those guys were crazy." Meanwhile, Dennis Murphy was crawling up the trail, exhausted, praying the enemy wouldn't see him. If he got hit again, he knew it would be over. He was praying out loud—"Hail Mary, full of grace!"—and making it to the log across the path, he somehow pulled himself over the top of it. "I could see my family. I could see my home. I could see my friends, and there was no way I wasn't going to go home. . . ."

Lieutenant Doyle, in the midst of his first heavy contact after three months at battalion and one month in the bush, had a furious grip on his radio handset. "The artillery just isn't coming!" he shouted to McGee, the acting company commander. "Where the fuck is it? In Infantry School, they promised me arty on the ground in two minutes. I need it and it isn't here!"

Doyle had previously helped his RTO out of his radio harness, telling the radioman to get up on line, while he dealt with the radio. Commo was such under the triple-canopy that Doyle couldn't talk directly with the artillery. He had to call the CP on the beach, which relayed his request to an element on higher ground able to get through to FSB Mary Ann. When the artillery finally reported that it was ready to fire, Doyle wanted the first round six hundred meters due north of his platoon, on the other side of the enemy ridgeline. He planned to walk the barrage back. He could not see the explosion when the round landed, but it sounded like it was a hundred meters left of where he wanted it. Doyle told McGee to have the fire shifted a hundred meters to the right, but the next round sounded like it had been adjusted by two hundred meters. Doyle looked at his map again. There was a draw through the ridge that opened up on the left side. He thought this terrain feature was playing tricks with the sounds of the explosions, making it even harder to determine where the rounds were really landing.

Jesus Christ, this is fucked up, he remembers thinking.

"Left one hundred," Doyle said into the handset, which should have brought the next round due north of Charlie One, "and drop four hundred." He reconsidered, remembering warnings that their maps were not entirely accurate. "Check that. Drop one hundred."

Lieutenant Doyle shouted to the troops hunkered around him, "Get everybody up on line, and I need two people to go down and get Gardner!" Eades and Sgt. Elmer R. Head said they'd try. "Everybody else put suppressive fire into the dinks. I've got a round coming in that's going to land five hundred meters ahead of us. That'll be the signal. When the shell explodes, you two take off—and everybody else open up over their heads to cover 'em!"

The grunts got ready, but when the round came in it exploded thirty feet up in a tree that was about twenty feet to the platoon's left-front. Doyle was convinced that his adjustments had been miscommunicated, given the extended link to the firing battery. If his initial command to drop the fire four hundred meters had not been countermanded as requested, and then the other hundred meters had been dropped in addition, that would have adjusted the fire right onto Charlie One.

The friendly fire resulted in instant pandemonium. "Add two hundred, left two hundred!" Doyle shouted, hoping to get the arty off their heads while he figured out what to do next. "Check the arty, check the arty, lieutenant!" Sergeant

Eades screamed. Eades had a chunk of red-hot U.S. steel embedded in the back of his right thigh, but he could still crawl, and he grabbed the handset away from Doyle. "Check the arty!" Eades screamed to McGee, thinking that Doyle was shell-shocked. Doyle took the handset back and explained to McGee, "Please be advised that we took friendly casualties with the last round . . ."

Lieutenant Doyle looked around amid the smoke and screams, aghast at the carnage. Eades, his best squad leader, was down, while to his rear Pfc. Alan B. Sanders and Pfc. Buss Moore had also been hit. Pfc. Herb Atkinson's arm was a bloody mess. Doyle glanced at Weinfurter, who was lying behind a tree just in front of him, bandages around his foot and leg, and realized that the back of the man's helmet had been caved in by what must have been a fist-sized chunk of metal. "Weinfurter, are you okay?" Doyle blurted.

"My leg hurts, but other than that I'm fine," Weinfurter replied.

"Do you have a headache, or anything?"

Weinfurter said that he did not, and Doyle thought that the colonel's policy of getting the troops out of their bush hats and into helmets had just saved a life. "Let's get the wounded out of here before something else fucks up!" Doyle shouted.

Meanwhile, point man Willie Gardner—a popular, twenty-one-year-old draftee from Alabama—had died. "Gardner did not moan anymore after the explosion," remembered Doyle. "There was a question of whether he was dying anyway, but that was it."

Lieutenant Doyle was devastated even though the commo problem that caused the disaster was not his fault. "All those casualties were a bitter pill to swallow, especially as I stood there without a scratch. I felt certain that the platoon had lost confidence in me." Previously, the grunts had responded to Doyle as a green but highly intelligent platoon leader who was coming along well under the wings of Carney and Eades. Shortly after the ambush, however, one of Doyle's NCOs told him to go to hell when instructed to deploy a mechanical ambush on a little trail meandering past the platoon laager. The sergeant angrily said that it was stupid, that the lieutenant was just going to blow up a wild pig. Doyle was so stressed out that he finally heaved the claymore onto the trail, screaming, "I want the fucking thing put out there!"

A few days later, Charlie One, moving down a trail, was within three hundred meters of the ambush site when Doyle halted the platoon and called Knight. Knight instructed him to continue through the shot-up area. Doyle called his squad leaders up to pass the word, but that same sergeant refused the order. "I didn't have the energy to persuade or reassure," recalled Doyle. He said he swore angrily at the NCO, turned away and headed back up to the point. One of the grunts, seeing how upset Doyle was, asked him what was wrong. "I was too angry to speak. I just shook my head and kept walking. I wasn't sure if it was going to be a patrol of one or if I was going to get a bullet in the back of the head." The patrol followed, but those were bad times for Doyle. "Perception is as important as reality, and the troops were convinced that I had screwed up big time with that artillery round," he later said. "They were good guys, but nobody wants to risk being led around by someone they don't trust, and decisions do get made that [force people to say], 'Hey, wait a minute, the most reasonable thing for us to do is get rid of this guy before he gets all of us killed.' There were times I was very frightened, not just of what was in front of me, but what was behind me."

When the company returned to Mary Ann, Lieutenant Doyle was interviewed by an artillery major who was investigating the friendly fire incident. According to the major, there had been no commo problem—the firing battery had received all the adjustments and had fired exactly where it was directed to. The first rounds that exploded on the other side of the enemy ridge had apparently been closer than Doyle estimated and because of his inexperience, he had adjusted the fire right onto his own men.

"Looks like I fucked up," Doyle mumbled to the major, waves of guilt crashing in. "What's your report going to say?"

"Well, it's going to say that a platoon leader was trying to do the best for his men," the major replied.

Doyle, who never forgave himself for Gardner's death, would have felt differently about the BSMv the army gave him for his leadership during the ambush had he been able to speak with Captain Conatser. "Doyle's coordinates were good," said Conatser, the battery commander on FSB Mary Ann. Although the artillery major had passed the buck to the infantry, Conatser himself felt that he was responsible for the friendly fire incident, if only indirectly. The round that had crested the ridgeline and gone long—four hundred meters past Doyle's correct adjustment—was still within the normal circle of error inherent in any fire mission. "There was no error in the infantry's coordinates, on the guns, or in the computations done in the Fire Direction Center (FDC). I was out on the guns, but when we got the check fire, I went into the FDC and looked at the map and thought, holy shit, we should have been doing a high-angle on this!"

The lieutenant running the FDC had done everything properly, but had not checked out the terrain on the map. "When you're shooting the regular low-angle and you crest a ridge because of the normal dispersion of the round, you go way past," explained Conatser. "That's what happened here, and the friendly element was right on the gun-target line. If we'd been firing high-angle, then when the round crested the ridge it wouldn't have gone as far. I was responsible because I had not brought that lieutenant to that level of sophistication. I didn't have a procedure that automatically called for the FDC personnel to look at the map and determine what kind of terrain we were shooting on. I did after that, but big fuckin' deal—we'd already lost a guy."

After the friendly fire slammed in, Lieutenant Doyle was alerted that he had a LOH and two gunships overhead, unseen above the canopy. It was 1730 on February 12, 1971. Popping smoke to mark his position, Doyle simply sat the smoke grenade in front of him so as to minimize the margin of error when the Cobras rolled in. It buried the platoon in smoke. "We can't see anything," guys started screaming. "For Christ's sake, Lieutenant, they could counterattack!" Doyle grabbed the red-hot canister and heaved it to their front, badly burning his hand from index finger to thumb in the process. The Cobras started working out. "That was a terrifying experience," Doyle recalled. The rockets made almost as much noise leaving their pods as they did exploding unseen on the jungled ridge. "I was trying to adjust by ear, but I was so disoriented that I finally just asked the scout pilot to adjust the fire. I didn't want to bring in any more fire on top of us."

"I can't see where they are," the LOH pilot replied.

"Well, look, let's just call it off," Doyle said.

The pilot agreed. "I think you might have broken contact. With all the shit you've dumped in, Charlie's probably long gone."

Lieutenant Doyle didn't know if the NVA had pulled back or were waiting with their sights on the dead point man. "Okay, we're going to try to get Gardner out of there one more time."

"The guy's dead, LT!" shouted Sergeant Salmen.

"I don't give a fuck, we don't leave people behind," Doyle answered, and with that he turned to Sergeant Head, who had volunteered to get Gardner before the friendly fire blew their plans to hell. "Jesus, are you still willing to do this?"

"Yeah," Head replied.

"Well, we need one more guy."

"I'll go," said Salmen. "Fuck it."

Under a barrage of covering fire, Sergeants Salmen and Head crawled down to Willie Gardner, and dragged his body back up the trail. There was no enemy fire. Salmen then rushed back to the platoon NDP to help clear a medevac LZ. "I had a machete in each hand, and I chopped trees until my hands bled," remembered Salmen. "I was taking my frustration out on the trees. I was mad at Lieutenant Doyle. I was mad at the whole world. I was shouting. I was really upset because I really liked Sergeant Carney, and it didn't need to happen. If Doyle had listened to Carney it wouldn't have happened. He tried to tell him. . . ."

* * *

Lieutenant McGee and Sergeant Calhoun had hustled up the mountainside with Charlie Two, which presently secured Charlie One's NDP. Sergeant Daniels had transferred up with Gardner from the 25th Division, and he stood before Calhoun, sobbing, "They killed Willie . . . they killed Willie . . ."

At 1814 a medevac arrived with a gunship escort. The sun was on the horizon, but it was dark under the triple canopy. The medevac pilot flipped on his spotlight as he hovered above the mini-LZ, tearing off branches all around. The Huey was lowering its jungle penetrater when an NVA 12.7-mm machine gun opened fire from another hill. Taking hits, the Huey banked away. The medic on board had been wounded. "Up to that point, I was doing really well," remembered Dennis Murphy, who lay on his side as Carmichael cut away his fatigues and slapped field dressings on his gaping wounds. Someone else got his army-issue rosary out of his pocket and put it in his hand. "I had lost a lot of blood, but I was awake, I knew that I was going to live. The guys were there, they were trying to keep me cool, but when the medevac took fire, I gave up hope, I went into shock." The pain, the noise, all of it just disappeared, and he felt completely at peace. He was no longer struggling. He knew he was going to heaven, so he just let go. "But then someone slapped me back and forth and knocked me out of the shock. I was back on earth again, and my first thought when I came to was why the hell did you do that?"

Murphy refocused and realized that it was Sergeant Daniels who was slapping him. "You're not going to die!" Daniels shouted.

Charlie Two GIs moved down the trail to the ambush site, and when Lieutenant Doyle suddenly realized that he had grunts all around him that he didn't recognize, he headed back up the trail to see how the medevac was going. Doyle had just reached the laager when his grunts started shouting at him to get down.

"What the hell's going on?" Doyle asked, dropping to one knee.

"The medevac just got shot up!" somebody hollered.

"Oh, God," Doyle mumbled, at the end of his rope.

Doyle got reorganized. "What direction do you think the fire came from?" he shouted. Doyle picked the direction that looked like a consensus and shot a compass azimuth. Looking at his map, he tried to pick out the piece of high ground that would have given an enemy gun crew a commanding view of the LZ. Doyle was requesting an air strike when Atkinson, one of the friendly fire casualties, called to him, "Jesus, Lieutenant, don't bring another one in on us!" Doyle felt about two inches tall.

The jets strafed the suspected enemy position with automatic cannons and plastered it with napalm and bombs. The concussion was mind-numbing, and fragments slashed the treetops above the laager. The air strike was completed at 1905. Another medevac hovered over the mini-LZ, its spotlight on as it lowered its jungle penetrater, which resembled a vertical torpedo with two foldout seats and handles for the wounded.

Dennis Murphy, who was the worst casualty, was in no shape for such a ride. "The guy's got groin wounds," a Charlie Two NCO told Doyle as they prepared Murphy for extraction. Murphy was in a litter made of two ponchos secured between two poles, and the sergeant planned to rig it under the penetrater with rope.

"Hey, look, you've got to put him on the penetrater!" said Doyle.

"It isn't going to work, Lieutenant. He can't sit up and hang on. It isn't going to happen!"

Doyle helped the sergeant with the rope, then prayed as he watched Murphy's litter going up, suspended horizontally beneath the Huey's jungle penetrater. The litter swayed back and forth, crashing into the trees as Murphy screamed in agony, unheard in the roar of the propwash. The penetrater stopped at the top of the winch beside the open cabin door. The crewman leaning out on the skid couldn't get ahold of Murphy's dangling litter, and finally shouted at him to just hang on. Bloody and half-naked, Murphy wrapped an arm around the skid beside him so he wouldn't spin as the Huey banked out of its hover. Looking through the hole in the jungle canopy, he saw his platoon in the sputtering light of a flare jammed in the ground and thought that he was leaving behind his buddies in that terrible world down there. Trying not to think about what would happen if the rig broke, he maintained a death grip on the skid as the helicopter flew through the night. They headed straight toward the firebase, which looked like a birthday cake to him—round and white with illume bursting over it.

8

Death
Was Among Us

Two days after the ambush, Companies C and D established a joint laager on almost the same spot the enemy had held on the ridgeline during the debacle. The ridge ran down from the mountain that dominated the area, descending to the southeast. The laager was halfway up the spine, a klick north of the tributary where the cache had been captured, and a klick west of the Nam Nim River.

This was the enemy's backyard. On the morning of February 15, Captain Kirkey had his map out as he briefed his platoon leaders about a patrol up the ridgeline toward the top of the mountain. The platoon leader assigned to take point tried to beg off. "Boy, I'm just not ready for this," he said.

"I've been here the longest," offered Lieutenant Schmidt of Delta Two. "I'll go ahead and walk point."

Lieutenant Schmidt made his point team wear flak jackets despite the two grunts' complaints about the terrible heat. "You guys, I really want you to be alert this morning," Schmidt said, an uneasy feeling in his gut. "We're catching a lot of shit right now—you've got to be really careful and pay attention."

Captain Kirkey called in artillery around the laager to discourage ambush, but Delta Two had just started uphill when it walked into one in the dark gloom under the canopy of the giant trees. The point man, Pfc. Donald L. Moore, got on a trail, stepped over a log—and was suddenly looking into the muzzle of an AK-47. Moore screamed, "Oh my God!" as he dove for cover. The enemy soldier opened fire and a round hit Moore's left shoulder and lodged in the small of his back. Private First Class David O. Ray was walking slack behind Moore. The first burst of enemy fire hit Ray's M16—which he had slung over his neck and held in both hands at the waist—disabling the weapon and spraying him in the face with metal fragments. Unarmed, Ray spun around and charged back down the hill, his face as white as a sheet.

Meanwhile, the third man in line, Sergeant Olints, was holding his M16 in one hand and pulling the quick-release clips on his shoulder straps with the other to get out of his rucksack. Seconds before the ambush he had whispered to Moore and Ray to get off the trail they had bumped into. Olints had just taken one step into the bushes to the left when the NVA opened fire. Not realizing anybody had been hit, he rushed toward the biggest tree in sight, unaware that he was going past his own point man and charging right at the ambushers. Unable to see the enemy, he didn't realize how close they were until their fire began tearing up the other side of the huge tree. The sound was so loud it hurt, the concussion so fierce against the tree Olints thought he'd been hit, but he blasted back around the side of the tree, expending six magazines even as enemy grenades exploded around him.

Lieutenant Schmidt, the fourth man, heard Moore scream—and the next thing he knew he was flying backward despite the rucksack on his back, shot through his left thigh. He landed hard, a fist-sized chunk of muscle blown away from the back of his leg where the round exited. Schmidt couldn't move—couldn't feel anything. He started firing his M16 uphill as the panicked Ray went screaming past. Suddenly the ground began jumping around him, the fire coming from above. He rolled away, swinging his rifle up and spraying the treetops.

"Get the pig up here!" Schmidt shouted.

Rushing forward, Private Meek opened up with his M60, inadvertently firing right over Moore, who was hidden in the brush. The point man screamed back, "I'm not dead yet!"

The firefight was over in moments. Afterward, Olints, almost doubled up with stomach cramps, had to sit on his rucksack with his head pressed between his legs. He couldn't move.

"You're white," someone said to Olints. "Are you okay?"

"I'm fine . . . I'm fine," he mumbled.

"Don't worry, man, it's all right."

Grunts patted him reassuringly on the shoulder. Sergeant Olints was embarrassed when subsequently awarded a Silver Star for this action. He should not have been embarrassed. His charge might have been an accident, but the heavy volume of his return fire had been real enough—as were the bullet holes in his tree.

Lieutenant Schmidt, who won another BSMv, was medevacked in a poncho litter. Delta Three's medic also had to be evacuated. "It was a case of shell shock," recalled Captain Kirkey, whose CP group had crouched behind the roots of the giant trees as stray rounds from the ambush up the ridge snapped past. The medic was with them. "Two of his best friends had already died in his arms during the previous ambush, and it just got to him," said Kirkey. The medic got up, shaking and crying, and the captain grabbed him before he wandered away from cover. "He was incoherent. I had to hold him. I had both arms wrapped around him and was just hugging him like a baby to give him some comfort."

Lieutenant Hugh Harrell, the Delta Company exec, helicoptered out to the joint laager aboard a LOH and took over Delta Three, whose platoon leader had recently rotated out. In the morning, Harrell told his platoon sergeant—who, like the grunts in his new platoon, he did not know—to get the guys saddled up for the day's push up the ridgeline. The platoon sergeant, however, came back, shaking his head. "Hey, we got a problem," he said. "The guys aren't going."

"What do you mean they're not going?" Harrell asked. "You go back and talk to them and see how far this is going to go."

"They ain't bluffin'," the platoon sergeant replied.

It was February 16, 1971, and the men of the 3d Platoon, Company D, 1-46th Infantry, Americal Division, had decided to survive this insanity by refusing to leave the laager. "Look, what's the problem?" Harrell inquired empathetically as he went to the little groups along the perimeter. "Nothing against you, LT," explained one grunt, "but this is just stupid. We move out and the point's getting ambushed before the rear squad's even cleared the laager. We've been hit day after day, and we're just not going."

Harrell reported the situation to Captain Kirkey. "Can you talk to them?" asked Kirkey. "Is this negotiable?"

"No, I don't think so."

Harrell walked back to Delta Three. "Hey, guys, there's no choice here," he said. "Either we sky up and go or we're all going to jail, it's as simple as that. I've talked to the captain, and the next step is to get the battalion commander out here."

Captain Kirkey, highly distressed, called Lieutenant Colonel Doyle on the radio. "The lieutenant and the platoon sergeant are kind of 'Mutt-and-Jeffing' it. One guy's the good guy, and one guy's the bad guy," Kirkey explained.

"What are *you* doing?" Doyle asked.

"Well, I'm going to go down there and start off as a nice guy, and then I'll kick their ass and see what happens."

"All right, I'm en route. . . ."

When Captain Kirkey talked with the Delta Three GIs, he learned that they were really uptight that it took medevac choppers forty-five minutes to reach them and another forty-five minutes to get back to Chu Lai. The grunts wanted a medevac on station above them at all times. "That's completely unrealistic," Kirkey told them. They also said they wanted a Cobra gunship on standby at Mary Ann, ready to provide immediate fire support. "That isn't going to happen either," Kirkey said. "It would never be able to take off. A fully loaded gunship needs to take off with its nose down almost like it's an airplane going down a runway. . . ."

Exasperated, Captain Kirkey finally exclaimed "When I tell you to do something, you're going to do it!"

"Yeah," a grunt barked back, "we've been listening to you—and look where we're at!"

Kirkey then threatened to court-martial them, but it meant nothing to men who felt they were in the middle of nowhere. Kirkey tried a different tack. "Well, we're going to leave your asses here," Kirkey said, reminding them that the NVA moved in to scavenge vacated NDPs. "You know my policy: we're gone about an hour and then we blow the laager site to hell with artillery. So you got a choice—you can move out or get blown up!"

Lieutenant Colonel Doyle finally settled the matter after being dropped off by a LOH. "I'm laying it right on the line," Doyle said forcefully. "When my chopper comes back, I'll put everybody in it and we'll go right to Da Nang. You're all going to jail. Amen. That's the end of it."

It was, almost. "We want scout dogs," a grunt said, breaking the silence that followed the colonel's pronouncement.

"Dogs don't work. Don't put your confidence in them," Doyle replied.

"We want dogs, sir," the GI insisted.

"Okay, you'll have dogs in two days. . . ."

Delta Three began to saddle up then, however sullenly. "Colonel Doyle was still real gung ho even though the war was winding down," remembered one grenadier. "We probably wanted to shoot him down a couple times."

Captain Kirkey said he never mentioned the incident again. "The troops were just scared. I could understand that." Officially, the U.S. Army was in a defensive posture around the major coastal installations of Vietnam. Officially, the ARVN were fighting the war. Soldiers frequently got clippings from home about Vietnamization, along with letters from parents who were so glad their sons weren't out fighting anymore. "Combat assaults were now supposed to be called airmobile insertions," recalled Kirkey. "Instead of search and destroy operations, we were now conducting defensive patrols. It didn't make it any easier. . . ."

Captains Kirkey and Knight had planned a joint patrol, and after the combat refusal had been quashed elements from both companies moved uphill toward the mountaintop. Charlie Two was on point, followed by the reluctant Delta

Three. As Charlie Two neared the scene of the previous day's ambush, three NVA opened fire at a distance of thirty meters, then disappeared as the jungle reverberated with return fire. Private First Class Gary W. Goble, a radioman, took a round through the meat of both thighs so high up that he feared his genitals had been blown away. When the medic started cutting away Goble's trouser legs to expose the wound, Goble grabbed him and said he had to find out for himself how badly he was hurt. Finding everything hanging where he had left it, he grinned widely and told the medic to get back to work on his nice clean wound.

The medic thumped him with morphine. "Million-dollar wound, man, it's cool," Goble called to his buddies as he was carried downhill in a poncho. "I'm going home—it's all over!"

More artillery was fired to cover the patrol's withdrawal, then a LOH bounced in to pick up Goble. "He was thrilled," remembered Sergeant Olints, "and I was envious." Two days later, Delta Two ran a patrol to a small, man-made clearing outside the laager that the platoon was supposed to secure as a resupply LZ. When Olints got clearance to recon by fire, Meek blasted the jungle on the other side of the clearing with his M60, then stepped behind a tree while a grenadier went into action. The grenadier's third round hit a tree, and Meek caught a fragment in his left hand, which was exposed as he held his machine gun up, ready to step out from behind the tree and fire again. The metal shard embedded in the bone between the first and second knuckle of his thumb. "It was burnin'-ass hot," said Meek. "My thumb was just going numb and wild, and I was cursing: goddamn, goddamn! I was just about at my wit's end anyway I was so tired."

The resupply Huey hovered over the tree stumps and debris of the clearing as the ammo and rations were unloaded. Meek, meanwhile, apologized to Olints as the medic wrapped his hand. Olints told him that it was okay, that he *had* to go. Olints was among those who helped Meek up on the skid of the resupply chopper. As the door gunner pulled him inside, Meek later recalled, he "felt real guilty about leaving Andy out there because a lot of the old guys weren't there anymore to take care of each other, but God, I was scared. I was scared to death. I just wanted to get on that helicopter and get the hell out of there."

There was more action the day of the combat refusal. To spread things out, Captain Knight moved several hundred meters south of the main laager to establish another patrol base with Charlie Two and Delta Three. "We hacked down some brush to clear some fields of fire, then set up our poncho hootches," remembered Private Creaven, a Charlie Two grenadier. Creaven was feeling good—after ten months in the bush, he was going on R&R. He was supposed to be lifted out on the morning resupply bird. To celebrate, Creaven—a tall, thin, middle-class kid radicalized by the '60s—smoked some dope at his position with several fellow heads. "I got a nice buzz," he said later. "I figured, well, I'm leaving tomorrow, I might as well finish my stash here. My squad was strictly freaks. We still had some gung ho idiots out there who would do stuff that freaked me out, but I hung with the group that was probably a little bit more educated. If it had been a different kind of war, I'm sure every one of those guys would have been busting his butt, but when you could see the total hypocrisy of the situation, why die? We just wanted to do our time and survive, then get the hell out of there and try and forget about it."

Sergeant Ledoux, who wore blinders when it came to the use of drugs in his squad, interrupted the going-away party at Creaven's position. He told them the lieutenant wanted a recon patrol to check out an adjacent hill and that Creaven had the point. The squad moved up the hill along a dried-out, gravel-bottomed creek bed. There were tracks in the gravel. Creaven followed the tracks but lost them where the creek went around both sides of a brushy knoll above them on the hillside.

Creaven halted. "Pass the word back," he whispered to the slack man. "We're going to walk into an ambush real soon."

Everything was hot and still. Creaven signaled for them to move out to the right, the way he thought whoever made the tracks had gone. "There was an ambush coming, I could feel it, but I figured, I'm good enough, I'm going to know where it's going to be—and I'm going to pop him first." Creaven had killed an NVA in a similar situation while with the 4th Division. He still had the man's bright blue hammock. Creaven's right hand was wrapped around the pistol grip of his XM203, and his left was on the grenade launcher under the barrel. He had a colored Montagnard scarf tied around his helmet, knotted so that its tail hung over the back of his steel pot—"just to show that you weren't willing to conform"—along with beads and bracelets, and a peace symbol the size of a silver dollar on a necklace. He never wore a flak jacket, but this time he had put one on at the suggestion of a grunt who said that Creaven was too close to his R&R to take any chances. "I thought the ambush was going to come from the right side of the fork, but I guessed wrong. I caught a flash of movement out the corner of my eye, up on the knoll to my left. I started to spin to my left to open fire, I was trying to move as fast as I could, but before I could even raise my weapon I saw this big orange ball—"

Creaven was looking into the muzzle flash of an NVA firing from behind a tree stump. The tracers seemed to float toward him in slow motion—so slowly that he recalls thinking he could duck between them. The burst hit him in his chest and arm, however, lifting him off his feet and slamming him down on his face. His weapon was gone, but, luckily, Creaven found himself sprawled behind the roots of a large tree in a little embankment.

Gravel sprayed him as the guerrilla tried unsuccessfully to depress his weapon into a killing angle. Creaven, unable to move, screamed desperately, "I quit, goddamnit, I quit!"

The bandolier slung across Creaven's chest had also been hit, and his slack man had been nicked by fragments from the mangled ammo magazines. The slack man rolled off into the bushes, but Ledoux and his machine gunner instantly rushed forward to take the heat off Creaven, and sprayed the area even after the enemy fire had ceased. The NVA was gone. It was another hit-and-run ambush. Creaven was not wounded as badly as he might have been. The rounds that hit his flak jacket had glanced away. Still, it looked like his right arm had been carved with a butcher knife. His triceps and most of his biceps had been blown away. He was lying on the arm in the same position he'd landed when help arrived. A medic rolled him over and a severed artery spurted blood into the air.

"I was pumping blood out like a fountain, but I was in no pain," remembered Creaven. "I was still pretty buzzed."

The medic clamped off the artery, bandaged Creaven's shattered arm and a minor frag wound in his right thigh, and administered morphine. Creaven, going into shock from blood loss, was vaguely aware of being carried back to the laager in a poncho. The platoon frantically cleared a landing zone with machetes and plastic explosives and Creaven was eventually strapped onto a jungle penetrater seat. He looked down at his buddies as he was being winched up and managed to flash them the peace sign.

Creaven passed out on the helicopter's metal floor after being pulled inside by a crewman. He woke up when they landed to refuel and realized that the wounded slack man was sitting beside him. The kid had a pack of cigarettes in his hands. "My God, this is crazy, we're taking on fuel and this asshole's going to light a cigarette!" Creaven said, recounting the scene. "I could see the fuel bladders. I remember him taking his cigarette out and doing the little tapping routine, and he was looking for his lighter, and I'm thinking, oh my God, what a way to go! I couldn't really talk by then, so I was trying to get the crewman's attention with my eyes. I was moving my head a little bit to make him look and then I remember him reaching over and snatching the cigarette away."

After the medevac, Sergeant Ledoux refused orders to take out a night ambush, telling the lieutenant that the enemy probably still had the platoon under observation. Ledoux had other worries besides getting overrun in the dark. "I always stayed awake on ambush," he recalled, "and it shocked me because I had guys actually snoring when they were supposed to be on watch. Some people just didn't realize that, hey, this is not a game, this is a life-and-death thing here."

Ledoux was in for a Silver Star. Knight had been with his squad when they spotted a VC with black pajamas and an AK in an irrigation ditch. They rushed him. Ledoux reached the ditch first and jumped in, his M16 set on automatic. The guerrilla was twenty paces away, crawling down the ditch, trying to get away. The man turned and tried to swing his weapon around. They were looking right at each other, and Ledoux, not thinking, not even aiming, blew him away. "The captain really loved stuff like that," Ledoux explained. "I don't want to give the impression, though, that I had my stuff together, because I didn't. When I first got there, they put me and two other replacements on a resupply chopper and dropped us off with the company out in the middle of the jungle, out in the middle of nowhere, pouring down rain at the time, and I didn't know anybody or anything. I was just scared to death. I was scared the whole time over there."

Sergeant Ledoux, then twenty-one, had a wife and baby son waiting for him in Orange, Texas. When Ledoux refused to take out the ambush, Captain Knight furiously told him that he would be court-martialed. After Ledoux explained himself, the company commander offered a compromise. "Well, what if I let you pick the people that you want from the whole platoon?" Knight asked, given some of the unreliable troops in Ledoux's squad. "I'll send another squad out with you. When you drop off into your ambush position, the dinks won't know you're out there because they'll be watching the other squad circle around and come back in like it was a recon patrol."

Sergeant Ledoux agreed and asked Sergeant Brandt, a fellow shake 'n' bake squad leader, for a good grenadier to replace Creaven. Brandt told Pfc. David G. Massich to saddle up for the ambush. Massich, who was heating up a can of spaghetti, looked up, outraged. "Wally Brandt was a good guy but it seemed to me that I was chosen for every patrol, and this time I snapped," said Massich. "I was so pissed off, I kicked the open can of spaghetti and splattered him. I hadn't meant to hit him, but I took some satisfaction when I looked back over my shoulder as I walked away and saw him brushing the mess off himself."

No one was willing to confront the captain directly, but there was a lot of loud complaining about the order to move out. Knight shouted that he wanted the names of everyone on the ambush, especially those of the "sorry sonsofbitches who say they aren't going!" Knight threatened to court-martial them, and the ambush finally moved out with all assigned members. "When we got out there, we didn't set up any claymores," remembered Ledoux, "because I wasn't about to make any noise and give the dinks any kind of idea where we were at. I kept the radio all night long. No one slept. If anybody had come along, definitely we would have opened fire, but nothing happened, thank God."

On February 18, Lieutenant McGee, back in command of Charlie Three, was working his platoon down a ridgeline when the point team heard ducks quacking farther downhill, somewhere in front of them. McGee radioed Knight, and reported that he probably had a Montagnard family up ahead. Knight, however, was taking no chances. "The captain told us to go down there and kill 'em all, kill everything," said Pfc. Tom Schneider, the Charlie Three RTO. He said Knight sounded cold and deliberate, angry about their recent casualties. McGee, a gung ho West Pointer, called back to explain again that he thought the noise was from Montagnards, not NVA. McGee, in the grip of malaria, shivered as he spoke. "McGee didn't want to do it," remembered Schneider. "My Lai was fresh on everybody's mind. McGee questioned the order a little, but the captain let McGee know firmly that that was what we were supposed to do." Charlie Three dropped rucks and started down on the trail, the men concerned that they were walking into an ambush. It was getting dark fast under the jungle canopy. "We got about halfway down there, and it's goddamn near pitch dark, and that's where McGee began using his head. He called the captain and told us we didn't find anything. Actually, we didn't even get there. He gave the captain a false report, then turned around and backed out. By the time we got back to where our rucks were and set up a night laager, he was freezing to death. He was in a sweat, but he was freezing. His teeth were chattering, and he was having a hell of a malaria attack, but he rode it out. He did not get medevacked."

Captains Kirkey and Knight, having pushed another klick up the main ridgeline, presently advanced toward the top of the jungled mountain on a six-platoon front that extended from the ridge down into the valley to their left, then up onto another ridge. They expected to find either a major cache, or the enemy headquarters for the area. But nothing was ever found on the mountaintop beyond a few abandoned hootches, which were uselessly destroyed.

It was February 20. The enemy supply trail on the right flank of the push followed the crest of the main ridge. The platoon on that flank, Lieutenant Harrell's Delta Three, walked into a claymore ambush on the trail. The platoon had moved downhill into a saddle and was starting up the next rise on the ridgeline. The NVA were above them on the slope, their claymore positioned so it would hit the heads and chests of anyone coming up the trail. The dog handler on point had already walked past the claymore when his dog alerted on the enemy soldiers in the brush to one side of the trail. The dog handler stopped in his tracks. The grunts, who had been moving in a spread-out formation, had become clustered on the trail behind the dog team as the vegetation, especially the bamboo, became thicker on the flanks, pressing them in toward the middle, pressing them into a perfect killing zone.

When the dog handler stopped, Lieutenant Harrell, fifth in the column, turned to Specialist Sutton, the machine gunner, and said, "Pass the word down the line to spread back out." As Harrell turned he stepped behind a tree—which saved his life because the unseen NVA blew their claymore at that instant. It knocked down everyone ahead of him. AK fire followed the explosion, and Harrell saw two enemy soldiers wearing pith helmets standing up in the brush. He turned and shouted at Sutton to fire.

"Where?" Sutton shouted back.

"Just out in front of you!" Harrell screamed.

"We'll hit our own guys!"

"No, man, they're *gone!*"

Harrell opened up around the right side of the tree with his CAR15, and Sutton cut loose with his M60 from the left as the two NVA rushed away. It was impossible to tell if they hit anything before the jungle swallowed the ambushers back up.

Lieutenant Harrell, blaming himself, held one of his mangled troops, trying to comfort him as he went under. The kid couldn't speak. He could only move his head and arms a little, and he died in Harrell's arms. The other two grunts in front of the claymore were killed instantly. "We could not pursue because there was mass chaos on the trail," remembered Harrell, who got on the radio and called for a medevac for the dog handler, who had gone past the claymore but was injured by the back blast. Harrell got the platoon into a defensive position in the bamboo on either side of the trail. He figured they'd only hit another ambush if they moved out, and he didn't think the men would go anyway. "They'd had it, they weren't functioning. We were all in shock, and I told them we had people coming up the hill from behind who would get this thing sorted out. We sat there until the support came up. No one said anything. They didn't have to. The looks on their faces were enough. It was all over their faces, probably mine as well. Death was among us. . . ."

Part IV

Countdown to the Storm

Concurrent with the bitter fighting along the Nam Nim, Lieutenant Colonel Doyle had Companies A and B employed in much more productive operations. By late-February, 1971, Company B, working north from FSB Mary Ann across the chain of mountains hugging the western bank of the Tranh River, had progressed to a point ten kilometers beyond the firebase, at the edge of its artillery fan. The NVA were especially active farther north in the Phuoc Chau Valley, which was on the eastern side of the Tranh and out of artillery range. To get at this sanctuary, Doyle helicoptered Bravo Company across the river, then lifted several mortar and two artillery tubes onto a small hill the company had secured in the valley, thus expanding the range of supporting arms. The mini-firebase was dubbed LZ Grunt.

The rest of Company B pushed on into the virgin territory. The results were encouraging. To get at other NVA sanctuaries, Doyle closed down the first mini-firebase in mid-March and had Bravo Company open another, LZ Mildred, almost seven kilometers southeast of FSB Mary Ann. Operations were then launched deep into the boondocks to the southeast and southwest, and again much damage was done to the enemy in quick, small meeting engagements. Troop morale soared. Mary Ann had never seemed so secure—or so removed from a war that was moving deeper and deeper into the jungle.

9

Body Counts

The LOH was flying at contour level under the low-hanging monsoon clouds when it popped over the ridgeline. There were six enemy soldiers on the other side, down on a sandy spit where a stream forked off the Tranh River. The NVA were butchering a wild boar. "They sure weren't expecting to see a helicopter drop down in the middle of their barbecue," said Capt. Peter J. Gallagher, who was taking the LOH out to join Company B, 1-46th Infantry, on FSB Mary Ann. He had just been assigned as company commander after having already served eight months down south with the 25th Division. The LOH was several klicks from Mary Ann when they encountered the NVA. Before the enemy could get to their weapons, Gallagher engaged them with his M16 as the pilot turned to put his door gunner on the enemy side. The door gunner raked the beach with M60 fire. "It looked like we left three bodies sprawled in the sand. We didn't hang around for a count. We hit fast and disappeared back into the fog."

Captain Gallagher took command of Bravo Company shortly after New Year's Day 1971. "Gallagher was a good man, and so were the platoon leaders and squad leaders," said Sp4 Steve Leventhal. "The other companies got their asses kicked. Bravo Company never did. Maybe we were lucky, or maybe we were good at what we did."

First Lieutenant Robert E. Moore of Bravo Three was out with a squad-sized patrol that bumped into five NVA. Surprised, the lead enemy soldier threw up his hands, but another NVA raised his AK-47. Moore's patrol returned fire—it looked like one NVA was shot in the chest—then moved out in hot pursuit, following a blood trail. The enemy soldier must have had his hand clamped over the wound because the grunts found bloody handprints on trees on which the man had leaned to catch his breath. The blood led to several deserted hootches, one of which was a primitive aid station where the wounded man must have grabbed some bandages before stumbling on. The grunts lost the blood trail at that point.

During another patrol, Bravo Three's point team spotted wet footprints upon crossing a small stream. Pressing on cautiously, they caught three NVA taking a break and opened fire. One of the enemy was wounded but the others bounded away. "Somebody grabbed the wounded NVA's AK," remembered Sp4 Ronald L. Shook. "He was pretty badly hurt, but they thought he made a quick move or something and shot him in the head on full automatic. I had the guy's skull and scalp and brains blown all over me."

Later, Shook was eating spaghetti and meatballs when the point man, a cocky little guy, wryly compared the meal to the enemy soldier's splattered brains. "I lost what I'd eaten of that can—but it was all in a day's work," sighed Shook.

Bravo Company took casualties only once while operating north of FSB Mary Ann. On February 10 Lieutenant Moore's platoon was humping back to rejoin Gallagher's CP, where a resupply helicopter was landing. The point man that day, Sgt. Jaime P. Acosta, who was also a great squad leader, could see the Huey about fifty meters ahead through the trees. He turned to the RTO behind him on the ridge-top trail to make sure the CP group knew the patrol was closing on its position. He didn't want anybody to get spooked and open fire. Acosta was still looking at the Huey when a booby trap suddenly exploded to the left, blowing him off the trail. He landed in a sitting position, his rucksack keeping him upright. His M16 was under him.

By the time he pulled it free and had it in his hands, ready to fire, he realized there was no ambush. The only sound was the moaning of the wounded radioman. Acosta himself had been peppered with fragments in the heel of his left foot, up along the leg, and around his left elbow, breaking the bone.

On that same day, Alpha One cut onto a supply trail with footprints on it eight klicks southeast of FSB Mary Ann. The platoon followed them to a creek running across the trail from a jungled hillside. The new lieutenant sent a recon patrol across. Pfc. Ed Voros took the point, followed by a black grunt, Eddie Williams, and their new platoon sergeant, who was also black. Williams whispered to Voros that he thought he heard someone talking, but Voros could hear nothing over the babble of the creek. He continued to a blind turn in the trail, stopped momentarily, and distinctly heard NVA coming their way. Backtracking toward the creek, they set up a hasty ambush to the left of the trail just as three enemy soldiers came around the bend, talking, weapons slung. One of them had a U.S. PRC-25 radio strapped to his back. Voros, on one knee behind three slender, bunched-up trees, swung his M16 toward the nearest NVA—but, before he could sight in, the man saw him and dropped and rolled off the trail. Voros fired on automatic, his barrel rising as he emptied the magazine. The burst went over the head of the prone enemy soldier. At that same instant, the platoon sergeant jumped up and ran back down the trail in a total panic. Voros and Williams scrambled after him.

Catching up with the sergeant back in the platoon position, Williams angrily confronted him. "Why'd you take off?" he barked.

"I was going back to the radio—" the NCO started to explain.

"What the hell?" Voros cut in. "When you got dinks right in front of you, you don't go runnin' back to the radio!" The career sergeant was later reassigned to the rear.

Meanwhile, Alpha One fired down the trail, then spread out to either side of it and swept forward, finding neither bodies nor blood trails. Captain Spilberg was "so pissed off I can't see straight," he wrote in a letter, noting that "when we get back to Mary Ann I'm going to make my whole company take marksmanship training . . . it is not the first time we've lost some kills due to poor marksmanship."

On February 14, Alpha One fired on a lone NVA walking along a path that paralleled the supply trail. The enemy soldier fled down an even smaller side trail. The grunts balked at pursuing him—it seemed the side trail was subtly marked by the enemy as being booby-trapped to prevent one enemy unit from wandering into another's kill zone—content to simply establish their assigned ambush on the main trail. Toward dusk, the Alpha One GIs, moving back to their laager, heard several NVA talking nearby. Everyone got down. Private Ed Gittens was getting his M60 ready when Doc Riley, the platoon medic, jumped over him. Riley landed to his right and pointed toward a creek bed where the NVA were ducking behind boulders. Gittens cut loose on them. Everyone else opened up, and the volume of fire was such that it was unclear if the enemy was returning fire.

"Cease fire . . . cease fire . . . !" someone shouted.

As Gittens released the trigger on his M60 he felt a punch to his left shoulder. His assistant gunner shouted, "Doc, Doc, Gittens done been hit!"

Gittens had taken a single fragment, presumably from a 40-mm grenade round hitting a tree. It didn't hurt until Doc Riley pulled out the three inches of shirt that had been pulled into the wound by the shrapnel. Again, the NVA had gotten away clean. "My people fired them up at about 50 to 75 meters and missed," wrote Spilberg. "When they got back to the patrol base I talked to some of the men and had them show me what they did. Every one demonstrated that they fire from under the shoulder or the hip position rather than use well aimed fire from the shoulder."

During another operation, Company A was in the courtyard of a French plantation house when it took fire from one of the hills overlooking the abandoned building. In response, Captain Spilberg headed through the hedge the first bursts had ripped through, and launched a one-man charge up the hill, firing his CAR15 as he ran. His RTO, Sp4 David J. Tarnay, ran for his radio. He passed four palm trees that were hit at chest level by the RPD machine gun tracking him, then scrambled after the captain. Blasting away, the two of them drove the enemy off even as friendly fire from where the rest of the company was sprawled in the courtyard buzzed over their heads.

When the fire petered out, Spilberg realized he was not alone. "Tarnay, what the hell are you doing here?" he exclaimed.

"Captain, I can't let you go run off by yourself!" Tarnay replied.

Tarnay said that the intense, chain-smoking Captain Spilberg was a fantastic company commander—especially in comparison to the one he replaced. "That other captain was a coward," recalled Tarnay. When NVA were sighted, the other captain would pull back. "That shot our morale to pieces, but Spilberg turned the company around. To show that he had no fear he took a grease pencil and drew a bull's-eye dead center on the front of his helmet. Our kill ratio picked up incredibly, and we went from having the morale of whipped dogs to being the best company in the battalion."

Many grunts considered Spilberg aggressive to a fault, however. Things came to a head during a combat assault off FSB Mary Ann on February 22. "I ain't going out with that crazy bastard, he ain't getting me killed," Sp4 Carl Cleek remembers saying to the other Alpha One GIs as they sat packed up and ready to go by the helipad. The choppers were already on the way, but the rest of Alpha One was in agreement. Spilberg sent his field first sergeant to get them moving. Sergeant Reed heard the grunts out, then said, "C'mon, you don't want to do this," and explained about conditions in the Long Binh Jail. Most of the men backed down. To get the rest in action, Spilberg finally marched down himself, embarrassed and furious at the timing of this stunt. "Now you sonsofbitches get off your asses, or I'm going to court-martial every one of you!" he barked.

Getting no response, Spilberg tried a calmer approach. "Doc Riley, you're a good soldier—you're in for the Silver Star."

"No, sir, I'm not going," Riley said.

Lieutenant Colonel Doyle then joined Spilberg. After some more pointed, no-nonsense conversations about courts-martial, everyone in Alpha One rucked up except Cleek, Riley, and a machine gunner named Osborn—country boys all. Doyle packed them off to Chu Lai aboard a resupply ship. Sergeant First Class Paul E. Davis, the company first sergeant, immediately called Cleek into his quarters behind the orderly room. Cleek said that when he started to light a cigarette, Davis snapped, "You light that, and I'll smack it out of your mouth."

Cleek was stunned. He thought the world of the first sergeant, a good old boy from Louisiana who carried an AK round near his spine, a souvenir of his first Vietnam tour. "I had high hopes for you," Davis said. "You were a leader. You were going to be a sergeant. Are you getting chicken-shit?"

"You know better, Top," replied Cleek.

"Then what're you doing refusing orders?" asked Davis.

"It's Captain Spilberg," Cleek said. "The man is incompetent. He's dangerous. He needs to be relieved!"

Sergeant Davis threw Cleek out of the orderly room at that point. The incident was allowed to die, however, when Cleek, Riley, and Osborn rejoined Company A on the next resupply ship. They were unwilling, in the final analysis, to spend six months in the LBJ.[1] "You either hated Captain Spilberg, or you loved him," reflected Tarnay, the radioman. "The guys who hated him didn't realize that deep down he really cared about us. He pushed us, but he pushed us for the right reasons. He was hard because he didn't want to see any of us die."

Captain Spilberg pushed himself hardest of all, running a good company but burning out in the process. "With the war almost over, leadership by example was paramount," he reflected. "It was 'Follow Me,' or they would not go." High-strung by nature, Spilberg was always on edge, his nerves unbearably frayed. There was an incident in the battalion rear which convinced Doyle that Spilberg was getting "flaky," as the colonel put it. It occurred the night Spilberg was medevacked with his wounded hand. Fuzzy with painkillers, he was just dozing off in a hootch used by several officers when there was a commotion outside. It was the headquarters company commander coming home from a night of partying, but Spilberg grabbed the .45 he kept under his pillow, saw a silhouette in the doorway, and had the pistol in the man's face before he realized where he was and who he had almost shot. "Being a company commander was extraordinarily stressful. I was pretty well exhausted, and from what I understand I was talking in my sleep and having nightmares out in the bush. The men were concerned that I was getting stressed out, and that might have been a factor in those troops refusing to go to the field."

Captain Spilberg went on leave during the mission that began with the combat refusal, and Doyle transferred him to brigade headquarters upon his return. Spilberg's last action with Alpha Company occurred on February 26. The column was on a ridge, following an enemy supply trail. Sergeant Joseph, a black, second-tour squad leader, was on point. The NVA were there—everyone could feel it—and Spilberg was right behind the lead squad. No one spoke, communicating instead by hand signals. The contact, when it came, was over in seconds. Joseph and two young, sharp-looking NVA—with AK-47s, closely cropped haircuts, green fatigues, pith helmets, and packs—walked right into each other. Joseph blasted one while the other dashed off down the trail and disappeared. According to Spilberg, Joseph—furious, scared, and overjoyed to be alive—emptied his M16 into the dead NVA on full auto, his eyes gleaming. They booby-trapped the kill, using a white phosphorous grenade and two frags, pins pulled and safety spoons held in place under the body. When the company moved back through the area several days later, the body was gone and the trail was scorched. The jungle was silent.

Given the light amount of action in the division area, these successful contacts by the Professionals drew much praise from Maj. Gen. James Baldwin, the division commander.

The general, in turn, was highly regarded by his officers. "Baldwin was a very analytical and thoughtful man," said Lt. Col. Crosbie E. Saint, G3 operations officer of the 23d Division. Baldwin was fifty years old, tall, bespectacled, and stolid. "Even when something went wrong, the general's modus operandi when he had a conversation with a subordinate was to provide insights on how to do better. He saw his role as that of a fatherly coach, as opposed to a taskmaster."

"General Baldwin was very much a gentleman," said Capt. John Strand of the 1-46th Infantry. "He was decisive when he needed to be, but also very thoughtful and approachable."

Destined for early retirement in the wake of the sapper attack, Baldwin had previously been considered a rising star in the army. The son of a Kansas farmer, he had originally been called to active duty from the National Guard in 1940. He was attending a teachers' college at the time. Baldwin won an OCS commission in 1942 and was awarded the CIB, BSM, and Purple Heart while serving as a regimental intelligence officer with the 99th Infantry Division in the European Theater of Operations in 1944–45. Baldwin missed the Korean War but successfully commanded a battalion and brigade in peacetime, prerequisite steps on a march to the stars. Furthermore, he excelled in several high-level Pentagon assignments, including a 1958–61 tour with the army's Office of the Deputy Chief of Staff for Military Operations; a 1962–64 tour as executive assistant to the Secretary of the Army; and a 1966–70 tour as director of U.S. Army Plans and Programs, and later Force Planning Analysis.

General Baldwin finally got to Vietnam in July, 1970. "Jim Baldwin was a brilliant staff officer who was obviously on a fast track to higher rank," wrote a fellow general officer. "Baldwin came to Vietnam to qualify for further promotions by demonstrating his ability to command in combat."

General Creighton W. Abrams, commander of the U.S. Military Assistance Command, Vietnam (COMUSMACV), thought Baldwin's troop experience was insufficient, and accepted him with the proviso that before getting his division, he would first get some experience in the theater as deputy commander of XXIV Corps in Da Nang. Major General Baldwin served at corps headquarters until taking over the 23d Division on November 23, whereupon he quickly established himself as a well-traveled, people-oriented division commander. After speaking with a grunt in the 91st Evac Hospital who had stepped on a punji stake, Baldwin wrote home that the trooper "was not happy to have a lovely wound which would keep him out of the war for a while . . . he was a quiet, well spoken, well educated young man. We have many, many really fine people who are doing a magnificent job. . . ."

Given the demoralization at the time, Baldwin also wrote that the simple "avoidance of disaster is an accomplishment," and he was exceptionally sympathetic to "the problems of the company commander who must face a group of young men who at best can be described as disgruntled—at worst, rebellious."

Whether Baldwin was a realist who did as well as could be expected, or a lenient defeatist, as his superiors contended, is open to debate. Following one serious contact, Baldwin and Saint flew to the firebase of the unit involved to speak with the battalion commander. It turned out that the engaged company had spent two nights in the same location, a complacent practice the company commander had been warned about. The enemy was able to organize an attack to coincide with the landing of a resupply ship, and inflicted heavy casualties.

During the return flight, Saint recommended that Baldwin relieve the battalion commander. "The battalion's not tactically sound," said Saint, who had served two combat tours with the division cavalry squadron. "The troops were really lousy looking, and the firebase wasn't very well kept-up or well-ordered."

Baldwin agreed, but said that "relieving the battalion commander probably isn't going to make a whole lot of difference." Saint, a future four-star general, recalled that he "looked at Baldwin, thinking, you're a hell of a lot nicer guy than I am. Baldwin handled the Mary Ann affair with the same compassion, which is probably what did him in. I don't think his attitude fit in with the war-fighter requirements of higher headquarters."

Lieutenant Colonel Saint described Bill Doyle as an "unkempt pro whose battalion had the best combat record in the division." Baldwin's best brigade commander, tall, rugged-looking Col. William S. Hathaway, was Doyle's boss. "Colonel Hathaway was a great man, and a great soldier's soldier," said one of the 196th Brigade's battalion commanders. Hathaway was a judicious, even-tempered southern gentleman known for his up-front, in-the-mud leadership with the 196th LIB. He had started up the ladder as an eighteen-year-old draftee in 1945. He earned an OCS commission, followed by three Silver Stars earned while serving as a platoon leader and company commander during the Korean War in 1950–51, and as a battalion commander with the 1st Infantry Division in Vietnam in 1966–67.

Colonel Hathaway commanded the 196th from October, 1970, until June, 1971, during which time he was selected for brigadier general—a promotion ultimately denied him because of the attack on FSB Mary Ann. The end of Hathaway's brigade command was marked by a certain controversy. "Hathaway was loyal to a fault to his subordinates," wrote Maj. Hugh T. O'Connor, S3 of the 196th Brigade. However, Alpha Company's Captain Spilberg was shocked by the difference in the efficiency reports rendered on him by Doyle and Hathaway after the sapper attack. "Col Doyle had just about 'maxed' me," Spilberg wrote home. "Col Hathaway slaughtered me." Whereas Doyle wrote that Spilberg was an "outstanding" and "courageous" officer who "prefers to lead by example," Hathaway gave him the lowest ratings possible. "What I believe but cannot prove is that there is a plot, purposeful or not to 'get' the principal people of Mary Ann," Spilberg's letter continued.

Captain Gallagher of Company B agreed. "In case there was any potential that Colonel Hathaway would be relieved, he made sure that plenty of blame got spread around," said Gallagher, who also got a glowing efficiency report from

Doyle and a career-stopping one from Hathaway. The brigade commander cited an incident that occurred after Doyle sent out a case of beer with Gallagher's resupply, taking a cue from the Australian army, which he admired. Gallagher rationed the beers two per man to be consumed in the ration line, but two troops managed to get hold of enough extras to get happily buzzed. The duo then got into a medic's bag and swallowed a handful of pills in an attempt to continue their party. "They went into convulsions and, despite the risk involved, I requested a night medevac," Gallagher said. "That was a major incident in brigade's eyes, having to get a night medevac out for some drug overdoses, and that was the incident Hathaway hung his hat on when he called me into his office and told me I was basically worthless as a company commander. If you want to hang me for that, I think that's pretty petty, but if your own career is in jeopardy you might do some petty things—and ultimately I still have the utmost respect for Hathaway."

The otherwise successful operations around Lieutenant Colonel Doyle's mini-firebases were marred by two tragic incidents of needless casualties. On March 12, Echo Recon was laagered on a jungle hillside overlooking a trail on which the platoon had rigged a mechanical ambush. When the claymore exploded, the new recon platoon leader, 1st Lt. Michael B. Good—formerly a top-rated platoon leader in Company A—took a patrol to check it out. The NVA who had hit the nearly invisible trip wire pulled taut across the trail at ankle level had been killed instantly, both his legs blown off. Another enemy soldier, missing one leg, had crawled away from the kill zone before expiring. The recon GIs dragged the bodies off the trail and set up another mechanical. Lieutenant Colonel Doyle radioed Good after the patrol returned to the laager and informed him that he was on the way out in his LOH to pick up the documents and two AK-47s recovered from the bodies. To secure an LZ, Good moved down the trail with another patrol, then headed left on a footpath that led to a natural clearing that would accommodate a helicopter. The area was heavily vegetated, the column well spaced, and the fifth man in line missed the turn off the trail. He had not been on the earlier patrol, and so did not recognize that he was walking right toward the new mechanical ambush.

When the claymore exploded, Good's patrol scrambled to the scene and found Pfc. William T. Lafield sitting upright, both legs ending in stumps at midthigh. "Everybody was real upset," remembered Pfc. Brad Brown, who helped load the body bag. Lafield, a gung ho, eighteen-year-old Texan, had spent four months with Bravo Company before volunteering to join Echo Recon in a search for more action. He was on his first mission with the recon platoon. "There was a lot of frustration," said Brown. "After the dust-off, they wanted us to continue the mission, and at first we was thinking about just telling them to kiss our ass. We'd done real good without losing anybody, and the way we lost this guy bothered everyone—but we finally saddled up and moved out."

Captain Gallagher had a similar mishap on the morning of March 15 when Company B was on LZ Mildred and the perimeter claymores were being disconnected and brought back so patrols could move out. The NVA were known to turn perimeter claymores around during the night, then to make an obvious noise, hoping a bunker guard would blow the claymore and take his own head off. In response, some troops booby-trapped their claymores with hand frags, replacing the regular fuse with a nondelay smoke grenade fuse, the pin pulled, the safety spoon held in place under the mine.

Gallagher had ordered his platoon leaders to put a stop to what he considered an "exceptionally dangerous practice." The grenade involved in the mishap belonged to Sgt. Charlie L. Lanier, a highly respected black squad leader. When it exploded, it killed Lanier and Sp4 Michael H. Richards. It was unclear who handled the booby trap, or which of the two was pulling security. It was also unclear if the former had accidentally knocked the frag out from under the claymore when he bent down, or if he had lost his grip on the dew-wet frag while trying to replace the pin. Lanier was "top-notch" according to his comrades, and the deaths of these good men under such tragic circumstances were a "substantial blow to all of us," recalled a grunt.

From LZ Mildred, Doyle inserted Gallagher's Company B into an enemy sanctuary eight klicks southeast of the minifirebase, a full fifteen klicks from FSB Mary Ann and thus out of reach of its artillery. The NVA had taken advantage of this isolation. Bravo Company's CA began late on March 18, using two lift ships. The insertion was "spooky"—despite the arty prep from LZ Mildred and the gunship cover—because as the Hueys descended toward the undulating, civilian-free terrain that rolled off toward the coast, the grunts could see hootches and little fenced-in rice paddies where the enemy enjoyed a garrison lifestyle. Bravo Company expected a hot reception from an enemy that secure. The landing went unchallenged, however. Apparently the NVA, upon hearing the helicopters' approach, had scrambled off to play wait and see. The company was reassembled on the ground two lifts at a time, with just enough daylight left to grab some high ground and set up an NDP.

In the morning, Captain Gallagher, saddling up with Bravo Two, was wearing not the anonymous shirt they usually got out of the laundry sacks, but one with his rank on one collar, infantry crossed rifles on the other, plus his Ranger tab on the left shoulder and other assorted patches. Gallagher's artillery spotter suggested he fold his collar under to conceal his subdued captain's bars. "Jesus, I've been here eleven months now," Gallagher replied. "You'd think if they were going to get me, they'd have got me by now."

"Well, they might try to get you and hit me instead," said the FO.

"Okay," Gallagher conceded.

Coming up against a jungle stream with open sandy banks, Bravo Two deployed two M60 teams, one facing upstream, the other downstream. The platoon then crossed one man at a time, each disappearing into the bamboo thicket on the other side. Gallagher made it across anonymously and safely. Sergeant First Class Thomas M. Kennedy, the platoon sergeant—a second-tour veteran with a great reputation for his good cheer and professionalism—brought up the rear. Before crossing himself, Kennedy motioned the M60 teams to pick up and move across. As soon as he revealed himself as a leader, an NVA sniper who'd been watching them, unseen and unheard, squeezed off his first and only shot. Kennedy was dead before he hit the ground.

After Bravo Company set up that evening, an ambush team with a dog handler slipped back down to a trail running along the stream. The team members were still discussing where to place their claymores when the scout dog alerted. Sure enough, an NVA came bopping down the trail, swinging an AK-47, his pack full of RPG charges. The ambush team fired him up before he realized what was happening, then packed up in a hurry and headed back in.

Captain Gallagher deployed ambushes along the supply trails that Company B cut into under the jungle canopy, but in two cases NVA supply squads got away unscathed because the grunts exploded their claymores too soon. Bravo Two's lieutenant finally did it right. He got out on the trail, the scene of a recent mishandled ambush, and went by the book, measuring exactly where the claymores would hit, making sure there was no dead space in the kill zone, pacing off where to put his machine guns, et cetera. The four NVA who subsequently came down the trail in broad daylight, carrying automatic weapons and humping packs heavy with medical supplies, paused when they saw the pellet-scarred trees from the previous ambush, but after much pointing and yammering they decided to continue on. The lieutenant pulled it off perfectly this time, patiently waiting until the enemy soldiers were in the middle of the kill zone before blowing the claymores and initiating the ambush. There were no survivors.

Notes

1. On May 4, 1971, then-Specialist Four Voros stepped on a mine while walking point during a platoon-sized Alpha Company patrol in the battalion's new Da Nang AO. Specialist Four Carl E.

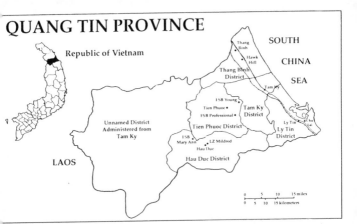

QUANG TIN PROVINCE

Republic of Vietnam

SOUTH

CHINA

SEA

Thang Binh

Hawk Hill

Thang Binh District

Tam Ky

FSB Young

Tien Phuoc

FSB Professional

Tien Phuoc District

Tam Ky District

Unnamed District Administered from Tam Ky

FSB Mary Ann

LZ Mildred

Hau Duc

Ly Tin District

Hau Duc District

LAOS

| 0 | 5 | 10 | 15 miles |
| 0 | 5 | 10 | 15 kilometers |

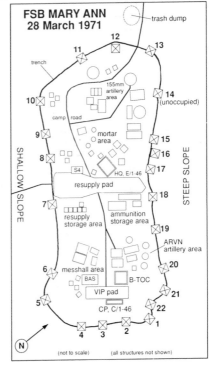

FSB MARY ANN
28 March 1971

trash dump

12

11

13

trench

155mm artillery area

10

14 (unoccupied)

camp road

9

mortar area

15

SHALLOW SLOPE

8

16

S4

HQ, E/1-46

17

resupply pad

STEEP SLOPE

18

7

resupply storage area

ammunition storage area

19

ARVN artillery area

6

messhall area

20

BAS

B-TOC

21

VIP pad

5

CP, C/1-46

22

4

3

2

1

N

(not to scale)   (all structures not shown)

Maj. Gen. James L. Baldwin, commanding general of the 23d Infantry Division (Americal), examines captured enemy weapons in the company of Lt. Col. William P. Doyle, commander of the 1-46th Infantry, at FSB Mary Ann, February 1971. Both Baldwin and Doyle would have their careers ruined as a result of the sapper attack on FSB Mary Ann the next month. *Courtesy Tim Baldwin*

Capt. Paul S. Spilberg *(center)*, commander of Company A, 1-46th Infantry, conducts a briefing in the FSB Young area, December 1970. 1st Lt. Robert J. Noonan is directly behind Spilberg, and S.Sgt. Max Braithwaite is on the right. *Courtesy Robert J. Noonan*

Sp4 Carl E. Cleek (bareheaded) and other members of the 1st Platoon, Company A, pose in a jungle clearing outside FSB Young, December 1970. *Courtesy Robert J. Noonan*

Lieutenant Noonan and his radio-telephone operator lead a joint U.S./ARVN patrol out of FSB Young in December 1970. *Courtesy Robert J. Noonan*

Pfc. William B. Meek, a machine gunner with Company D, 1-46th Infantry, throws the peace sign after boarding a truck at the end of a patrol for return to FSB Young. Although injured, Meek would kill two sappers during the attack on FSB Mary Ann on March 28, 1971. *Courtesy Andrew H. Olints*

Capt. Richard V. Knight, shown here outside the battalion tactical operations center at FSB Mary Ann, commanded Company C, 1-46th Infantry, from October 18, 1970, until killed in the sapper attack on March 28, 1971. *Courtesy Paul S. Spilberg*

1st Lts. John L. Hogan *(left)* and Peter K. Doyle *(right*, wearing glasses) of Charlie Company during the February 1971 operation southwest of FSB Mary Ann. *Courtesy Peter K. Doyle*

Lieutenant Colonel Doyle (sitting in center with forearm on knee and knife on web belt) during a visit to a Company C laager position in the FSB Mary Ann area. Captain Knight is second from left, wearing glasses. *Courtesy Paul S. Spilberg*

Sgt. W. Allen Eades, a Company C squad leader, poses at FSB Mary Ann with part of a weapons cache he discovered on February 1, 1971, the day before this photograph was taken. *Courtesy Andrew H. Olints*

During an awards ceremony on the resupply pad at FSB Mary Ann after the sapper attack, General Baldwin pins the Silver Star on Sgt. Elmer R. Head, who ended up in command of Charlie Company because of the heavy casualties. *Courtesy Tim Baldwin*

FSB Mary Ann as seen from a helicopter, with the northwest end of the base in the foreground and the southeast end in the background. The sappers came up the shallow slope on the right side of the photograph while ignoring the sharp drop-off on the left side. *Courtesy Carl D. Hewitt*

Captain Spilberg received the Silver Star and his third Purple Heart as a result of the attack on the B-TOC at FSB Mary Ann. He is pictured here while temporarily commanding Company A, 2-1st Infantry, in June 1971. *Courtesy Paul S. Spilberg*

1st Lt. Edward L. McKay, S2 of the 1-46th Infantry, with enemy prisoners at FSB Young in December 1970. *Courtesy Paul S. Spilberg*

This interior shot of FSB Mary Ann, looking northwest from the southeast side of the base, shows the ammunition storage area *(right foreground)*, the S4 hootch *(left center)*, and Company E's HQ building *(middle center)*. *Courtesy Ervin E. Powell*

Cleek won the BSMv at this time, shouting at everyone to stay put in case there were more booby traps in the area while he himself dropped his ruck, had the others toss their medical packs to him, and then cautiously made his way up to Voros. Voros calmly asked Cleek to straighten his legs out, but his right leg was actually gone at the knee, and his left was bent grotesquely below the knee. Cleek removed Voros's web gear, using the pistol belt as a tourniquet around the stump. Voros was lifted in a poncho to the medevac that landed in the tall grass. His left leg was amputated in the evac hospital.

Part V

The Massacre at Firebase Mary Ann

"On 28 March 1971, a small number of sappers, through surprise, made a successful attack against a superior US force on FSB Mary Ann. . . . The sapper force was not detected prior to entering the fire base. . . . To put the matter of the attack on FSB Mary Ann into the proper perspective, consideration should be given to the fact that this incident could very well have happened to other units of the 23d Infantry Division or to like combat units in Vietnam. . . . The reduced level of combat activity and the increasing publicity by the news media focused upon ending of the war tend to create complacency among both the troops and their commanders."

—From the confidential report into the sapper attack prepared by the Deputy Inspector General, U.S. Military Assistance Command, Vietnam (MACV).

10

Another Quiet Night

Lieutenant Scott Bell, the new Alpha Company commander, was decidedly uptight during his last night on FSB Mary Ann. Something was going to happen. He could feel it. The line companies rotated on and off the hill according to a fairly consistent schedule, and Bell always hated it when Alpha Company was lifted up to Mary Ann for its three or four days on the bunker line after walking the bush for two weeks. The troops wanted to relax. To them the firebase was a rear area, but Bell, looking at the foggy, jungle-covered mountains around them, knew better, and during that last nervous night, March 25–26, 1971, he organized the Big Rat Kill to keep his people awake and at least semialert. Mary Ann had a substantial rat population. The vermin thrived in the trash dump at the north end of the firebase, and even made their homes in the wooden ammo crates that the grunts had lazily not filled with dirt when constructing their hootches and bunkers. Bell had his troops make booby traps with C-ration cans, blasting caps, and cheese, and there were little explosions all night long as the platoons competed for the highest body count. One hundred and thirty VC rats were eliminated, and the KIA Romeos—dead rats—were brought to the command post and laid out in rows by each platoon.

During Lieutenant Noonan's abbreviated tour with Company A, he frequently found guards asleep when he walked the bunker line at FSB Mary Ann. He also smelled marijuana at night. During the day, the grunts would balk at conducting security patrols around the hill. "Hey, LT, you don't know what the other platoons do," one grunt said after they cleared the wire. "They don't really go on patrol. They just come down here and then sham for a while."

"We're going on patrol," Noonan said. "We're going to see if there's any bad guys. You just can't sit on top of a hill . . ."

Following the Big Rat Kill, Bell and Company A were replaced on Mary Ann by Captain Knight and Charlie Company, which had been on stand-down in Chu Lai. The next morning, March 27, they policed their positions in preparation for an inspection by Colonel Hathaway. The brigade commander usually made it out to each of his firebases three times a week, and had been on Mary Ann four days earlier. He had not been overly impressed. Company C had been on the hill at the time, prior to its stand-down, and Hathaway had spoken with Doyle about numerous small shortcomings in the general appearance and alertness of the troops. Hathaway had emphasized to Doyle and Knight that they really needed to keep their people awake now that they thought the war was over. He'd also talked with the grunts on the bunker line, answering their questions about upcoming operations and preaching about wearing helmets, digging in, and staying alive by staying alert—even on the hill. The colonel had given the same talk to every one of the companies he visited, for the no-sweat attitude of these troops was apparent throughout the brigade given the long lulls between contacts.

When Colonel Hathaway choppered back to FSB Mary Ann on March 27, he walked the bunker line with Doyle and Knight, who had formal responsibility for security on the hill. Each of Knight's platoons had its own sector on the bunker line, and each platoon leader reported to Hathaway with a sharp salute when the colonel entered that sector. "It was a big improvement over what I had seen before," the brigade commander later testified, ". . . the troops were alert . . . the area was policed, their weapons were clean. . . . Now I did not go down and make inspections down into the tactical wire because somewhere along the line you have to put the trust in the company commander."

Colonel Hathaway would have been well served, however, had he played squad leader and checked the wire, for there was much left undone behind the facade. Charlie Company's new 2d Platoon leader, 1st Lt. Jerry W. Sams, recalled that

> The sergeant major was on everybody's ass about policing the area before the inspection, and they had my platoon out there picking paper off the wire. Those helicopters would come in and kick up all kinds of crap. I had to send the guys out two or three times, and it was one of those typical army things where everybody's bitching and raising hell. We were accidentally setting off trip flares in the wire—all our early-warning devices that would have come in mighty handy later on that night.

The trip flares were supposed to be disconnected each morning and relaid each evening to avoid such mishaps, but that ritual was rarely observed. Numerous trip flares were also triggered when Chinooks landed on the hill—the propwash was that strong—and, given the never-ending nature of the chore, there was no sense of urgency among the troops to replace them immediately. Knight's grunts had left other details undone, their complacency the result of a false sense of security because they had never encountered the enemy in greater than squad strength. Hathaway also thought a certain cockiness was involved. He later stated: "Doyle was the most aggressive battalion commander I had . . . and Charlie Company, commanded by Captain Knight, was certainly the best company in that battalion, and probably one of the best companies in this division . . . one of the problems was that they were so good that they were a little contemptuous of the enemy . . . they were the hunters, not the hunted."

Major Alva V. Hardin, the 196th Brigade intelligence officer (S2), later testified that "we had no intelligence to indicate that there would be an attack on LZ Mary Ann."

Lieutenant Colonel Doyle noted that "during the entire time we were at Mary Ann there was . . . no indication of any enemy activity on the Mary Ann side of the river." In accordance with brigade and division policy, Doyle had organized a reaction force among the firebase support personnel in case of ground attack, and the line companies conducted occasional practice alerts complete with siren, flares, and live fire from the bunker line. Mad minutes were not commonly employed, however, because the entire division was under pressure to reduce ammunition expenditures. Doyle did not fire a lot of random illumination at night for the same reason, and he did not employ listening posts around the perimeter. "Listening posts were not a policy," said Hathaway, mostly because the troops were undertrained. "I considered listening posts outside the wire . . . a hazard. . . . I considered the danger of people getting wounded, either by defensive fires or somebody getting excited and firing on the perimeter, to be greater than the necessity for the listening post."

Meanwhile, after the inspection, Knight and Captain Spilberg, who had become brigade training officer, conducted marksmanship classes with Charlie Company at the firing range outside the wire on the southwestern side of the firebase. The troops also test fired their machine guns, knowing that the company would be moving out in a day or two. The marksmanship training ended at about four in the afternoon and a beer call was held in one of the mess halls. It was payday, and the company executive officer, who handled such administrative matters, helicoptered out to the hill that evening.

Firebase Mary Ann, which looked like a shantytown, was built on the bulldozed crest of a ridge running northwest to southeast, and occupied two camel humps with a shallow saddle in between. The ridge was 200 meters high. The firebase, approximately 500 meters long, was 75 meters wide across the saddle, and 125 meters wide at either end. The outer perimeter was defined by a trench that was knee-deep in certain stretches and waist-deep in others. Twenty-two bunkers were set into the trench line; most were metal, room-sized shipping containers (called "conexes") with firing slits cut into them. The conexes had been slingloaded up under Chinooks during the post-monsoon rebuilding of the firebase. Thirty or more hootches, bunkers, and buildings of various shapes and sizes dotted the two low hills inside the base. The saddle between the hills was used as a resupply pad. The B-TOC was located on the southeast half of the base, adjacent to a smaller VIP helipad used by the battalion commander. The rifle company CP was also on that side, as was the artillery liaison bunker, the battalion aid station, a communications center, a sensor monitoring station, mail room, three mess halls, two ammunition storage bunkers, a fuel storage area, a resupply storage area, and three parapets for the medium artillery platoon presently assigned to the base.

The southeastern half of FSB Mary Ann was divided by a dirt road that ran from the VIP pad to the resupply pad, where it exited the perimeter to the southwest and continued down to the firing range and the base water point, which was fed by a spring. Another dirt road traveled the length of the northwestern half of the base, where there were hootches for the supply personnel and a headquarters for the battalion support company that doubled as an FDC for the Mortar Platoon, plus mortar firing positions and the parapets for other artillery pieces on the hill.

The second dirt road exited the perimeter at the northwest end of the firebase where the trash dump was located. Both roads interrupted the trench line and the three aprons of double-concertina wire, but Doyle had been unable to get chain-link fencing to secure these openings because the Professionals were preparing to turn FSB Mary Ann over to the ARVN. All construction projects on the hill had been halted, and the process of packing up had begun. The entire 196th Brigade was, in fact, preparing for redeployment north to Da Nang to relieve the 1st Marine Division, which was pulling out of Vietnam. Doyle's staff estimated that it would take ninety Chinook sorties to clear Mary Ann, and Doyle planned to backhaul their supplies and building material to the battalion rear in bits and pieces as Chinooks were made available over the next two weeks. Doyle planned to gradually reduce Mary Ann, which seemed to have outlived its usefulness, to a mini-firebase with two mortars and a small supply section. All conexes were to be lifted out, including those used as perimeter bunkers, with the troops living instead under culvert halves and sandbags.

Such a position could be evacuated on short notice with only five Chinook sorties.

Doyle was one day away from moving his B-TOC to LZ Mildred, where most of Mary Ann's mortars and artillery had already been lifted to support the mission against the enemy sanctuary in the area. LZ Mildred, an elephant-grass-covered hillock, was a temporary position with culvert-and-sandbag bunkers. When the time came, it would be easy enough for the artillery battery to expend all its remaining ammo and slingload its pieces out under four Chinooks. The infantry would follow in an additional five sorties.

In preparation for the move north, both ground radars on Mary Ann, and all the night-vision starlight scopes, had been sent to the battalion rear for maintenance. On March 27, Lieutenant Colonel Doyle was still on FSB Mary Ann, while his new operations officer—Maj. Stanley J. Wisniewski, who was usually in command of LZ Mildred—was in Chu Lai, on his way back from reconning their new Da Nang AO. The battalion was deployed as follows:

- Company A, 1-46th Infantry (1st Lt. R. Scott Bell) was in the LZ Mildred AO.
- Company B, 1-46th Infantry (Capt. Peter J. Gallagher) was in the LZ Mildred AO, with one detached platoon securing LZ Mildred.
- Company C, 1-46th Infantry (Capt. Richard V. Knight) was securing FSB Mary Ann.
- Company D, 1-46th Infantry (Capt. Charles D. Kirkey) was in the LZ Grunt AO.
- Reconnaissance Platoon, Company E, 1-46th Infantry (1st Lt. Michael B. Good) was on FSB Mary Ann, having been lifted up that morning from stand-down with the mission of launching a CA into the LZ Mildred AO.

At the time of the sapper attack, Lieutenant Colonel Doyle had 231 U.S. and 21 ARVN personnel on FSB Mary Ann, to include the 18-man Recon Platoon and 75-man Company C. Also present were the brigade training team; the battalion intelligence officer, sergeant major, and interpreter; 22

members of Companies A, B, and D, mostly grunts in transit between the bush and the rear; 34 assorted medics, radiomen, cooks, et cetera, mostly from Headquarters Company (HHC); plus:

- The HHC Support Platoon Leader and nine supply personnel from the letter companies.
- The commanding officer, executive officer, and supply sergeant of the battalion support company, plus an 8-man detachment from Echo Company's 4.2-inch Mortar Platoon. (There were no heavy mortars on FSB Mary Ann; this detachment had been left to backhaul ammunition after two tubes were sent to Chu Lai for maintenance, and the other two were sent to LZ Mildred with their crews and Echo Company's Mortar Platoon Leader.)
- One 81-mm mortar with an 8-man crew from Bravo Company, and another 81-mm mortar with a 4-man crew from Delta. (The medium mortars from Companies A and C had already been lifted to LZ Mildred.)
- A 4-man liaison team from Headquarters Battery (HHB), 3-82d FA, and a 6-man detachment from Battery B, 1-14th FA, under the operational control (opcon) of the 3-82d FA. (The latter was backhauling ammunition; Bravo Battery's four 105-mm howitzers had moved from FSB Mary Ann to LZ Mildred on March 17.)
- The 2-man crew of a searchlight jeep from Battery G, 29th FA, and the 4-man crew of a quad-mounted .50-caliber from Battery G, 55th FA.
- Two 155-mm howitzers commanded by the battery executive officer and manned by 20 members of the 1st Platoon, Battery C, 3-16th FA (which moved to FSB Mary Ann on March 20).
- Two 105-mm howitzers and 20 crewmen from Battery B, 22d FA, 2d ARVN Division (which had moved to FSB Mary Ann on March 25 to support ARVN operations ten kilometers south of the firebase).
- Three ground-sensor operators from HHC, 23d Division who acquired targets for the artillery and mortars. (Five strings of electronic sensors emplaced within

fifteen hundred to forty-eight hundred meters of FSB Mary Ann had been detecting the nocturnal movement of small enemy groups several times a week since the firebase had been reopened. Depending on the range, each unseen target was engaged with mortar or artillery fire, or both. Ground patrols then checked the area. The results were always negative, and the sensors had detected no unusual activity prior to the sapper attack.)

Lieutenant Colonel Doyle, who once remarked to his new operations officer that no one in his right mind would attack FSB Mary Ann, was more concerned at the moment with the security of LZ Mildred. During both of Colonel Hathaway's recent visits they had discussed intelligence reports indicating that the VC in Quang Tin and Quang Nam Provinces were going to conduct some sort of coordinated surge operation during the last week of March to disrupt ARVN pacification projects in the foothills and lowlands near the coast. The ARVN would probably be rocketed and hit by sappers, and the roads between their outposts mined. LZ Mildred was not a suspected target, but given the mini-firebase's relative proximity to the ARVN, Doyle had deployed two of his companies east of Mildred as much to disrupt the enemy logistics in the area as to screen for any approaching sapper units.

LZ Mildred, however, was never attacked. The surge against the ARVN never materialized into anything but harassing attacks.

The night of March 27–28 began routinely on FSB Mary Ann. Doyle had Knight's Charlie Company at 25 percent alert, meaning that one out of every four troopers on the bunker line was supposed to be on guard. Given that Company C was so understrength that it had recently been reorganized into two-squad platoons instead of the usual three, the alert status meant that each of the twenty-two perimeter bunkers would have a single guard on top with weapon, ammunition, grenades, flares, and the firing clacker attached to the claymores. The troops assigned to each bunker were to have deployed six to twelve claymore mines and a like number of trip flares on the slope in front of their position. In addition, most of the bunkers had a tear gas dispenser on top of them, plus a fougasse drum out in the wire filled with napalm and wired for command-detonation. The squad leaders were supposed to act as so-called bunker boppers, moving from bunker to bunker at different times during the night to check on the guards. To ensure that the bunker boppers made their rounds, they were required to sign in at the B-TOC, but that was viewed merely as a formality by some, just as guard duty itself seemed a waste of time to most of the guards.

Specialist Wise, then with HHC, stated:

> There had never been any enemy action against FSB Mary Ann, and things became so relaxed it was unreal. The bunker boppers would usually just come into the TOC to talk and play cards, and by two o'clock in the morning you couldn't call up a bunker for a sitrep because you wouldn't get an answer. You might get three out of twenty-two. I don't think Captain Knight had a clue as to how lax the security was, and I know the battalion commander was never informed because in that area, and only that area, Knight wasn't diligent. He left it up to his lieutenants and sergeants to check the bunker line. Some of the lieutenants would make rounds, and people would get chewed out for sleeping on guard duty, but nothing would ever come of it. There was never any formal punishment that required the captain's attention.

On the night of the attack, understrength Company C left one perimeter bunker unoccupied, although the many transients on the hill could easily have been used to man it.

Mary Ann was not just a place to relax from the hardships of the bush, said Wise, it also was a place to party for those so inclined. According to Wise:

> Thirty percent of the guys on the hill were heads. Marijuana, heroin, whatever you wanted. The three guys in the sensor hootch next to the TOC were potheads, and a lot of people congregated there to buy stuff, but unless they knew you, you didn't come in. They had locks on the door of their hootch. Nobody did it in the open. It

wasn't brazen. If an officer saw someone doing it, he'd bust the guy. Some of the officers and sergeants knew what was going on, but as long as you did your job, they didn't say anything.

Some bunker guards were awake no matter what the time, and some had properly deployed their claymores and trip flares. Given that the ARVN planned to take over FSB Mary Ann, however, a real let-the-ARVN-fix-it attitude had developed toward the perimeter defenses. The morning after the sapper attack, the brigade public information officer would find and photograph claymore mines that had not been deployed to kill the enemy but which had been thrown down into the wire after the troops had removed the plastic explosives from each to heat their rations with.

Sergeant Russell J. Burns of Charlie Three stated that a "lot of people don't even go outside on guard. They just get up for the lifers (slang for career soldiers)."

"The hill was not the bush to the short-timers in the company," remembered Lieutenant Sams of Charlie Two. "The squad leaders had responsibility for guard, and one the responsibility to be the bunker bopper. We discussed that night who was doing what, but at the same time I never thought it was imperative to double-check because by then I had the same laid-back attitude."

Lieutenant Colonel Doyle should have increased security regardless of the tranquil intelligence picture. It was a moonless night, and low clouds had rolled in over the mountains, socking the firebase in so that even when flares were fired the bunker guards could barely see the concertina wire twenty meters away. "I had considered increasing the alert status," Doyle later wrote, but "decided against doing so" because of the "extreme state of fatigue and the low foxhole strength" of the company on the perimeter. "Many soldiers had been involved in tearing down . . . bunkers to retrieve salvageable timber, steel culverts and other construction material then in short supply. Others were moving these heavy items to the resupply pad and rigging them for extraction by air. On the morning of the 28th we were planning to complete the move to LZ Mildred of the battalion command group. In order to have sufficient manpower available to complete the move, I decided not to increase the alert status. . . ."

The fog was ghostly, the silence eerie. There was not even the usual chorus of screeching insects. The fog, thinning as the clouds pushed along, was relatively clear at two in the morning when the searchlight crewmen started their jeep to power the twenty-three-inch Xenon device mounted on the back, then swung the infrared beam out across the wire. The jeep was parked at the edge of the resupply pad, adjacent to the exit to the firing range. The searchlight was employed at least once a night. The crew, using the infrared light and a pair of infrared binoculars, spent about twenty minutes scanning the gentle slope, which had been cleared of all trees and major brush for over a hundred meters but which was dotted with tree stumps and boulders—plenty of places to conceal a skilled sapper. Had they spotted anything, the searchlight crew would have hit it with white light, but seeing nothing they shut their equipment down and slowly walked back to their sleeping bunker in the dark. The attack started ten minutes later.

11

Sappers

At least fifty sappers moved silently through the wire that moonless night. The sappers, bareheaded and naked except for green shorts, were covered with charcoal and grease so that even in the shimmering light of explosions and burning bunkers they would be only half-seen shadows to the stunned grunts—wraiths, specters who were here, there, and everywhere, methodically slinging grenades and satchel charges into position after position, then coldly shooting the survivors as they tried to scramble out.

The attackers were later identified by a battalion Kit Carson Scout as belonging to the 409th VC Main Force Sapper Battalion. The scout had been a member of this elite unit before coming over to the other side, and he recognized a former comrade among the handful of enemy dead left on FSB Mary Ann.

The 409th usually operated against softer ARVN targets in Quang Nam Province, though not under provincial control, receiving its missions instead from Military Region (MR) 5, the headquarters for all enemy forces in the first five provinces below the Demilitarized Zone (DMZ). The sapper battalions were used selectively. Perhaps the 409th was sent into action against FSB Mary Ann to grab big headlines at minimal cost. Perhaps MR 5, unaware that the 1-46th Infantry was packing up for new hunting grounds, wanted to slow down an aggressive foe that was uncovering caches and ambushing supply parties on the trails that were the logistical heart of communist operations in Quang Tin and Quang Ngai Provinces.

The allies possessed no firm intelligence on any sapper units, but they suspected that the 409th had recently slipped south from Quang Nam into Quang Tin Province to join the 402d, a sapper battalion already known to be in the area. At the time of the attack, the S2 map in the 196th Brigade TOC had the 402d and 409th plotted fifteen to twenty kilometers east of FSB Mary Ann, preparing for the anticipated surge against the ARVN. During the nine months since Mary Ann had been reopened, the NVA had studied the position in detail and had presumably prepared a sand table model for the newcomers of the 409th. Sappers sometimes rehearsed their attacks on mock U.S. positions built in their own jungle base camps.

At Mary Ann, local NVA probably served as guides for the sappers during pre-assault recons and the attack itself, after which they evacuated sapper casualties, covered their withdrawal by fire, and led them quickly away from the area. It was the sappers alone, however, who negotiated the wire obstacles and infiltrated the base. That was their specialty. With weapons slung tightly across their backs, grenades attached to their belts, and faces and bodies blackened, they slid snakelike through the brush, silently, patiently, an inch at a time, listening, watching, gently feeling the ground ahead of them. They neutralized trip flares encountered along the way by tying down the strikers with strings or strips of bamboo they carried in their mouths. They snipped the detonation cords connected to claymores, and used wirecutters on the concertina, careful to cut only two-thirds of the way through each strand, then breaking each noiselessly with their hands, holding it firmly so the large coil wouldn't shake.

The sappers ignored Mary Ann's northeastern side, where the slope dropped steeply to the river. They came instead from the southwest. The outer apron of double concertina was one hundred meters from the bunker line, and the sappers cut four large gaps in it, two to either side of the camp road that exited the perimeter from the resupply pad. They cut four identical gaps in the next barrier fifty meters ahead, though in places the wire was in such a state of disrepair the sappers could walk right over the rusty, mashed-down junk. It was another thirty meters to the third and final barrier, which was only twenty meters from the bunker line, and instead of risking the snap of wirecutters the lead sappers opened the way by tying the wire back with more bamboo strips. The sappers then spread out along that half of the bunker line, ready to dart into the perimeter when the mortar rounds that were to signal their attack slid down the tubes set up on the high ground north of the firebase.

Even veteran sappers were known to tremble when worming their way though a firebase's inner wire. They were completely vulnerable there. Sappers were not supermen, and on numerous occasions alert bunker guards—the best defense against sappers—caught the infiltrators in the wire. It helped if the wire was festooned with rock-filled cans that rattled when brushed against, and included trip flares cleverly placed under the rocks the sappers would probably pick up and move aside on their way in. It also helped if the defenders placed mock trip wires in the concertina—the more the better, for the sappers had to stop and waste time checking each one. Then there was illume and mad minutes.

Nevertheless, enemy sappers enjoyed a record of chilling successes during the Vietnam War. Air bases were a favorite target, and in February, 1965, the VC employed mortars and demolition teams to reduce the army's Camp Holloway near Pleiku to a shambles. The shelling hit barracks buildings, and eight Americans were killed, another 126 wounded. One sapper body was left behind near the flight line where twenty-five planes and helicopters had been damaged or destroyed. Records do not indicate ARVN casualties at the base, but they were presumably substantial.

In October, 1965, a ninety-man VC raiding force penetrated the Marine air facility at Marble Mountain near Da Nang. Almost a quarter of the sappers were killed or captured, but not before they and their comrades had killed three Marines, wounded ninety-one, and practically destroyed a helicopter squadron. Nineteen choppers were blown up on the airstrip, and thirty-five damaged.

Even the elite Green Berets were given a black eye by the sappers. On an August night in 1968, sappers suddenly materialized inside the headquarters compound of the 5th Special Forces Group's Command and Control North (CCN), on the outskirts of Da Nang, tossing satchel charges through windows as they raced through. The secret ground war in Laos was run from CCN. Given the security clearances involved, the raid received little media attention, but a dozen Green Berets were killed, along with an unknown number of their Nung mercenaries.

In May, 1969, sappers infiltrated the 101st Airborne Division's FSB Airborne in the A Shau Valley. Twenty-six GIs were killed and sixty-two wounded in the horrific night action. Forty enemy bodies were found. Most of the enemy casualties were regular infantry who tried to follow up the sappers' successful penetration and were chopped up in the wire by the embattled defenders.

In January, 1970, the 409th Sapper Battalion used the cover of night and a heavy monsoon rain to get into FSB Ross, even though 1st Marine Division intelligence had been tracking the unit's movements and had reinforced the firebase in expectation of attack. Thirteen marines were killed and another sixty-three wounded. The casualties would have been worse, but most of the sappers' water-soaked ordnance failed to explode, and the marines were able to organize a stunning counterattack. Artillery fire blocked the enemy infantry that was to have followed the sappers in, and at least thirty-eight enemy soldiers were killed and four captured. Several sappers were blown up by mortar fire from the infantry backing them up. The sappers had not been informed that a mortar barrage was part of the plan, and it threw them into some confusion after their classic penetration of the firebase defenses.

During the first week of February, 1971, a sapper force walked right into a hilltop perimeter manned jointly by the ARVN and a reconnaissance platoon from the 198th LIB, American Division. The VC entered through the ARVN side of the hill and demolished the position from inside out, killing five GIs and numerous ARVN. Given the timing of the raid, it was later speculated that the enemy force involved was the 409th and that the attack had been launched as something of a live fire drill in preparation for the upcoming attack on FSB Mary Ann.

In March, 1971, sappers went through 101st Airborne Division units on the perimeter of the Khe Sanh Combat Base, which had been reopened to provide helicopter support to the ARVN in Laos during Operation Lam Son 719. Three GIs were killed and fourteen wounded during the fight on the bunker line. Fourteen sappers were killed and one was wounded and captured, but the rest made it to the airstrip. The base rocked for hours with burning fuel and exploding munitions from two ammo storage areas; helicopter rockets went up like roman candles.

Less than three months later, in May, 1971, a small sapper team that got in and out without a fight blew up 1.8 million gallons of aviation fuel at the army's huge logistical complex at Cam Ranh Bay.

The sappers of the 409th, waiting in darkness and silence between the inner row of tactical wire and the bunker line on the southwest side of Mary Ann, carried with them lessons from FSB Ross. This time the support fires would be better coordinated. This time there would be no follow-up wave of infantry to get chewed up in the wire. The sappers were spread out, probably in three- and six-man teams. Each sapper knew the plan and his part in it. They would strike from the north, south, and west, and exit through the trash dump at the northwest end of Mary Ann. Most carried folding-stock AK-47s. Some were armed with RPG launchers, and carried wicker baskets with shoulder straps on their backs filled with rocket-propelled grenades like arrows in a quiver. Each had a dozen hand grenades around his waist, many of which were simply beer and Coke cans stuffed with explosives. The sappers also carried satchel charges—twenty-five pounds of C-4 in a flat canvas bag with a pull-type fuse and a strap on top for throwing. The 82-mm mortar crews of the support element were to initiate the assault with a short barrage of HE and CS tear gas shells. The enemy rarely used gas, but in this case even some of the satchel charges were wrapped with dry CS to further confuse and disable the defenders. The shelling, which would prove uncannily accurate, was targeted against the B-TOC and company CP on the southeast half of the firebase, and the mortars and heavy artillery on the northwest half. Those were the primary targets. Under the cover of the mortar fire, the sappers would quickly cross the trench line that connected the bunkers. The six-man teams were to rush up either hill to take out the primary targets, while the smaller teams would step up to the perimeter bunkers—one team per bunker—where shocked grunts would be cowering inside under cover, unaware that the mortars had stopped firing and all the explosions were being caused by grenades and satchel charges.

12

B-TOC Burning

Specialist Harold Wise was probably the first casualty of the sapper attack. The former Charlie Company radioman was assigned to the B-TOC on FSB Mary Ann. He had the afternoon shift in the radio room, but had stayed behind that night to play cards with the guys on the graveyard shift. After half a dozen cold ones, Wise, normally not a drinker, had a slight buzz by the time the card game broke up at 0230. Wise said he had to get some sleep because he was supposed to be on the first chopper out in the morning to start his R&R. The B-TOC radiomen were quartered behind the battalion aid station, which was directly across the camp road from the command bunker. Wise, beery and bleary, slowly followed his flashlight to his hootch, barely able to see where he was going after stepping into the pitch black from the fluorescent lights in B-TOC.

Wise was a few steps from his hootch when there was a sudden, brilliant flash between his hootch and another one nearby. Knocked to his ass, Wise at first thought he had kicked one of the little rat traps—until he heard more explosions and the AK-47 fire. He could hear no return fire. Unarmed and blind without his missing glasses, he tried to get up to run—but his legs weren't working. He had kept a grip on his flashlight and, sitting up a little, he was stunned to see blood all over. He had taken fragments in the top of his head, up the front of both legs above the knees, in the testicles, and in his left arm—which hung useless, a hole in the muscle the size of a silver dollar. He could see the bone, but was feeling no pain. Using his good arm to drag himself, he inched laboriously to the door of his hootch, pushed it open, and crawled inside the sturdy little sandbagged structure, which was built with dirt-filled ammo crates and roofed with steel planking.

It was dark inside. Wise roomed with Private Detlef, another former field RTO assigned to the B-TOC. Detlef was out cold on his stretcher bunk—already asleep, he had been hit in the head by something when the first round came in—but Wise shook him awake. Detlef helped Wise onto the floor at the back of the hootch and Wise grabbed the M16 leaning beside his cot, fumbling a magazine in one-handed. Detlef went to the door—and was stunned to see that the B-TOC was on fire. Looking the other way, he spotted a shadowy silhouette standing between two engineer stakes. The shadow threw something that had sparks at the end of it.

Terrified, Detlef saw another sparking grenade land beside his hootch, its fuse hissing loudly. The explosion that followed an instant later blew the door atop him. Something else went off on the roof, shaking the whole place. Wise used his reel-to-reel tapedeck as cover as he lay propped against the wall, legs stretched out, holding his M16 up with his good hand toward the open doorway.

Having left the card game before Wise, Sgt. Nolan G. Bingham, a radioman, and Sp4 Dennis A. Schulte, a grunt headed back for R&R, were in Bingham's hootch behind the aid station when the attack started. They got into their helmets and flak jackets while lying prone on the plywood floor, then slipped their gas masks on when they realized there was CS in the air. They thought they could hear someone outside, so they trained their M16s on the closed door—which suddenly blew in on them. Schulte was slightly wounded in the arm, while Bingham was thoroughly peppered with wood fragments and knocked unconscious.

Just as the sappers had hoped, the attack stunned many of the base personnel into confused inaction. One radioman simply rolled off his cot in his one-man hootch, pulled his mattress down on himself, and did not come out from under it until the firing had petered out.

Sp4 Charles D. Mullikin, on duty at the battalion switchboard, was seriously wounded in the leg when the sappers hit the commo conex next to the aid station with satchel charges.

Sergeant Danny T. Foster, chief of the radioteletype team, thought the base was on practice alert when he heard the mortars. He was puzzled that the alert siren wasn't wailing—then debris from a near miss rained on the hootch he shared with Sp4 Thomas F. Meinzer, and he realized this was no drill. Private David J. Karkoski, also with the radioteletype team, opened the door of his hootch, turned on his flashlight, and saw somebody throw something at him. Sparks bounced across the ground, and Karkoski dove to the rear of his hootch just as the door disappeared. Meinzer went outside with his M16 and immediately ran back inside, eyes smarting, shouting at Foster to get his gas mask. They both went out just as two mortar rounds exploded on the road in front of them. Ducking back inside, they left the door open so they could see a little of what was happening, maybe enough to save their lives as they lay on the floor, weapons ready.

Because the battalion aid station was being shut down and relocated, Sp4 Frank Brown was its only occupant. Slapped awake by a mortar explosion on the sandbagged roof, the black medic hurried to the door just in time to see five or six sappers on the move between the aid station and the B-TOC across the road. Another sapper was setting a charge against the aid station door. Brown dropped down a second before the explosion. Regaining consciousness, he felt a slight wound on the forehead, and his eyes were burning from tear gas. He found his helmet and flak jacket in the dark and rushed outside with his M16, where he encountered a black-pajama-clad sapper placing a charge against a hootch. Brown swung his weapon toward the man, but the M16 misfired. He hurriedly snapped another round into the chamber, but it misfired again because, as he discovered later, it had been damaged by fragments. He bolted back into the aid station to find another weapon, and was scrambling around inside the blacked-out building when he saw the sapper coming in the door after him. Thinking fast, he grabbed his poncho liner and covered himself with it as he curled up in a corner. The sapper looked around, but could not see him. The enemy soldier finally left the aid station, turning to toss a grenade back inside before darting off into the darkness.

The B-TOC was a fat target. Contrary to brigade policy, Lieutenant Colonel Doyle posted no guards at the two entrances leading down into the rectangular, half-submerged bunker. He considered it a waste of manpower. Of the seven personnel inside the B-TOC when the attack started, four were asleep: Doyle, the sergeant major, and two captains. The other three were on duty in the radio room: 1st Lt. Edward L. McKay, the battalion S2 and TOC night duty officer; Sp4 David Tarnay, who monitored the infantry radios; and Sp4 Stephen G. Gutosky, who monitored the artillery radios. As a GI entered the B-TOC through its north entrance and proceeded down the hallway that divided the bunker along its length, the radio room was the first room to the right. The other half of that side of the bunker was occupied by the map and briefing room. There were four additional rooms across the hallway, and the battalion commander was quartered in the last one where the hallway made a left turn and exited onto the helipad.

Shortly after the card game in the B-TOC broke up, Lieutenant McKay and his radiomen heard shots down on the bunker line. They had not been given clearance to fire, so while Tarnay got on the internal net to find out who had fired and why, Gutosky alerted the FDC of the supporting artillery battalion to "Stand by, we may be getting hit."

Seconds later, there was an explosion.

"What the fuck was that?" they asked simultaneously.

There was another explosion, then another, and another.

"Holy shit, it's incoming!"

"Be advised," Specialist Gutosky said, gripping his handset, "We are taking incoming at this time. Stand by and I'll see if I can get a direction on it."

It was approximately 0240 on Sunday, March 28, 1971, and the battle for the 1-46th Infantry B-TOC had begun.

Lieutenant Colonel Doyle came awake when three mortar shells impacted with heavy, muffled thumps around the B-TOC and the Company C CP directly across the VIP pad. Doyle was still on his cot when his quarters suddenly filled with CS, almost blinding him. In the radio room, McKay flicked the switch to sound the alert siren, as did Tarnay, but neither could get it to work. It had already been damaged. One of the captains previously sleeping across the hallway rushed into the radio room and cranked the field phone for Gutosky, who was trying to contact the mortar section via the landline running to the firing pits on the other side of the base. The mortars went unmanned in the chaos, the call unanswered.

The radio crackled as someone in the FDC of the supporting artillery battalion asked, "How many rounds have you taken?"

"Beaucoup—too many to count!" Gutosky shouted.

"Where are they coming from?" the caller inquired.

"No way to tell!" Gutosky answered. "There's too much incoming. I can't get outside to see where it's coming from!" Unaware that they were also under ground attack, Gutosky did not request that the artillery fire the defensive targets plotted around the base, calling instead for counterbattery fire: "Just fire all the countermortars, and all the counter-rockets you got ASAP!"[1]

Meanwhile, Doyle's room had just filled with tear gas when he heard Captain Spilberg choking and coughing in the hallway. Awakened by the shelling, Spilberg had picked up his .45, but left his M16 by his cot. He couldn't imagine needing either weapon. It was simply a mortar raid, and he planned to scoot out the east hatchway and join Knight's CP, partly to see if they needed any help, mostly because a show of officers was important—especially since most of the men had never been under mortar fire before.

Spilberg was taken totally by surprise when he walked into the tear gas. "Sir!" he sputtered. "They're using CS!"

"No fuckin' shit," Doyle coughed in reply.

Captain Spilberg, blinded, unable to breathe, was seized by panic, and he charged back down the hall, screaming, "CCC-SSSSS!"

Spilberg threw himself onto the stairs of the north entrance and crawled out into the fresh night air. He collapsed near a conex, trying to get control of himself. There were explosions everywhere. As his eyes began to clear he could see things moving—figures going through the smoke like phantoms. He was suddenly aware of AK and RPG fire. We're being overrun! he recalls thinking. Spilberg was a survivor of the sapper attack on the CCN headquarters, and as he lay in the dark reliving that nightmare he was too scared to check the .45 he still gripped in his hand to ensure he had chambered a round. He didn't want to draw any attention to himself. To move could bring death. It was an impossible situation, he remembers thinking as he lay there. The troops couldn't counterattack because they didn't know where to go. The sappers were all over in small teams, and anyone who emerged from his bunker to fight them had a better chance of getting fired up by his own side than of finding sappers to shoot. The sappers went in one side and out the other, setting charges along the way, and by the time the troops grasped who was where and what was what, it was all over.

The only way to beat the sapper was to catch him in the wire. Lieutenant Colonel Doyle, thinking one of their own CS dispensers had been ruptured, was going for the door of his quarters when a satchel charge exploded in the hallway, throwing him violently to the floor as it blew the door away. The sappers had made it to the B-TOC's east entrance, where the passageway made a right turn into the hallway. Doyle got up, grabbed his .45 from its holster, and started for the doorway again just as one of the sappers rushed around the corner, ready to sling another satchel charge into the room—or perhaps prepared to run inside with it in a suicidal attempt to eliminate the enemy commander.

The colonel shot the sapper with his .45—just as the satchel charge exploded, knocking Doyle unconscious.

When Doyle regained his senses, he started to his feet again only to have a third satchel charge explode in the hall, knocking him out again. (The subsequent charges against Doyle included the fact that he had left the entrances to the B-TOC unguarded.) The satchel charges exploded inside the bunker at 0244, four minutes into the attack. The time was recorded by the FDC when Gutosky, thinking they were still under mortar fire, reported that the B-TOC had just taken direct hits. Dust rained down from the rafters. The whole bunker felt like it was going to shake apart. Gutosky also shouted that they were being tear gassed. A noxious yellow cloud had made its way down the hall from the east entrance and flooded the radio room. McKay, Gutosky, and Tarnay—none of whom had their gas masks with them—stampeded up the stairs of the north entrance. They were joined by the captain from across the hall and a radio repairman who had left after the card game but dove back in when the shelling began. He had his helmet on, but left behind his weapon, ammunition, flak jacket, and gas mask in his haste.

It was pitch black outside. Eyes blurry from the tear gas, they couldn't see anything anyway. But the sappers could see them and an AK-47 burst kicked up dirt in front of Gutosky and the unarmed radio repairman, Sp4 Dennis S. Sikora, and blasted the wooden bunker wall between them. The captain became separated from them in the confusion, but Tarnay, clamping a green towel over his nose and mouth, led the way back into the gas-filled command bunker, followed by McKay, Gutosky, and Sikora.

It was easy to panic when hit by tear gas, and Gutosky, whose weapon was back in his living quarters, dove under his desk in the radio room. Tarnay dragged him back out, shouting at him to get some illume going. Calming down, Gutosky requested that the artillery start firing illumination, but did not explain that the base was under ground attack.[2] Meanwhile, Lieutenant McKay and radio repairman Sikora made their way down the hallway, which was littered with wood paneling blown off the walls, and found the colonel lying semi-conscious in his demolished quarters with his gas mask on. McKay was getting Doyle to his feet when two Coke-can grenades were tossed through the east entranceway, blowing them back against the wall. Next, a satchel charge was heaved in. It bounced off a wall and onto a case of white phosphorous grenades. McKay was deafened by the explosion, and his back badly burned as he was lifted off his feet and launched backward down the hallway like a rag doll.

Sikora was hit near the left eye. Thinking his eye was

gone, he rushed back into the radio room and rolled under one of the radio racks. Tarnay, who had been leaning over the room's Dutch door, looking down the hallway, was knocked flat by the blast that sent McKay flying past the doorway as though a giant had flung him. Tarnay rushed to McKay, thinking him dead, but the lieutenant was able to stagger back with him into the radio room. Tarnay reached for his M16, which had been leaning beside the door, but instead found it lying on the floor, the butt missing, the fiberglass hand guard blown off, the exposed barrel twisted like a pretzel.

The white phosphorous grenades set the south end of the command bunker on fire from the inside out. Those not set off by the satchel charge continued to detonate one at a time in the fire. Meanwhile, Lieutenant Colonel Doyle had made it to the radio room, where he discovered that the power had failed and Tarnay's four AN/VRC-26 radios were dead. The main mast of tall, rigid RC-292 antennas on the roof had apparently been damaged. Gutosky's artillery net was still open, however. The arty antenna was not set up with the main mast, but was in the artillery area on the other side of the base, and the cable strung into the B-TOC.

"Alright, get some gunships," Doyle said. "Get some illumination going over the hill and what artillery we can. I'm going out to see what's going on!"

As he headed out the door, Doyle thought he had suffered only superficial wounds, but the adrenalin rush he felt masked the true extent of his injuries. He had a concussion and was semideaf. His eyes were slits—he could barely see because of powder burns and the tear gas—and he had multiple fragment wounds in one arm and both legs that would take months to heal.

There were two sappers in view outside the B-TOC. Lieutenant Colonel Doyle, wearing a flak jacket, didn't have a chance to bring his Swedish K to bear because there was another sapper on the roof of the artillery mess hall about ten meters from the northern entrance. As soon as Doyle hit the top of the steps leading up and outside, that sapper threw a grenade at him. It landed at Doyle's feet, the fuse sparking in the darkness. Doyle stared at it blankly, still a little punchy from the other blasts. Finally realizing what it was, he spun and dove back into the bunker just as the grenade exploded, blowing him down the steps.

The attack was visible from a distance as orange flashes against the low clouds in the mountains. Lieutenant Schmitz, currently assigned as an assistant operations officer, was in command of the 1-46th Infantry's Jump CP on LZ Mildred in the temporary absence of the S3. Schmitz was asleep on a cot behind the CP—which was simply a dug-in, sandbag-layered conex—when he was awakened by the Mortar Platoon leader, who had heard muffled explosions and then monitored the report of enemy fire on the artillery net between FSB Mary Ann and Hawk Hill. Schmitz scrambled into the CP with Sergeant First Class Davis, senior NCO on the mini-firebase, and Sp4 Gary L. Noller, the senior radioman. They made contact with Tarnay in the B-TOC on Mary Ann, then lost him. "What the hell's going on? When you're under attack, you stay on your radio," Noller lectured when Tarnay came back on the radio minutes later. Noller did not know that the radio mast at the B-TOC had been hit, or that Tarnay had just scrambled to slap a fresh battery into one of the spare PRC-25 field radios stacked on a shelf in the radio room. "Listen," Tarnay answered urgently, "we got dinks inside the perimeter. They just tear-gassed the TOC!"

Schmitz and Davis and Noller looked at each other in shock. They had assumed the hill was being mortared, maybe probed. Then Doyle came on the net. "Call for a flareship," the colonel told Schmitz, who was in direct contact with the 196th Brigade TOC. "We need gunships and medevacs and a doctor, and we need artillery support right away. Give me artillery fire all around the hill!"

Although arty had initiated the illumination and counter-mortar program with alacrity, there was considerable delay in firing the defensive targets (DTs) Doyle requested to help break up the ground attack. The reasons were numerous. In case of ground attack, the mortars and howitzers actually on Mary Ann were supposed to fire the DTs. Those crews, however, were presently fighting for their lives and could not man their guns. A number of DTs had also been plotted for the big guns at FSB Pleasantville. It was not until 0250, though, that Gutosky, the artillery radio operator in the 1-46th Infantry TOC informed Captain States of the 3-82d FA at Hawk Hill, that they were under ground attack in addition to the mortar attack. Gutosky and States lost contact at this point because of the fire in the B-TOC on Mary Ann. States should have ordered Pleasantville to commence firing the DTs, but in the confusion—and without a specific request from Gutosky—he hesitated to do so. The only other arty in range of Mary Ann was Conatser's battery, which was firing illume and counter-mortar grids. Conatser knew from Schmitz that the DTs had been requested. Although Conatser had plotted DTs around Mildred after his battery moved there, he had not thought to plot them around Mary Ann also, and he now had to select targets and work up the firing data in the middle of the battle.[3]

Fearing an attack on his own position, Lieutenant Schmitz pulled his listening posts in and had his Bravo Company platoon go to 100 percent alert on the perimeter. Meanwhile, 1st Lt. Robert D. Trachsel, the Echo Company Mortar Platoon leader, fired LZ Mildred's DTs with his two attached 81-mm mortars and the two 4.2-inch mortars from his own heavy mortar platoon. Trying to do something, anything, to help Mary Ann, the heavy mortar crews also fired illumination in that direction even though the four-thousand-meter range of their mortars was still three thousand meters short of the battle.

Captain Victor A. Ferraris was the officer separated from the rest when the CS originally flushed everyone out of the B-TOC. Having previously served as Doyle's artillery liaison officer before transferring to the infantry, Ferraris was supposed to take over Company A, and was on the hill that night in preparation for undergoing on-the-job training with Company C. Ferraris had donned his flak jacket and steel pot and grabbed his M16 before following the radiomen up the stairs, but by the time he got outside he was in a bad way from the tear gas and he immediately lost track of the rest, assuming that each had headed in a different direction to find cover.

Not realizing that everyone else had scrambled back into the bunker, Captain Ferraris started off, not sure where to go or what to do. Luckily, he went right past Captain Spilberg, who called to him in a hoarse whisper, "Vic, here I am!" Spilberg, armed only with a .45, was glad to see the M16 in Ferraris's hands, and without a word they crawled into a small hole in front of the artillery mess hall. Hand flares had been fired from the bunker line, and Ferraris and Spilberg could see straight across the saddle to the opposite hill, where there were numerous explosions around the mortar pits on the slope facing them, as well as at different points all around the bunker line. They also watched the big antenna mast come tumbling down from above the northern entrance of the command bunker when what sounded like a grenade exploded next to it.

Captains Ferraris and Spilberg had been lying side-by-side for maybe five minutes, not speaking or moving, when a grenade exploded behind them.

"I've been hit," Ferraris whispered.

"Me, too," Spilberg added, grunting in considerable pain.

The grenade had apparently been thrown from the mess hall roof. Unable to get completely below ground level in the small hole, Ferraris was hit in the heel through the bottom of his boot, and in the back of his leg. Spilberg caught three burning, quarter-sized fragments in his buttocks and the left side of his lower back.

Command Sergeant Major Carl N. Prosser, the battalion sergeant major, had come out of the B-TOC with a towel over his face but without his M16, which was lost somewhere in his demolished room. Trying to reach the bunker line, Prosser headed downhill across the road. He had only gotten as far as the infantry mess hall when an AK-47 opened up on him. Prosser hit the deck, then sprinted back towards the B-TOC to find a weapon. Spilberg grabbed him as he went past, pulling him down into cover with him and Ferraris. Moments later, Prosser saw a green star cluster flare explode brightly over the south end of the base. It had been fired not from the bunker line but from a hill down toward the river. The enemy was apparently using flares as signals.

* * *

The B-TOC was made of wood and weatherproofed with tar, so it burned rapidly. Captain Spilberg could hear shouting inside the bunker, and when he saw flames leap out the northern entranceway he left his cover and ran back inside. Doyle, Tarnay, and Gutosky were juggling radios, trying to get fire support. McKay and Sikora were also in the radio room. The rest of the B-TOC was ablaze. The eastern entranceway was on fire and caving in. The plywood hallway was on fire. The plywood quarters across the hall were on fire. The plywood wall dividing the radio room from the briefing room, which was also on fire, had been blown down, and the heat was intense, the smoke thick. The fire had also spread along the ceiling, and blazing timbers were collapsing into the hallway and the briefing room, along with sandbags and steel planking.

"We gotta get out of here!" McKay shouted.

"Not yet!" Doyle shouted back.

Painfully wounded, Lieutenant McKay's eyes were hysterical behind his glasses as he shrieked, "We're all going to die!"

Doyle delivered a resounding, open-handed smack across McKay's face, shouting, "Shut the fuck up, lieutenant!"

Captain Spilberg picked up a radio handset and said, "I want artillery fifty meters out, three-hundred-and-sixty degrees around our position." He added that the whole hill may have fallen. "On my command be prepared to fire on the firebase!"

It was now about 0251, and the command bunker was an unbearable oven on the verge of total collapse. Doyle informed Lieutenant Schmitz on LZ Mildred that they were being forced to evacuate the TOC and they would probably lose commo—then he shouted for everyone to get out and head for the aid station. Tarnay loaded Gutosky up with radio handsets and antennas, and the artillery operator took off while Tarnay paused to pull the pins on the thermite grenades in place atop their radios. The superhot grenades, which looked like smoke canisters but with different colored bands to identify them, burned straight down through the metal radios. Tarnay had no intention of leaving the enemy a radio they could use. Spilberg and Gutosky and Sikora had already dashed up the north steps.

Doyle tried to shove McKay out of the radio room behind them, but the lieutenant was incoherent. Tarnay put his shoulder into McKay's gut, lifting him over his shoulder, and followed the colonel up the stairs. He had one arm around the lieutenant's legs and a radio in his free hand. Timbers crashed behind them in blizzards of sparks as they went into the night.

After getting reorganized outside the B-TOC, Captain Spilberg dashed across the road to the blown-up aid station, ready to shoot any sapper he encountered along the way. He saw none. The level of fire had decreased dramatically on that side of the base. Spilberg went back to Doyle's group and, communicating in quick whispers, led it across. Tarnay was wounded when a shadow suddenly appeared to throw a grenade. They piled into the aid station, where Brown was hunkered down holding a poncho across his face to ward off the gas and laid McKay on a cot. Brown worked on him while Gutosky and Sikora picked up the medical gear scrambled all over the floor, and Tarnay started to set up his radio.

Doyle and Spilberg left the aid station and cut across the helipad to the Charlie Company CP, which served as the alternate B-TOC. As they approached they saw it was also on fire, its sandbagged entrance caved in. There were figures sprawled there, none of them moving. . . .

Notes

1. Gutosky was speaking with Capt. A. E. States, fire direction officer in the 3-82d FA FDC on Hawk Hill. States had a target list with fourteen counter-mortar grids around FSB Mary Ann—specific locations in the surrounding high ground where an enemy mortar team was likely to set up to shell the base. States relayed this firing data to Captain Conatser, commander of Battery B, 1-14th FA (105-mm) on LZ Mildred. Five minutes after the enemy lobbed their first shell Conatser's four howitzers were booming in reply. Conatser subsequently received an official admonition, however, because his howitzers should have been firing sooner. Conatser,

who was responsible for the counter-mortar program, had registered the target list while still on FSB Mary Ann, but had not computed the firing data after moving to LZ Mildred. States's FDC therefore had to recompute the data during the attack itself, which they did quickly enough, making the rationale behind the admonition more technical than material. After Bravo Battery fired the fourteen-target series, Conatser, in the absence of target information from FSB Mary Ann, went into his FDC and selected targets closer to the perimeter, which were then fired on. In all, his guns expended six hundred rounds during the night.

2. Given this lack of information, the artillery did not fire its defensive targets around the base. Captain States in the 3-82d FA FDC had two illumination on-call missions over FSB Mary Ann that were the responsibility of a two-tube platoon from the 3d Battalion, 16th FA (155-mm) on FSB Pleasantville, twelve kilometers northeast of FSB Mary Ann. The request for illume came in at 0245, and by 0247 one of Conatser's Bravo Battery tubes was putting the light in the sky while his other three continued firing the counter-mortar program. The heavy artillery commenced firing illume shortly thereafter.

3. Doyle's artillery liaison officer received an official admonition for not having gotten together with Conatser before the attack to plot DTs from LZ Mildred to FSB Mary Ann. The CO and S3 of the 3-82d FA were also censured for this oversight, as was the CO, 23d Division Artillery.

13

Primary Targets

Captain Virtus A. Savage, the new artillery liaison officer (LNO), was quartered with his team from Headquarters Battery, 3-82d FA in a rectangular, half-submerged bunker to the left of the aid station, across the road from the B-TOC. Savage was on his third combat tour, and had been Doyle's arty LNO for one month. Sitting up on his cot when the mortaring began, Savage, who'd been sleeping in his shorts, could see flashes all around through the cracks in the dirt-filled ammo-box walls as he pulled on his jungle boots and grabbed his .45 pistol. He did not waste time getting dressed or looking for his helmet in the dark, but went straight out the door and headed for the B-TOC. Savage, crouched low on the steps leading up to ground level so as not to present a silhouetted target, was getting ready to crawl across the road when he was shot in the left leg, which was bent under him, ready to spring forward. The bullet hit the calf muscle in the back of the leg, about three inches below the knee. It went straight into the bone, hot but painless, and at such an angle that whoever fired the shot must have been aiming straight down from the roof of the bunker.

The sapper had apparently been going for a head shot, but Captain Savage had moved slightly forward the instant the sapper pulled the trigger on what sounded to Savage like a pistol. Savage jumped back into the bunker, closing the door behind him. Sitting on his cot, he yelled that he was hit, hoping one of the radiomen quartered on the other side of the wall that divided his room from the larger part of the bunker would hear. He was tearing open a bandage when the sapper jerked open the door to throw in a Coke-can grenade. The sapper slammed the door as the grenade rolled to within a few feet of Savage. Time seemed to slow down as he started to get up—and he was looking right at the burning fuse when the thing exploded, throwing him back against the wall and knocking the wind out of him. There was a light in his head. It was going out, and he knew that if it did he was dead. It pulled back into a pinpoint, but then started back out again.

Captain Savage, coming back to reality, found himself sitting against the wall on his cot, a heavy collapsed beam to either side of his head. The roof of pierced-steel planking and sandbags had sagged on his side of the bunker until it was almost touching his head. It was going to collapse any moment, and Savage quickly bandaged his leg wound and then scrambled over several fallen timbers to get out the door. He was moving on adrenaline, hardly aware of how banged up he was even though the concussive force of the grenade had been defused through the slits in the bunker walls. His eardrums had burst, and his eyes were peppered with tiny fragments. One of his front teeth was missing. He'd been hit in the nose, the face, in the abdomen—where a big piece of metal had gone in several inches to the right and down an inch from his navel—and just below the knee of his wounded left leg, the fragment hitting the front of the bone, fracturing it.

Outside, Savage saw that the B-TOC was ablaze. Pistol in hand, he crawled to the back door of the bunker. "Get out of there!" he yelled down the steps to the radiomen inside. "The last place you want to be during a sapper attack is in a bunker!"

"No! Captain Savage is dead!" someone shouted.

"No, I'm not, I'm right here!"

Captain Savage had three RTOs in his liaison team, including Gutosky in the B-TOC. The other two, Sp4s Steven E. Webb and Stephen W. Whitson, asleep when the attack began, rolled out of their cots and frantically tore apart their bags, which had been packed for the move to LZ Mildred. Both found their M16s and ammo, and both got hold of their helmets and flak jackets. They were still trying to get their stuff together when the tear gas hit them, so they pulled their gas masks on.

Whitson came out of the bunker as ordered, just as a grenade with a sparking fuse came flying at them. Savage and Whitson dove back into the bunker, hitting the floor as the grenade exploded outside the hatchway. Enough of this shit! Savage recalls thinking. He returned fire then despite his multiple wounds and the army later gave him a Silver Star—along with the official admonition for not coordinating with Conatser regarding the DTs. Savage rushed outside with his .45, convinced that the sapper who had already shot and grenaded him was still out there, intent on finishing the job. Each sapper had a mission, and this one was apparently supposed to eliminate the artillery officer on the base. Savage saw the bareheaded, bare-chested sapper standing up about fifteen to thirty feet away, looking toward the bunker. The Vietnamese was silhouetted in front of a fire, a faceless outline, and Savage opened fire with his pistol. He grabbed an M16 from one of his radiomen and pumped a few more rounds in the sapper's general vicinity. He never actually saw the man go down, but no more grenades came their way. The sapper having been either blown away or scared away, the liaison team members were able to take up positions in a shallow trench that ran along the edge of their bunker.

Captain Knight had stayed up until two in the morning talking with his exec, Lieutenant Mack, who'd helicoptered out at dusk with the company payroll. Knight was sitting on a cot inside their bunker. Mack, who was in a hammock, had been with the company for seven months, mostly as a platoon leader. He had been their best one, and Knight told him that as soon as he took the payroll receipts to the rear in the morning, he was to catch the next chopper back out to the hill to take over Lieutenant Doyle's platoon while Doyle was on leave. Knight told Mack he would brief him on their upcoming mission when he returned. When Knight turned in, Mack lit a last cigarette. The only other man awake was the trooper on radio watch. The rest were asleep—the company commander, the forward observer, the field first, the commo sergeant, and two other radiomen—eight men in all. Four would survive.

Captain Knight, who had said that he didn't want to be anywhere near FSB Mary Ann during Tet '71, given the communist's reputation for spectacular assaults during that season, had been slightly off in his timing. The first two or three mortar rounds of the sapper attack landed almost atop the CP of Company C, 1-46th Infantry, which was built with ammo boxes and sandbags on the slope directly below the B-TOC, and marked by two antennas. The AK-47 fire began immediately thereafter. Knight rolled out of his cot and, while still at the prone, grabbed a radio handset and tried to make contact with the bunker line. There were rectangular windows cut horizontally into the bunker's wooden walls, and before the captain could even get an answer on the radio, a grenade was pushed through one on the left side of the bunker. The grenade, unseen in the darkness, landed with an audible thump, causing a scramble for the door.

Specialist Four Carl D. Carter, a radioman, was hysterically fighting his way through hammocks when the grenade exploded like a fireball in the blacked-out bunker. The concussion was devastating, and Carter, scorched across the arms, was so dazed that he couldn't find the doorway. His weapon too was lost.

Lieutenant Mack had just swung out of his hammock and was reaching for his jungle boots when the explosion filled the bunker with smoke, blinding them. Mack was hit by fragments in his left foot. Captain Knight's CAR15 was missing in action, so he grabbed Mack's .45 from under the lieutenant's hammock, while Mack, not knowing what had happened to his weapon, rushed barefoot for the open doorway. He wasn't thinking about sappers. He thought that they'd taken a direct hit from a mortar and that the sandbagged roof was going to collapse. He'd no sooner hit the bunker hatchway than two more grenades came through the window and exploded behind him, blowing him out in the direction he was going. He landed about fifteen feet from the bunker, fragment wounds and abrasions across his lower back and right buttocks.

Mack realized that the B-TOC was aflame as he regained his bearings. Seconds later, what sounded like a rocket-propelled grenade slammed into the Charlie Company CP. The explosion collapsed the roof and the bunker caught fire. The company commander never got out. "Captain Knight did not fulfill his responsibility on the firebase," Colonel Hathaway later testified. "That night, Captain Knight, and Colonel Doyle to some extent, were both negligent in that they did not do what the SOP for firebase defense called to do. The SOP was very firmly established. Captain Knight, as the responsible officer for the immediate security of the perimeter of the firebase, did not implement this SOP. I think this is the primary cause for the enemy attack being as successful as it was."

In the glare of the fires, Lieutenant Mack saw sappers coming over the wire to the south. The radio inside the demolished CP was still operational. Mack could hear the Charlie One CP trying to raise Knight—"Bunker 18 calling 42"—and he scrambled back to the bunker. He tried to get inside but was blocked by flames. Mack heard Vietnamese voices then and hit the ground, landing in a small dugout. He found himself face-to-face with the radioman Carter, who had gotten outside just before the RPG blew up the CP. The east wall had fallen on Carter, completely burying him with sandbags. He could see through a space three inches in diameter, and was telling Mack that they had to get away from the CP, that it was taking too many direct hits. But the sappers heard them talking and stitched the dugout with a burst of AK-47 fire. Mack caught a round in his right leg, which blew away the inner calf muscle. Whispering to Carter to be quiet, he played dead as at least one sapper dropped in the dugout with him. He could hear more moving around the bunker, speaking to one another, but he never saw any of them. He had his eyes closed and his head down as he played dead. He was unarmed. The sapper in the dugout stepped on his back, and Mack knew to expel the air in his lungs, but not to inhale when the sapper removed his foot. While the man crouched down to frisk him, Mack breathed like a bird, rapid and shallow, knowing that he dared not permit his upper body to contract and expand. The sapper checked his right arm first, then pulled on his bloody left foot before grabbing his left wrist. The sapper wanted Mack's watch and, unable to get the double-backed leather band unfastened, finally ripped it free of the band.

The sappers never saw Carter under the sandbags.

Lieutenant Larry Hogan, the forward observer, got out of the CP but was apparently wounded seconds later when the RPG blew the bunker apart.

Hogan, a mustached, dark-haired, twenty-three-year-old ivy leaguer from New Hampshire, was lying wounded and probably unarmed by the burning bunker when a sapper shoved his AK-47 into his chest and finished him off with a squeeze of the trigger. Hogan had been as green as grass when he joined the company four months earlier. He had been a nervous wreck. But he had known his artillery and learned fast about the bush. He had always been there when needed.

Captain Knight's commo sergeant, Sgt. Ronald J. Becksted, was also killed after scrambling out of the CP. He had been one month away from the end of his tour, a few days away from reassignment to the rear. "Knight didn't like anyone that wasn't aggressive, and troops that were short and trying not to make waves really annoyed him," recalled Mack. Knight had never liked the timid, easy-going Becksted, and had dragged him out to the firebase one last time after the stand-down as punishment. Becksted was supposed to have caught a chopper to the rear when the company humped off the hill.

Sergeant Calhoun, the field first, had been sleeping in his fatigues. Thinking they were only under mortar fire when the attack began, he had rushed out the little doorway barefoot, with neither his helmet nor CAR15. Calhoun and two radiomen, Sp4 Thomas Simmons and Pfc. Michael S. Holloway, had just gotten outside when the RPG hit the CP, causing the sandbag walls to either side of the hatchway to cave in on them, pinning them at the waist. Suddenly aware of the sappers, they frantically shoved the sandbags away, trying to get free. Holloway pulled Calhoun loose, and the two were just taking off to find cover when a burst of automatic fire chopped them down.

Specialist Simmons tried to get back into the burning CP to find an M16 but ran right into what looked like a dozen sappers. He went down, shot in the chest, his back broken.

Sergeant Calhoun, shot in the left knee, right thigh, and through the biceps of his right arm, landed beside Holloway. The twenty-one-year-old draftee radioman was nicknamed "Hardcore" because although he was a terrible soldier—a clumsy, blond kid with thick, black-rimmed glasses—he was also a great guy and would uncomplainingly hump a tremendous load in the bush, to include his weapon, ammunition, and rucksack, plus the radio with whip antenna, the big RC-292 antenna, a scrambler device, a hundred feet of coax cable, et cetera, et cetera.

The pain was excruciating when Calhoun tried to move. He touched his trouser leg and discovered it was soaked with blood. "Hardcore," he whispered, "see if you can get a tourniquet around my leg."

Calhoun and Holloway, who had been shot in the leg too, were curled up on their sides, each with his head almost touching the other's thigh. They were each trying to bandage the other man's leg when Calhoun spotted shadows approaching in the weird shifting light of the illume rounds coming down under parachutes.

"Hardcore, they're comin' back! Lay still, play dead!" hissed Calhoun.

Several sappers stood above them. One rolled Calhoun over and pulled his wallet and radio codebook out of one of the baggy cargo pockets on his trousers. Calhoun was terrified. He tried to mask his breathing and tried not to move even as the sapper tugged at his plastic army-issue watch and nylon band. Calhoun had seen at least one grunt use his knife to whack off the finger of a dead, swollen enemy to get his ring, and he was convinced that the sapper was going to chop off his whole hand to get his cheap watch. Luckily, the clasp finally gave way. The sapper searched Holloway next. Holloway groaned in pain. The sapper grabbed a large rock and Calhoun watched in silent, incredulous horror as the man bashed Holloway's head in with it. Holloway died without a sound. The sappers moved away in the flarelight then, but turned to spray Calhoun and Holloway with another burst of automatic weapons fire. Calhoun saw rounds hitting the ground all around him, but he was going into shock and it took him a few moments to realize that he had been hit two more times—one round grazing his left side, the other hitting the lower part of his right buttocks, splitting the cheek wide open.

14

Dominoes

The perimeter bunkers were numbered one through twenty-two. Lieutenant Sams's platoon, Charlie Two, manned Bunkers 1 to 8—the part of the line starting at the south end below the B-TOC and the Charlie Company CP and wrapping around the southwest side of FSB Mary Ann. Five troops were supposed to be assigned to each position, but the platoon was so understrength that only two or three men were in most of the bunkers. Most slept through their guard duty.

Private First Class James C. Barnes was probably the only man in Charlie Two who saw the sappers coming. When the mortaring began, Barnes, who'd been sleeping atop Bunker 8 in the saddle by the resupply pad—it was the first bunker to the right of the break where the road ran down to the firing range—looked across the road toward Bunker 7. He saw two sappers, then spotted ten to fifteen more coming up the gentle slope. Starting from the inner barrier of concertina, they were already two-thirds of the way to the trench that connected the bunkers. Barnes jumped down to the back door of his own, hollering that they had "beaucoup dinks coming through the wire!"

The sappers, coming in under their own mortar fire, got into the trench line before the grunts got out of their sandbagged conex bunkers. "We didn't have a chance," said Sp4 Gary D. Webb, a machine gunner in Charlie Two, when interviewed by the division inspector general in the 91st Evac Hospital. "There wasn't a man out there that wasn't a good man in our company. We'd been in firefights before and we had a lot of kills credited to us. I got kills credited to me, but that was one time that I was just helpless."

Webb was in Bunker 7 with Pfc. Druey L. "Buck" Hatfield, who was from a different squad in Charlie Two, but who bunked with Webb because both were from West Virginia. Webb went out the door with his M60 after quickly pulling his jungle boots on. As he reached for the ammo belts hung up outside the bunker, he got a faceful of CS. Half blind, Webb fumbled around in the dark, feeling for the ammunition. Hatfield, who had grabbed his M16 and rushed into the trench, hollered at Webb to follow. Unable to find his own ammo, Webb finally dropped his machine gun and scooped up a bandolier of magazines lying in the bunker doorway before taking off after his buddy.

Stunned and knocked down by an explosion, Webb crawled into the trench. Buck Hatfield was already inside, moving toward Bunker 6. Several figures, unidentifiable in the dark, were moving toward them in the trench. Hatfield held his fire, thinking they were friendlies. Two wore gas masks.

Another explosion knocked Webb backward. Hatfield also went down, and the figures coming down the trench were on him before he could get back up. "I heard him holler, 'Oh God!' and then I heard a volley of shots," Webb recounted. "I saw figures up there around Buck and I knew the dinks were already in the trench line before we even got there."

The body of Private Hatfield, a twenty-year-old draftee with nine months in country, was stripped of its watch and valuables by the sappers. The ones in the trench turned their AK-47s on Webb, and as he spun around to run back to his bunker he realized there were several squads' worth of sappers coming up the hill between Bunkers 5 and 8. "All I could see was shadows," he later said. Webb reclaimed his M60 and made one last frantic grope for his ammo. It was gone, scattered by the explosions, and "in the meantime, I could hear them shooting and coming up the hill . . . coming from everywhere." Webb dropped his machine gun again and ran up to the old mess hall, where he bumped into two GIs. He asked if they had weapons, but they shouted, "No, no, no!" and took off into the darkness. Webb proceeded to the rear of the mess hall just as someone else came running around the corner. The figure was six feet away. "I hollered, 'Friendly,' but it was a dink. They made it up that far, that quick. He threw a Chicom [hand grenade] or something at my feet, and it blew up. It put holes all over me. Maybe I was unconscious for just a few seconds, I don't really remember, because I started crawling away. I finally realized that I was bleeding real bad everywhere."

The sappers were all over Charlie Two. Private First Class David Massich, a grenadier, went to the back door of Bunker 2 just in time to see an RPG explode in the company CP on the hillside behind his position. Massich could hear sappers outside speaking to each other in calm, conversational Vietnamese, and then a grenade thumped down on the bunker floor behind him. Massich started to turn, but a big flash filled the darkened bunker and he was blown out the doorway and into the blast wall of dirt-filled ammo crates. His glasses were broken and his face cut up. Everything was fuzzy, but when he reached for his grenade launcher it was right where he'd left it, leaning beside the doorway only an arm's length away.

Specialist Four Richard R. Carson also slept in Bunker 2, and he was calling for help when a second grenade exploded inside the position, killing him. Private Massich jumped into the trench, a single magazine in his XM203. His ammo vest with his grenades was still inside the bunker. Wearing only his olive-drab (OD) undershirt, fatigue pants, and socks, Massich ran toward Bunker 3, making it about halfway before a grenade hit the back of his leg and bounced between his feet. He threw his grenade launcher out of the trench and scrambled up after it.

The grenade exploded just as Massich rolled away from the edge of the trench. Massich, his head ringing, was badly shaken and he couldn't get his feet back under him to run. Another GI tripped over him in the dark, then asked if he had a weapon. As Massich reached for where he thought his grenade launcher was they heard a Coke-can grenade rolling toward them. The other GI took off. Massich, lying there with his face pressed into the crook of his left arm, was knocked unconscious by the explosion. He was hit in the top of the head by rock fragments and a lot of little metal bits. It felt like he'd been whacked with a hammer, and as soon as he could focus he realized there were three or four sappers standing around him. He froze, his face still buried in the crook of his arm as one of the sappers said, "Are you okay, GI? Are you dead, GI?" before giving him a couple of semihard kicks to his left side to see if he would move. The sapper pulled his arm out from under his head and took his watch. The sapper then shook him, and Massich, holding his breath, felt a rifle barrel against his back and a foot on his buttocks as another sapper removed his wallet from his pants pocket.

Massich had been trying to get to Bunker 3, where his squad leader, Sgt. Jerry Ledoux, had gotten out of his hammock just before a grenade exploded in the submerged position. Ledoux—stunned, wounded, and unable to find his M16— went to the doorway that opened up into the trench toward Bunker 4 and caught a glimpse of two shadowy sappers in position right beside the entrance. Ledoux bolted past them unarmed and half dressed, running up the hill as quickly as he could with wounds in his leg, nose, ear, and lip—feeling nothing, his adrenaline pumping.

Sergeant Ledoux hollered at his RTO to get out of the bunker with him. "He never answered," Ledoux later recalled. Ledoux's dead radioman, Sp4 James E. Edgemon, a twenty-year-old draftee, was a fellow Texan with only two months left on his tour. "All he talked about was he had a new pickup truck at home his daddy had bought him, and he couldn't wait to get home and drive it. He was easygoing, one of those guys you never had a cross word with."

The sappers also hit Bunker 1, killing two more of Ledoux's grunts: Pvts. Steven D. Plath and Clark V. Shawnee. Ledoux, meanwhile, stopped to get his bearings as he ran uphill. He saw a muzzle flash and took two AK-47 hits that threw him backward. One round went through his right shoulder, the other his right lung, collapsing it. The sappers ran up to Ledoux, who played dead as he was kicked around and searched. He had nothing to take. He passed out, numb and in shock.

Lieutenant Sams had spent a few minutes talking with the colonel in the B-TOC during his first day on FSB Mary Ann a little over a month earlier. Doyle assigned him to OJT with Company D, then saddling up for a CA off the hill. Sams got back into his helmet in a hurry when he emerged from the B-TOC, half-expecting mortar tubes to start coughing from the jungled hillsides around them. The grunts cracked amused grins. He was overreacting, they said. The hill was the safest place around.

The men always occupied the same positions on FSB Mary Ann. Lieutenant Sams bunked with his platoon sergeant, S.Sgt. Terry H. Price, in a sandbagged, half-submerged conex behind Bunker 5. Sams, a farmer's son from West Salem, Illinois, had enlisted for OCS after college, knowing he would be drafted anyway. He was twenty-four, a husband and father. Sams had seen no action during his week with Delta Company, nor during his month with the 2d Platoon of Company C, 1-46th Infantry. His only prisoners were an old Montagnard couple they choppered out of the jungle. His only kills were some hapless water buffalo the platoon was ordered to slaughter. Sams was asleep when the mortars started blasting the base. It was his first time under fire, and he sat up from the floor, boots off. Price, rolling out of his hammock as AK-47 fire stitched the conex, shouted that they had to get out of there. Sams agreed, but before he could get up he heard something clunk beside him in the dark. He reached down instinctively and put his hand right on the Coke-can grenade that had just been thrown in. He threw it back toward the door even as he kicked his feet up in the air, trying to turn away from the blast, trying to cover his face with his arm.

The grenade exploded in the doorway. The concussion was terrible, and Lieutenant Sams, his eardrums ruptured, caught multiple fragments in his heel, his buttocks, and the backs of his legs, which had been exposed as he rolled away. He was also peppered in the side of his face, permanently blinding him in his right eye. Sams shook off the pain, as did Price, who had also been hit, knowing they had to move if they wanted to survive. Sams reached in the dark for his M16, which should have been right there where he had been sleeping, but he couldn't find it. The next thing he knew, a firebomb was thrown down into the conex.

Lieutenant Sams was suddenly sitting in a pool of fire. He jumped up screaming and ran right into the blast wall. He passed out. When he awoke, he was wearing only his OD undershirt. He assumed that Sergeant Price—who was gone—had ripped his flaming trousers off him and saved his life. As it was, he had second-degree burns on both feet, his left leg, and on his hands and arms. The pain had not yet caught up with him as he lay unarmed and in shock inside his conex. Outside, the sappers rampaged with grenades and automatic weapons.

"I could hear 'em killing my people in the trench," Sams later recalled with great anguish.

Lieutenant Sams's radiomen, Sp4s Ronald M. Gourm and Donald M. Stotts, who slept in a conex next to the platoon CP, emerged into a hail of AK-47 fire. Stotts was killed instantly; Gourm got a concussion from a grenade explosion.

Lieutenant Sams's 1st Squad, led by Ledoux, was wiped out in Bunkers 1, 2, and 3. Sergeant Earl W. "Moose" Shelborn, the 2d Squad leader—a Nebraska farmboy—had no sooner scrambled into the trench line from Bunker 4 than a sapper fired his AK at him, emptying the magazine. Shelborn stopped five bullets in his massive frame, but survived. Private Bruce L. Ordoyne made it to the trench, too, but was immediately hit by a grenade. Everyone in Bunker 5 was killed, including Sgt. Michael L. Crossley, a team leader from Texas; the platoon medic, Pfc. Dallas D. Robinson of Tennessee; and machine gunners Sp4s Richard J. "Kraut" Boehm and "Chief" Johnson, who were both from North Dakota. Crossley, Robinson, Boehm, and Johnson were all draftees, and all close friends. Their bodies were found afterward spread out for twenty feet from the door of their bunker down the trench line toward Bunker 4, along with three dead sappers who had been stripped of all weapons and grenades by their comrades.

Sergeant Price was also killed in the trench, shot in the head. Price had served four tours as an aircraft engine repairman and part-time door gunner with the 1st Aviation Brigade in Pleiku from 1965 until he joined Company C in June, 1970. "Price was just a fabulous guy," said Ledoux of the unmarried, twenty-six-year-old Mormon from Salt Lake City. "He was a country boy and a mama's boy. His mother was always sending him packages with country-and-western tapes. He was a down-to-earth guy that you'd go to for answers 'cause he had been there so long." Price actually felt that he'd been there long enough. He had earlier requested and been granted reassignment to the rear, and was replaced by a fat Regular Army sergeant first class. The platoon made contact on a steep hillside shortly thereafter, getting one kill, and the choppers kicked out an ammo resupply at treetop level. One ammo can bounced from limb to limb down a tree right at the platoon sergeant, who spit out his false teeth as he jumped backward. The ammo landed on the dentures and the sergeant was sent packing. Price was brought back out, uptight and somewhat short-tempered, afraid that his number was finally up. "He told me of this premonition the very night we were overrun," said Sams.

Specialist Fours Scott E. Campbell and Donald J. Grant of the 2d Squad, and Sp4 Robert G. Davis, a grenadier from the 1st Squad, were in Bunker 6. Tear gas suddenly filled the bunker, then a grenade was thrown in. Grant's eardrums were burst by the explosion and the three piled outside as more grenades were thrown at them. Campbell suffered a bad cut across his hand. He dropped his M16 and bolted up the hill toward the aid station, followed by the barefoot Davis, who had been peppered with fragments in his chest and arms. Davis had a magazine in his XM203, but he was half-blinded by the gas and barely saw the three or four sappers who grenaded them again as they reached the mess hall area. Davis took a fragment in his throat, and he and his buddy flung themselves prone, petrified amid the flames and explosions all around them on the hill.

Campbell finally headed toward the aid station, hoping to find a spare M16. He couldn't find a weapon—he couldn't even find any GIs around the blown-up aid station—but he did walk right into a sapper in the dark. The VC, who was holding a grenade, wasn't looking in his direction, and Campbell shoved him before running around the corner of a bunker and disappearing.

Specialist Campbell, crossing the VIP pad, spotted three more sappers in flak jackets and Russian-style helmets down by Bunker 2. Meanwhile, Grant, who had just gotten outside when Campbell and Davis originally took off, saw six sappers coming down the trench from Bunker 6. Grant emptied the magazine in his M16, the only one he had on him, then turned to run. The quad .50 was positioned between Bunkers 5 and 6, and the gun crew and searchlight team were bunkered twenty meters behind it. Grant rushed into their position, shouting that the enemy was right behind him. The gun crew couldn't get out to man the quad .50 because their ammo bunker was on fire, thousands of rounds cooking off into the night. The crewmen thought a mortar round had hit the ammo bunker, but in the morning they dug the tail fins of a rocket-propelled grenade out of the wreckage. The enemy, knowing what the quad .50 could do to them, had made the bunker a priority target.

Behind Charlie Two, the battalion mess section, which operated two mess halls between the resupply pad and the aid station, was in a state of mass confusion. Tear gas had filled the old mess hall. "Everyone started screaming for their gas masks, turning everything inside out," remembered Sp5 Carl Cullers, one of the HHC cooks who bunked in the old mess hall next to the new semisubmerged one where their field ranges were set up. Pro, the unit's Montagnard mascot and kitchen policeman, also slept in the old mess hall, along with the battalion's ARVN interpreter. Cullers, not having a gas mask, pulled the blanket off his bunk. Something exploded at the front door of the mess, then at the back, blowing part of the wall away. There was fire and smoke, and little Pro crawled over to Cullers, totally lost without a gas mask. Cullers held his blanket over Pro's face, too.

After masking, Sp5 Robert H. Coles was lying prone with his M16 when the first grenade exploded at the front door, blowing his weapon out of his hands. Unable to find it in the dark, Coles spun around and headed for the back door, just in time to be wounded and burned when the next grenade exploded.

Amid panicked screaming from the cooks, S.Sgt. Ngoc Chau, the ARVN interpreter, told Cullers that they should move to the dug-in mess hall. Cullers jumped up and grabbed his M16 off the wall as Chau crawled out the front door. Cullers was right behind him, patting Pro on the shoulder to follow. Outside, he spotted two or three sappers in a prone position next to the mess hall. Cullers attempted to fire, but realized that he had no magazine in his weapon at the same time he saw the sparking fuse of a grenade one of the sappers was preparing to throw.

Cullers shouted a warning and kept crawling. Private First Class James W. Wiggins, a brand-new black cook, was following Cullers out the door when the grenade exploded. Wiggins was peppered with small metal fragments in his hands, arms, neck, and face—including his left eye which swelled shut—and by bigger chunks in his legs.

Separated from Cullers, Pro followed several cooks as they bolted for the artillery mess hall across the base, but they only ran into more tear gas and sappers. Private First Class Larry Sumlin, a black cook, had his foot blown off by a grenade that rolled under a cot in the artillery mess hall. Pro was greviously wounded in the same explosion.

Meanwhile, Wiggins lay in a bloody heap, screaming for help, but by then Cullers and Sergeant Chau, the interpreter, were already scrambling into the new mess bunker. Chau, who had been wounded himself—he was the only ARVN casualty of the battle—wanted to head for the aid station, but Cullers restrained him, trying to explain that they were not simply being shelled, but that there were sappers out there and that if they didn't kill him, the grunts probably would in a case of mistaken identification.

Lieutenant Colonel Doyle and Captain Spilberg made it to the Charlie Company CP, which was ablaze and belching smoke on the crest of the helipad. The ammo inside was exploding, and Dick Knight was nowhere in sight, not even among the bodies sprawled there. Doyle had his Swedish K, but only one clip. Spilberg, who was able to secure the radio hanging inside the bunker entrance, had his .45, plus a beat-up M16 he had just found lying on the ground. The weapon's hand guard had been blown off and he doubted it would work. The two moved into Mack's dugout on the left side of the CP and put a short whip antenna on the radio. Doyle again requested illumination, plus flareships and gunships and medevacs.

Lieutenant Schmitz on LZ Mildred recorded that Doyle reestablished contact with him at 0305. Lieutenant Mack, unable to walk, crawled to Specialist Carter and dug the radioman out from the wall of sandbags that had fallen on him. Specialist Simmons, the other wounded radioman, was also recovered. Spilberg could hear someone else moaning on the slope below the CP and, after asking Doyle to cover him, moved down there and found Calhoun, the field first sergeant.

"Can you get up, Sarge?" Spilberg whispered.

"I can't move," replied Calhoun.

Captain Spilberg grabbed Calhoun's collar, but the shot-up sergeant screamed with each tug. "You gotta shut up!" Spilberg whispered frantically. It was too late, several grenades landed around them, and Spilberg quickly hauled Calhoun into the dugout on the crest of the helipad. The grenades were duds. There was plenty of illume up, but smoke obscured the hillside so they could not see the sappers they heard scuttling around on the rocky slope below.

It sounded like a second wave was forming up. "They're comin' back," Spilberg whispered to Doyle. "Let's fall back!"

"Fall back to where?" answered Doyle, his legs no longer working. "Paul, this is where we're going to die."

Having no ammunition to waste on sounds in the dark, Doyle and Spilberg held their fire. Calhoun asked Spilberg for his spare .45—he wanted to take the next sapper that appeared with him—but he was too banged up to even chamber a round. Spilberg took it and did it for him, then put the weapon back in Calhoun's hands.

The battle still raged on the north side of the base, but the relative silence on the south side was eerie. There was no movement in the trench there, ten members of Charlie Two having already been killed, and eleven wounded. There were only three unscathed survivors in the platoon: Private Barnes, who had seen the sappers coming, and Sp4s Michael J. Holmes and Charles D. Velard who were with him in Bunker 8 by the resupply pad. "They were allegedly the platoon potheads, but nice guys and competent," recalled Sams. "The story was that they were up smoking when the shit hit—and they immediately started lobbing grenades all over so nobody could get close." Holmes, Velard, and Barnes—who told the inspector general for the record that they had gone to sleep before the attack started while listening to music with their tape player turned low—had two cases of grenades in their bunker, which they had made into a bench by placing a board across them. They threw the frags down into a gully where rainwater drained off the hill, into all the other blind spots on the slope, and at intervals right outside their windows in case a sapper managed to get close without being detected. They could see the silhouettes of what were presumably sappers moving past the burning bunkers and exploding ammo to their left but, concerned about hitting friendlies, only fired when they had clear targets. Velard spotted a sapper squatting in front of a conex to their right as he shoved a grenade through the firing port. When the VC started back toward the wire, Velard and Holmes opened fire. The sapper ducked into the shadows, but when he reappeared several minutes later, again trying to slip away, Barnes pitched a grenade practically into his lap. They found the sapper lying dead in that spot at dawn.

Specialist Steven Webb of Charlie Two, who was completely disoriented in addition to being wounded in his head, shoulder, and left arm, crawled toward an above-ground sleeping bunker across the camp road, shouting, "GI, GI!" He saw a Vietnamese approaching from the bunker. He thought it was another sapper, but it turned out to be one of the ARVN artillerymen on the base. The ARVN helped Webb inside and bandaged his wounds. Webb tried to get an M16 away from one of the ARVN guarding the door, but the man would not let go, and Webb, who wanted to help but didn't know what to do, could only wait anxiously in position as illume went up and the light flickered through the cracks in the bunker walls.

Specialist Webb was the only GI with the ARVN during the battle, and despite rumors that the ARVN fired on U.S. positions during the sapper attack, he never saw it.

Nevertheless, most grunts were convinced that the ARVN artillerymen had betrayed the base. "It was an inside job," said Sergeant Calhoun. The ARVN were located in Battery B, 1-14th FA's former positions behind Charlie One on the steep northeast side of FSB Mary Ann. The ARVN did not man their howitzers during the attack and because the sappers bypassed their area they suffered not a single casualty. However, as was noted in a division-level investigation, that entire side of the perimeter was "generally untouched, including the battalion ammunition storage area. The actions of the ARVN soldiers were no different from many US soldiers in taking cover until the attack was over."

There was some circumstantial evidence of ARVN collusion with the VC. "That morning before the attack, an ARVN officer came up to our bunker and asked how we got out of the perimeter," said Sp4 Edward L. Newton of Charlie One. "We asked him why he wanted to know. He said because he and his men wanted to go down there fishing. We thought it was kind of peculiar. We said we did not know for sure." The ARVN officer, who wore the two-chrysanthemum insignia of a first lieutenant, asked around until some grunts finally explained that the easiest way down the hill was at the south end and on the road running past the rifle range to the water point. Later, Specialist Cullers, an HHC cook, said he observed "an ARVN going behind the rifle range. It was more or less a joke at first. One of the cooks said, 'Hey, Cullers, there's an NVA down there,' and I said, 'Quit joking.' . . . and he said, 'Wait, and I'll point him out to you.' I knew it was an ARVN by his size. He had gone out beyond the rifle range, and down the slope for about twenty minutes. I took it for granted that he had gone down to defecate."

Did certain ARVN meet the VC near the water point and

exchange information about the base for a promise of sanctuary during the attack? Sergeant Olints of Company D was on the resupply pad at dusk before the attack (he was returning to the bush after R&R), when "an ARVN chopper came out, and fifteen of those little suckers got on. They were thrilled to death, jumping on, pushing each other. I didn't think the thing would take off it was so overloaded. We had no idea what was coming, but, in retrospect, it sure looked like they did."

During the sappers' withdrawal, S.Sgt. Domingo Lopez of Company E held his fire when he saw "one man in jungle fatigues go into the wire. I thought he was a GI—but he went along with the sappers." Perhaps some VC were outfitted as ARVN to cause confusion, but several ARVN were reportedly missing after the battle.

"I remember carrying dead and wounded past the ARVN near the end of the attack," wrote Pfc. Brad Brown of Company E, "and they just stood and watched. They didn't even help with security. We were very angry, and there was talk of shooting the bastards up."

Private First Class John A. Bruno of Company A testified that when he passed the ARVN bunker the next morning, the ARVN were "standing around their guns, just laughing and joking like it was all a big joke." The ARVN artillery platoon was pulled off the hill within forty-eight hours of the attack, but an ARVN infantry company was then brought in to reinforce the firebase. "I remember an incident where a GI came to the TOC and said that an ARVN was signaling with a flashlight to someone outside the wire," wrote Specialist Noller, a B-TOC RTO who, upon checking, "did encounter an ARVN with a GI flashlight near the east perimeter wire. I told him not to use it, in English which he probably didn't understand, and then reported this to an officer. The incident was not treated seriously by the officers, but added credence as far as the GIs were concerned that some of the ARVN were not on our side."

Behind Charlie Two, the bunker known as the battalion barbershop because it had a padded barber's chair mounted on top was a shambles, one wall gone and part of its steel-plank roof caved in by a nearly direct mortar hit. Inside were Pfc. Thomas N. Pruitt, an Echo Company sniper, and Sp4 Elixsandro C. Rios, a Delta Company mortarman. Both were in an ear-ringing daze, as well as being barefoot and clad only in their underwear. With them was an anonymous, shell-shocked GI who had stumbled into their wrecked bunker for cover. Pruitt had to slap the man to calm him down. The GI was sitting on the floor when he mutely pointed toward the doorway. Pruitt and Lopez—back in the shadows unsuccessfully digging around for their M16s, ammunition, and jungle boots—saw a sapper standing there, sighting his AK-47 on the shell-shocked soldier, who was too stunned to move. Enraged and terrified, Pruitt grabbed a board, the only weapon available, and was rearing back to throw it when the sapper ducked away from the doorway, apparently startled by the commotion.

Pruitt demanded they get out of the bunker, and the three had no sooner rushed out the door than the whole place went up, destroyed by a satchel charge. Pruitt and Rios decided to head for the B-TOC—the shell-shocked GI didn't want to go that way, and disappeared—and as they were walking Rios suggested they pick up something in case they encountered another sapper. Rios picked up a rock, as did Pruitt. It was all they had. They crossed the camp road, went past the burning B-TOC, and took cover for ten or fifteen minutes at the rear of the artillery battery's orderly room. Pruitt's eardrums were leaking blood. Rios's were bleeding even more heavily, and they slipped into the artillery shower so they wouldn't be seen as they checked each other's injuries. Small-arms fire began anew down by the resupply pad, so Pruitt peered through a crack in the shower. He spotted two sappers sprinting up the road in the direction of the B-TOC, firing away and slinging satchel charges to either side. They ran right past the shower.

Because the sappers did not come up the steep side of the base overlooking the river, they ignored the positions along that crest. In fact, when Sp4 Timothy Carmichael, the junior medic in Charlie One, looked out the rear window of his conex—he had been sleeping alone in Bunker 17—he thought the white flashes down by the resupply pad were the result of somebody stupidly lighting up a cigarette in the ammunition storage area. Carmichael collected his medical gear, assuming that there would be casualties from the accident, and only after walking over to the platoon command post for instructions did he realize that the base was under attack.

With Lieutenant Doyle on leave, Sgt. Elmer Head, a cheerful black shake 'n' bake, was the acting platoon leader for Charlie One. Sergeant William G. Walker, normally the 2d Squad leader, was acting platoon sergeant. Head and Walker were in Bunker 18—the platoon manned Bunkers 15 to 22—along with their RTOs, Sp4 Kenneth M. Gates and Pfc. Brian T. Pappizo. Originally sleeping in a hammock outside Carmichael's conex, Pfc. Larry J. Vogelsang, the senior platoon medic, scrambled into Bunker 18 when the shelling began. Head kept everyone down on the bunker floor for several confused minutes, then led them out into the trench line when there seemed to be a lull in the fire. Head fired into the wire, but there was no return fire, only stray tracers that buzzed overhead from the fight behind them, and the tear gas they smelled was only what had drifted over from the primary targets on either hilltop. It did not require them to mask.

Charlie One had been spared, and because it had been bypassed the platoon survived its initial confused inaction and was able to get organized in the trench line. The sappers did not touch any of the positions from Bunker 15 on the far left flank of Charlie One's line—where Pfc. William G. Cahill began lobbing frags downhill and Sp4 Marshall H. Turner, a team leader in the 1st Squad, began pumping HE grenades into the wire and illume overhead with his XM203—to Bunker 19 on the right—where Sergeant Neill, the 1st Squad leader, got his two bunkmates out into the trench with a case of fragmentation grenades, which they proceeded to heave down the black hillside, taking no chances.

Meanwhile, the medics—Vogelsang and Carmichael—were stunned to find Sgt. David H. Thompson, the support company supply sergeant, lying in the trench between Bunkers 15 and 16 with his legs blown off. Vogelsang got tourniquets around the stumps while Carmichael started an

IV. When the attack started, Thompson had been in the Echo Company headquarters north of the resupply pad and directly behind Charlie One. Joined by Sergeant Lopez, the heavy mortar platoon sergeant, and Sp5 Thomas G. Sklaney, a support company radioman, Thompson made a dash to the trench line. A grenade exploded beside them, superficially wounding Lopez. Moments later, Sklaney heard someone yell, "Are they dead yet?" Perhaps the sappers were speaking in English to add to the confusion, or perhaps some grunts had mistaken the sudden arrival of the three support personnel for sappers. Whatever the case, the next thing Sklaney saw was a U.S.-issue baseball grenade sailing toward them, silhouetted by the flames in the background.

The grenade landed right next to Thompson.

Charlie One did not come through the attack completely unscathed. "I was blown out of my bed by a satchel charge," recounted Sp4 James M. Leach, sole occupant of Bunker 22, the first position to the left of the decimated Charlie Two. The sappers tossed a second charge into the sandbagged conex. "I took off running for the door," said Leach, who, knocked dizzy by the first blast, was shot in the hip as soon as he got outside. Unarmed, he took cover in a hole where a hootch had recently been dismantled, only to have a sapper drop into a hole right in front of him. "I started screaming. He jumped out of the hole and took off running. After that, I kept running and hiding."

Private Avery W. Blevins, previously on guard atop Bunker 21, hollered for everyone to get out into the trench line. Sergeant Michael Shell, the acting 2d Squad leader in Charlie One, was asleep in the bunker with Sp4s Charles L. Gilliland and Robert J. Schumacher. Alerted by Blevins, the three were still scrambling for weapons and ammunition when a grenade landed in the trench right outside the doorway. The bunker was "blown all to hell," Gilliland, a country boy, wrote in a letter to his buddy Dennis Murphy, "the sappers did us a damn job man." Schumacher survived the blast unscathed because he was behind the doorway, but Shell caught it in the face. Gilliland's eardrum was ruptured, his side and arm riddled with fragments. He couldn't find his M16, which had been hanging on the bunker wall.

His letter continued, "Shoe got out of the bunker and I got out and the E-5 [Sergeant Shell] was still in it, yelling he couldn't see so I went back in the bunker to get him and the dinks threw in some explosives and they hit me in the back but I was able to get down on the floor before they went off. I got the E-5 and carried him up to the next bunker."

Brutally awakened by the shrill descent and conex-shaking impact of the mortar shells, Pfc. Dennis Ziems of the 1st Squad scrambled to pull on his jungle boots, then grab his M16 and ammo. He, Sp4 Gene Ratliff, and Pfc. Philip S. Nichols had all been asleep when the attack began. "The bunker was filled with panic and confusion," noted Ziems—they were in Bunker 20—describing the common dilemma. "You didn't know what to do—stay in the bunker because the mortars were landing so close, or go to the trenches and defend yourself and your bunker?" Ziems and Nichols, followed by Ratliff, headed outside when they heard the AK fire to their rear, but the trench smelled of CS. Ziems told Ratliff and Nichols to crawl back into the bunker one at a time to find their gas masks, then followed them in to pull his own out of his rucksack. They were able to take their masks off five or ten minutes later when the gas dissipated. "We couldn't see what was going on at the bunkers on each side of us. We just hoped they were holding their own. There were a lot of small explosions and gunfire coming from everywhere, and we could see a few people moving around back in the perimeter. They were too far away to see who they were. We decided not to fire back into the perimeter unless we had positive identification of our target."

Private Ziems saw three figures crawling down the trench from the right. "Who's there?" he shouted, raising his M16.

"Don't shoot!" called back Schumacher, who was in the lead. "It's me, Shoe, and I got Sergeant Shell and Gilliland with me!"

In front as usual, the sandy-haired, devil-may-care Schumacher was the best grunt in Charlie One. He was also one of the battalion's few paratroopers and sported tiger-stripe fatigues. Meeting Schumacher in the trench, Ziems helped pull the wounded Shell and Gilliland into Bunker 20.

Schumacher and Ziems then started up the trench line to their left to find and bring back the medics. They didn't make it. The trench had been dug deep for about twenty feet to either side of the bunker, but as soon as Ziems crawled into the stretch where it became shallow and wide between Bunkers 20 and 19, an AK-47 cracked from somewhere up the hill and a round hit the trench wall just a few inches above his head. Dirt came down on him. Ziems immediately backed up to Schumacher, telling him there was no way they could go in that direction. The shot seemed to have come from the vicinity of the artillery mess hall and latrine, but they could see nobody there in the light of the adjacent and burning tactical operations center, and they could not simply pump away on automatic for fear of hitting their own guys.

Schumacher could not have returned fire whatever the situation. "I didn't bring my rifle from my bunker," he told Ziems. "I'm going after it."

"Don't go—just use Ratliff's!"

"No, he might need it himself!"

Schumacher took off. Private Ziems, raising his head a little, got the sniper's attention again, but this time the rounds were not quite so close. Ziems saw Schumacher make it back to his demolished bunker. Telling Nichols to watch the area, Ziems then ducked into Bunker 20 to check on Gilliland and Sergeant Shell. Ratliff said that Shell was shaking all over, so Ziems flicked his lighter—drawing sniper fire—and grabbed the bandages and medical pack in his rucksack. Shell was screaming that he couldn't see as Ziems leaned over him with the lighter. More shots thumped into the sandbags outside. Ziems got Shell to lie down and put his feet up on the ruck he pulled over, then put the bandages in his hands and told him to hold them tightly over his eyes and face, which had looked like a red mask in the glow of the lighter.

"It doesn't look that bad," Ziems told Shell. "I think you just have blood running in your eyes is why you can't see."

Ziems moved to Gilliland, who said quietly despite his wounds that he was okay, merely numb. Ziems told Gilliland and Shell to hang in there, they'd get help as soon as they could, then whispered to Ratliff, "Watch Shell—if he goes into shock again, talk to him and get him calmed down. Keep him lying down."

Back in the trench, Ziems and Nichols, keeping low to avoid any more green tracers from the sniper, who may or may not have still been in position behind them, started throwing frags down the hill in front of them just in case. Schumacher should have been back already, so Ziems shouted to Blevins and Leach, asking if they had seen him. Blevins answered that he had heard shots when Schumacher reached his bunker, adding that he hadn't answered when they yelled to him earlier.

Doc Vogelsang, crawling on his belly down the shallow trench and drawing no fire, finally reached Ziem's position. Vogelsang said that medevacs and gunships were on the way, and that everyone was to sit tight and hold what they had. The medic then called over to Blevins and Leach to ask if they were all right. Blevins answered that he was okay, but that they still hadn't heard anything from Schumacher, and volunteered to go with the medic to check on him. Blevins and Vogelsang headed toward the silent bunker. They returned moments later to report that the best soldier in the platoon was dead, shot down in the doorway of his bunker before he could find his weapon in the debris and fight back.

15

Hand-to-Hand

Specialist four Joe M. Lowry, a grenadier in Echo Recon, saw the attack begin while on guard atop Bunker 9. The CP was calling for situation reports (sitreps), and Lowry, waiting his turn to call in, had just checked his watch when the quad .50 ammo bunker exploded down the line to the left. He saw a nearby position take another direct hit in almost the same instant and, thinking they were under mortar fire, jumped into the trench seconds before his conex took a direct hit from a rocket-propelled grenade.

Sergeant Gordon Kitts, 2d Squad leader in Charlie Three, and the other men in Bunker 9—Sp4s Terry L. Felt and Dennis H. Hunt, and Pfc. Eugene E. Erickson—had piled outside just before the RPG hit. Felt came out last, having paused to grab their weapons and ammunition. Kitts was hit in the back of the head, his lower back, and buttocks. Hunt also caught some RPG fragments.

From the trench, Felt and Lowry returned fire against snipers behind a boulder in the wire, while other nearby grunts began screaming that they were hit. The casualties included Sgt. Russell Burns, the other team leader in 2d Squad, Charlie Three, plus the four GIs in the conex they used as a sleeping position to the right rear of Bunker 8. The conex was halved by a dividing wall. Burns and Pfc. James A. Johnson bunked in one section; Pfc. Laymon Palmer and

Sp4 Bernard E. Coleman, a platoon medic, were on the other side with Pfc. Calvin Dukes of A Company. All were black. Burns awoke to the sound of AK-47s, then was wounded in the face and right arm by a grenade. Burns and Johnson crawled outside. The sappers got two other grenades into the other side of the conex, and Dukes emerged wounded and stunned to make a run for better cover. Palmer was pinned inside by a beam across his back, and Coleman wrestled with it until a rocket-propelled grenade hit the roof. Coleman scrambled out then, joining Burns and Johnson, the only one of them who had grabbed his M16.

Another grenade came out of nowhere. Sergeant Burns caught fragments in the back and Johnson's elbow was shredded and his M16 knocked from his hands. The sappers sprayed the area with AK fire, and Doc Coleman, burned across the back by the grenade blast, bolted off to find Sergeant Head of Charlie One.

The closest cover was actually Bunker 8, occupied by Holmes, Velard, and Barnes of Charlie Two. Johnson saw two shadows rushing toward them, and he retrieved his weapon and hastily crawled with Burns into the bunker—almost getting fired up by their own men in the confusion as they reached the rear doorway.

The casualties also included the Charlie Three command group. Lieutenant McGee was asleep atop Bunker 10 when his radioman, Pfc. Gaven M. Monoghan, who was pulling guard, actually saw the first enemy mortar rounds flash from their tubes in the still darkness. Monoghan didn't know what he was seeing until the explosions began seconds later because the mortars were to the northwest, higher up on the firebase ridgeline. As soon as he realized an attack was in progress he woke the lieutenant, grabbed his radio, and jumped off the left side of the bunker into the trench. Monoghan saw someone coming his way, but assumed it was a grunt from the next bunker—until a grenade landed hissing beside him. Scrambling out of the trench, he was able to dart around the back of his bunker just before it exploded.

Charlie Three manned Bunkers 9 to 13. Lieutenant McGee scrambled into his CP, joining Sgt. Warren P.

Ritsema, his platoon sergeant, and Sp5 Carl E. Patton, the senior platoon medic. Monoghan followed McGee in, shouting that they had sappers on the hill as he secured his M16 and helmet, and grabbed the ammo bandoliers hanging from a nail in the doorway. Monoghan handed out the other M16s leaning there, but had no sooner gotten set up to cover the doorway when two mortar rounds hit the bunker, blowing the radioman against the back wall and dislodging a ceiling beam, which slammed into the lieutenant's head. Patton, who wrapped the wound, later testified that when the explosions began to peter out some fifteen minutes later:

> The lieutenant stood up and said, "Alright, let's go" . . . and he started running through the door. A Chicom came through the front door and landed at his feet. He and I both spotted it at the same time. He said, "Grenade!" I saw a small twinkling of a light like a cigarette in the dark. I reached out and picked it up and threw it toward the door which I was leaning against . . . it went off, not hurting anybody except my platoon sergeant an· me. I got some fragments in my arm and it skinned m hand up. I thought I'd lost my arm and the concussion blew me back against my lieutenant, who grabbed my weapon at this time, stood up, and started heading for the door. When he reached the door, I saw another Chicom land between his legs and come skidding into the room . . . and real fast I tried to kick the Chicom over into the corner, but I couldn't make it in time. It blew up right next to my legs. I received fragments in the left leg, and in the left buttocks.

Within seconds, a satchel charge detonated on the roof, caving in the corner where Ritsema was kneeling. "I saw a beam come down and hit him in the back, and I knew then that he'd had it," stated Patton. Big, blond Sergeant Ritsema, age twenty-two when killed, was a married draftee from Michigan, described by one grunt as a "helluva nice guy who always took care of his people."

Doc Patton spoke of his own close call in the bunker:

The roof was falling on me, and I tried to curl up and protect myself when I was covered with sandbags. . . . I started piling sandbags off me with my one good arm. . . . The beam that had fallen and hit the lieutenant had held up and made most of the sandbags fall away from me. I crawled out that way and had just about crawled out where I could get my head out when my [wounded left] foot would not come out the rest of the way. . . . I lay there. I could hear movement all around outside.

Monoghan, crawling out into the trench, was knocked unconscious by a grenade, while Lieutenant McGee ran into a sapper right outside the demolished CP and wrestled him to the ground. McGee, who was short, wiry, and powerful, locked his hands around the sapper's throat, choking him to death. Patton then stated:

I heard my lieutenant cuss at somebody. . . . I heard him scuffling with somebody. . . . It got quiet again, and I heard an AK going off right outside the bunker, and I heard my lieutenant groan out there. . . . I couldn't get out because of my foot. . . . I couldn't reach my bandages. I had a tourniquet in my left pocket, but my left pocket was gone. I grasped my left arm with my right arm and squeezed it real tight to cut off the flow of blood so I wouldn't bleed to death. I was hoping that somebody would hurry up and come up that way.

When help finally arrived, Lieutenant McGee was found lying dead atop the sapper he had killed, shot from behind by another sapper. McGee had been a Golden Gloves boxer at West Point (Class of 1969), and his hand-to-hand exploit became one of the legends of FSB Mary Ann. The lieutenant was a complicated hero, however. "People didn't respect McGee," recalled Lieutenant Bell. McGee, twenty-three at the time of his death, was Detroit blue-collar, airborne qualified, and had attended jungle warfare school in Panama before shipping out to Vietnam. He was initially assigned to lead the battalion reconnaissance platoon, but his curt and precisely military manner did not fit in. "He couldn't read a map," said Lieutenant Schmitz, whom McGee replaced. "It was very difficult to read a map out there, but he wouldn't pay attention to anybody. He was a hard-chargin' little guy, and he knew it all. He had NCOs who I'd thought were terrific, but he came and told me what lousy guys they were. They came to me too and told me that the guy didn't know shit and wouldn't listen to any suggestions. He'd be lost and wouldn't admit he was lost."

Lieutenant McGee took over Echo Recon in September, 1970, but was relieved after his men killed one of their own in a friendly fire debacle. McGee decompressed on the battalion staff, then requested reassignment to the line. "He wanted to go back, much to his credit," said Lieutenant Bell. McGee assumed command of the 3d Platoon of Company C, 1-46th Infantry, in February, 1971; he got his second chance in part because Captain Strand, then the battalion operations officer, still had faith in him. "McGee was his own man, and probably didn't listen as much as he should have," said Strand, "but he was a tough, tough kid. He was a little crazy, but extremely brave, and he didn't try to be a buddy with his soldiers like a lot of other lieutenants during that period. I frowned on lieutenants who were buddies with their troops because when they decide that they don't want to do something dangerous, what do you do then? McGee didn't have that problem."

Private Tom Schneider, a Charlie Three RTO, recalled:

> We thought Lieutenant McGee was just a gung ho bastard at first, but we found out he had a good head on his shoulders. The platoon was moving down a trail with a dog handler on point. The dog went on alert, pointing uphill on our flank, and that crazy McGee had us conduct an on-line assault up that hill. Well, it worked because the NVA saw twenty grunts coming at them spread out and ready, and they took off in the opposite direction. We found a little spot of crushed brush that would have fit two enemy soldiers, plus the palm fronds they'd been sitting on as they waited to ambush us.

Sergeant Burns, however, said that their perimeter defenses were never inspected ("when I was with the 4th Division, somebody was always checking"), and Private Johnson stated for the record:

> We didn't have any claymores or trip flares out for the whole time we were on that hill. . . . After we went into LZ Young's AO, and went back out to FSB Mary Ann's AO, we never put them back out. . . . No one ever mentioned it since they were tearing down that hill. The [concertina] wire was so rusty. The claymore wires were rusty, too. Nobody ever mentioned anything about policing them up or putting out brand-new ones. . . .

Most of the sappers slipping unhampered through Charlie Three headed for the 155-mm artillery atop the northwest half of FSB Mary Ann. Several teams, however, hit the supply section alongside the resupply pad. Specialist Four Anthony Jorgensen and Pfc. Paul E. Newburn, the Company C supply reps, were confronted by a sapper as soon as they opened their hootch door. Newburn grabbed his .45 and shot the sapper, who threw a grenade as he fell backward. The explosion blew Newburn through one of the hootch walls, knocking him out. Jorgensen was also catapulted outside, wounded in the chest and legs, and though he passed out then under a layer of debris, he thankfully discovered when he woke up that he had kept a grip on his pistol. He was lying on it.

There were fires everywhere, and no one seemed to be returning fire. Jorgensen wondered in horror if he was the only one left alive. Thankfully, he heard Private Palmer calling for help from the trench line, having finally gotten out from under the beam that had had pinned him inside his conex. The sappers also heard him. Jorgensen, crawling toward Palmer, saw two of them coming around the little chain-link compound in which rations were stacked behind Bunker 8. The sapper who approached Palmer was wearing a GI steel helmet. The Vietnamese asked in English if he was wounded and Palmer mumbled a reply. When he started to rise, the sapper shot him dead in the ditch. The other sapper went straight for Jorgensen, who froze and played dead until the sapper kicked him in the back, at which point he flipped over and shot the sapper with his pistol, touching off one of the man's grenades. Jorgensen was knocked unconscious again, splattered with enemy blood. . . .

The officer who controlled logistical activities on the resupply pad, 1st Lt. Rafael C. Rivera, the HHC Support Platoon leader, was headquartered at the northwest edge of it, directly behind Bunker 8. His S4 office faced the camp road, which ran up from the pad to the artillery parapets atop the hill. Rivera bunked with his black supply sergeant, Sgt. Louis J. Meads, and Sp4 William Meek, the machine gunner who had been rewarded after being wounded with reassignment as Delta Company's supply rep. Rivera thought their own arty was firing when he awoke, but Meads shouted that it was incoming. With that, Meek, who had heard nothing, instinctively grabbed his weapon from where it rested on two nails at the head of his bunk bed, rolled over without looking, and hit the floor with a crash. He jumped up in his underwear, without a clue.

Lieutenant Rivera turned the light on so they could dress quickly—no one was thinking of sappers—and amid the continuing incoming, he said to Meads, "Go outside and turn my radios on."

"Are you kidding?" Meads blurted.

"No, go on back outside!"

Sergeant Meads opened the door and a grenade landed inside the hootch. Rivera screamed, "Get down, get down, get down!"

Meek hit the deck against the left wall and Meads landed on top of him. The grenade exploded an instant later, blowing the door and the lighting fixtures away and plunging them into total darkness. Half of the wall facing the resupply pad was also demolished. Meads, hit in the head by a beam, was blown to one side of Meek, who was also stunned and injured by the blast. The former machine gunner was brutally cracked across the shins, perhaps by the same beam, and although he was too shaken up to notice, a burst eardrum bled down the side of his face.

Moments after the explosion, Lieutenant Rivera, formerly a grunt platoon leader, headed out the door with his .45 just in time to see a U.S.-made frag coming his way. He saw the spoon pop off and stumbled back inside two or three steps before being wounded and temporarily knocked out by this second blast. Meads was hit by fragments in his leg. The supply sergeant found his M16 in the debris then and lay down beside Meek in the back corner. They didn't even whisper to each other because they could hear sappers talking outside. One slid right past the missing wall of their hootch to take up a position near the open doorway. The sapper eased up to look across the road, then sank back down and was joined by another who appeared from the direction of the bunker line. They talked, unaware they were being watched from the demolished hootch.

Illume was up, lighting the scene as one of the two sappers made his move to get across the road. "I gut shot him," recalled Meek. "He fell down, and I put a few more rounds in him." Sergeant Meads also pumped an M16 burst into the sapper as he crawled down to the edge of the resupply pad. The sapper swung his arm and moaned and the other one stepped into view as he went to rescue his dying buddy. The VC moved in a slow crouch, silhouetted by the fires behind him. "He got right where I wanted him to be," said Meek, who had been expecting another grenade, "so I pulled a bead down on him, and when I squeezed off the only thing I saw was a chunk of his skull flying up over the sights. I felt so good because I knew that sonofabitch wasn't going to get me. If I could have seen the one that was moaning, I would have shut him up with another burst."

Having demolished Rivera's hootch and the one to the left occupied by Jorgensen and Newburn, the sappers then hit the hootch across the road—where Pfc. Lonnell A. Thompson, the Alpha Company supply rep, bunked with two fellow blacks, Sp4s David Mays and James E. Fletcher of Company D. There was an explosion on the roof, then one in the doorway, and Fletcher, wounded when that grenade flashed in his face, ran outside, trying to get away.

Inside, Mays, wounded in both feet, hunkered down with Thompson. "I was just scared to death," Thompson later told the inspector general, but the next blast never came. The sapper at the door was dead, according to Capt. Donald Sampson, who was watching from his nearby headquarters. "We didn't see him until he actually blew himself up throwing a satchel charge or Chicom. He was too close to it and he rolled out in front of us."

Captain Sampson guarded one of two doors leading into the Echo Company headquarters with 1st Lt. John M. Clark, his exec, and Lieutenant Good of Echo Recon. Two mortarmen guarded the other door, while a third went into the FDC room, waiting in vain for the call to fire from the B-TOC. (Sampson and Rivera were later admonished for not getting outside to organize the reaction force, which was their responsibility, but probably a suicidal task given the circumstances.) Good, lying in the doorway, had the best vantage point, but he held his fire for fear of missing the few sappers he spotted and shooting up the S4 hootch across the road. Good sighted in on one sapper who rushed right toward the headquarters, but before he could fire, his target disintegrated, apparently blown up by his own explosives. The headless, limbless torso was still lying on the pad in the morning.

Facing the road to the right of the headquarters building, Sgt. Thomas L. Bush, and tow of his gunners, Sp4 Harry M. Honaker and Pfc. David A. Rogillio from Company E's 4.2-inch Mortar Platoon had pushed the door of their hootch open and were watching from either side of it when they spotted a sapper sneaking through an evacuated gun pit across the road. Honaker aimed his M16 at the sapper and squeezed off five quick shots—but in return, an RPG hit the hootch about two feet above his head, blowing most of the roof away. Honaker and Rogillio were wounded. Honaker had hit the sapper, though, and the man bled to death in the gun pit, lying beside his launcher and a second round he had not had the energy to load and fire.

Given that the heavy mortars had already been lifted out, the sappers bypassed the rest of the Echo Company mortarmen while making a beeline for S.Sgt. Vincent Young's 81-mm mortar section, which was in position halfway up the slope from the headquarters building on the same side of the road. Two of Young's mortars had already been lifted out, but he still had two others in position. When the shelling began, Young, a black NCO, ran into a vacated mortar hootch occupied by two fellow Bravo Company GIs—Sergeant Shook, who was on his way back to the bush after appearing before a promotion board in the rear, and Sp5 Kyle S. Hamilton, a grunt medic recently reassigned to the battalion aid station. Young shouted that there were sappers all over the hill. Shook pulled on his jungle boots and reached for his M16, but Hamilton got to it first. Young extinguished their kerosene lantern in the same instant—and a second later, a satchel charge blew the door away. Young, Shook, and Hamilton were just picking themselves off the floor, trying to get their bearings, still trying to find weapons in the dark, when what felt and sounded like a mortar shell exploded on the roof, setting it afire.

Sergeant Young was hit in the buttocks. Limping badly, he stumbled from the burning hootch to the Company E headquarters. "He looked pretty scared," recalled Captain Sampson. "I didn't want him to upset too many people there, so I sent him into the back room."

While being bandaged, Young told Sampson that Shook and Hamilton were still in the burning hootch. There was no way to rescue them. Hamilton was, in fact, already dead. The body of the popular, nineteen-year-old country boy medic was burned beyond recognition. Shook had been knocked unconscious and peppered with wooden splinters, and he woke up with a burning poncho liner on his back. He suffered second-degree burns. Assuming the others had already escaped, he crawled from the blazing hootch. His eardrums had been ruptured, fluid ran down his cheeks, and when he called out, he couldn't really hear if there was any reply. He felt like his head was in a bucket.

When the shelling began, Sgt. Johnny L. White, who ran Bravo Company's 81-mm mortar squad, shared a startled glance with the guys playing poker with him at the ammo-box table inside their sleeping bunker. They assumed the arty was firing—but just seconds later White was stunned to see a grenade come flying through their open doorway. As he dove to the floor everyone else scrambled for cover too, whether they had actually seen anything or not.

Sergeant White was burned on the face when the grenade exploded, blowing out their light. The five other wounded men in the bunker included Pfc. Robert Stainton from Delta's 81-mm team; he had turned sideways behind the edge of the doorway when White hit the deck but, unable to get completely behind it, had caught fragments in his buttocks and the back of his right calf.

The only occupant of the sleeping bunker next door was Sp4 Donald L. Rice, who ran the 81-mm mortar squad from Company D. Rice had been a point man with the company for almost nine months—most of the mortarmen were ex-grunts—and with the mortars for the last four, having extended his tour. Better known as "Snowflake" for his shock of whitish-blond hair, he was a popular wheeler-dealer type who always made sure his old platoon had ice and sodas whenever it was lifted onto the firebase. He was king of the hill as far as the enlisted men were concerned.

Specialist Rice was asleep in his hammock wearing jungle boots and a pair of cutoffs. He snapped awake at the whistling rush of an incoming round—only to be thrown to the floor an instant later by a direct hit on the roof of his bunker. Sandbags and timber caved in on him. Rice was deafened and blinded. He thought he had just been dazzled by the flash, but in reality his right eye was gone and his left punctured by minute fragments. Because he was suffering little pain, he also did not realize that he was gouged and burned across his face, chest, arms, and legs. Rice groped around in the shambles before crawling out through a hole, barely escaping the flames that were quickly engulfing the bunker.

Rice blindly crawled into a crater, then hollered for help when he heard two people approaching. They didn't do anything. Rice screamed again and the two figures bent down, grabbing his arms and legs. They were sappers. Rice tried to push them away but, given his wounds, one sapper had no trouble holding him down while the other took his gold watch, ring, and necklace with its peace medallion. The sappers spoke urgently to each other, anxious to get moving, and the next thing Rice knew they started dragging him down toward the wire, apparently intent on taking him away as a prisoner.

Rice was screaming, and Sgt. David P. Arias, who was coming out of the Bravo Company mortar bunker, swung his M16 on the sappers. Arias squeezed off a burst, and the sappers stopped and crouched down. It was now or never, and Rice grabbed the arm of one of the sappers and bit into it as hard as he could. When the man jerked away, Rice rolled to his right, determined to pop up and make a run for it, blind or not.

The sapper, however, turned his AK-47 on Rice and emptied the magazine as he screamed furiously in Vietnamese. Bullets hit Rice in the right leg and shattered his right forearm. The sappers then disappeared into the darkness. Arias was joined by Sergeant White and three other mortarmen, and they dragged Rice into their bunker like a sack of potatoes, moving as quickly as they could. Rice was convinced that he was dying, that he would never survive the time it would take to medevac him. It didn't matter anyway. He didn't want to go home blind. Arias cradled Rice against him as he moaned, "Please just put me out of my misery, please, the pain is so bad!"

Specialist Four Victor R. Bennett, Charlie Three's 1st Squad leader, and Pfc. Paul A. Sheer were in Bunker 12 to the left of where the camp road exited the perimeter through the trash dump. Bennett had four GIs from his squad in Bunker 11, and three more across the road in Bunker 13. Private First Class Robert J. Reed in Bunker 13 thought their own arty was firing until "one hit real close. All the time, I was swinging in my hammock and I just rolled out [and] crawl[ed] down inside our bunker . . . it seemed like AK fire was coming right over my head. Everything was happening so fast, it was just like I was in a daze. I was still half asleep."

Privates First Class Frederick G. Ramirez and Dennis M. Womack hastily grabbed their M16s and were just starting out of Bunker 13 when Ramirez caught a glimpse of two sappers running past from the rear. A grenade thumped on the bunker floor near the doorway and Ramirez was knocked cold by the explosion. Womack was caught trying to get behind the blast wall in the bunker, and was deafened and half-blinded by the flash, his weapon wrenched from his hands.

Womack couldn't find his M16 and thinking Ramirez dead, he crawled out of the bunker through a firing port. "I didn't want to go out the door without a weapon. All I could hear was dinks talking, AK fire, satchel charges and Chicoms going off. I didn't hear too much M16 fire, every once in a while sporadic fire. . . ."

To the rear, the 155-mm artillery area was going up in flames.

To the left, Bennett was screaming for a medic—then another blast in Bunker 12 silenced the squad leader. Bennett died inside the bunker and Sheer was later found dead outside.

Private Reed played opossum inside Bunker 12, unable to get to his M16 beside the doorway "because I heard the enemy over there." The sappers, having blown up the artillery, were heading down toward the open gate by the trash dump. "[T]here must have been at least nine or ten of them," Reed later said. "They were quite loud. We could hear them above the explosions . . . they were yelling and they were on the move."

The artillery platoon atop the hill had two howitzers. The sappers destroyed both. The sappers also trapped both gun sections in their sleeping bunkers before they could get out to the parapets, where they had two machine guns and cases of grenades. When the shelling began, 1st Lt. Evan W. Layton, the battery executive officer, and S.Sgt. Easton M. Rowell—who was chief of smoke in Battery C, 3-16th FA (155-mm), 23d Division—were asleep in the exec's office, which was attached to one of the sleeping bunkers. Specialist Four Richard E. Lowe, who was on radio watch and the only man awake in the position, thought the first explosion was in the 81-mm mortar section below them and ran to the door. The next explosions were all around them. Rowell pulled on his flak jacket and secured his M16 as he shouted for everyone else to do the same, but before he even had time to head for the door, the sappers were already in position there and along the six-inch-high firing port that ran like a seam around the entire sandbagged bunker. They had plenty of grenades.

The first one landed next to Rowell and Layton. "It knocked our weapons out of our hands, pretty well demolished them," stated Rowell, who was wounded. Lowe had just been joined by Pfc. James B. Kelley, the gun section radioman, when that first grenade bounced in. "The explosion blew me back across the room," testified Kelley, who was badly burned. "I had the handset and about a foot of cord left, and that's all."

Lieutenant Layton bolted out the door in a panic, his shirt on fire. The grenades kept coming. "We took a screwin' because the grunts on that hill were a bunch of potheads," said Staff Sergeant Rowell, who, peppered with fragments in the first blast, was wounded five more times. Weapons and ammo were scattered in the bunker, lost in the darkness. Rowell and Sgt. Michael T. McGreevy, chief of Section 4, ended up crouching defenseless behind a blast wall along with Lowe, Kelley, and Pfcs. Eugene Cloud, Arnold C. Diedrich, John D. Mahoney, and Richard J. McCormick. Cloud and McCormick were also wounded. "Lowe found his weapon, and we had one bandolier between us," stated Kelley, who had also recovered an M16 and his sawed-off carbine. Kelley threw his flak jacket atop one grenade that rolled near them. The explosion blew it apart. "I had a steel pot in my hand," Kelley testified. "Something came in the door, and I just threw my steel pot at it. There was another guy right beside me, and he was facing it. I was afraid it would probably blow up in his face, so I took the steel pot and knocked it over against the wall."

Private First Class Allen H. Coughtry had made it outside. He later told investigators:

> I jumped out of bed. I didn't grab any clothing or anything. I just grabbed for my ammunition, my M16, and out of instinct I headed straight for the door. . . . Then there was an explosion of a Chicom or something behind me, and I was more or less propelled out of the doorway of the hootch. . . . From there, I low-crawled around the side of another building for cover. Then I

decided I should go back and get my weapon because I had lost it when I was blown outside.

Coming around one corner of the building, Coughtry saw Pfc. Larry M. Pickering, who had also made a narrow escape from their bunker, crawling around the other corner. Coughtry and Pickering both went for the M16 lying on the ground between them. Coughtry got it, then a grenade landed between them, and they headed downhill toward the 81-mm section. Looking back, Pickering could see two sappers grenading their bunker while others "started working over the guns, blowing them up."

Like the other position, the sleeping bunker of Sp4 Roger D. Whirlow, chief of Section 5, had only one exit, which the sappers had covered. Being a one-room structure, however, it had fewer walls. There was no place to hide. "I knew if I got up, I would never make it out alive," stated Pfc. Lonnie G. Robinson, who squeezed flat and didn't move. He survived, along with Pfcs. Michael L. Hardy and Michael F. Moulds—though all three were wounded and suffered from shell shock. Specialist Four Larry D. Austin scrambled out of the bunker and was killed. Whirlow was killed in the bunker, as were Sp4 Clifford W. Corr and Pfc. William W. Kirkpatrick, who was blown in half. Private First Class Donald C. Bennett, in the gun pit on phone watch, was killed there. The bunker caught on fire and the M79 CS tear gas rounds stored inside began to burst. "I had a hard time breathing," stated Moulds, whose bare feet were a bloody mess. "We just crawled around. We were trapped. I can't talk about that . . . I just ran . . . I decided to get out, so I ran . . . I was just fortunate enough that at the time I went running out there, they didn't lob a Chicom. I ran into the pit. I started screaming for a medic, then decided to shut up."

Lieutenant Layton, unarmed and wounded, tried to get back into his bunker past the sappers. He was in the doorway when a grenade exploded behind him, wounding him again and blowing him inside. The bunker caught on fire then, apparently when a Chicom ignited two U.S. thermite grenades among the ammo scattered on the floor. The whole place started to go up and, with no options left,

Lowe charged to the door with his M16. He caught the sappers off balance and opened fire on their half-glimpsed silhouettes, covering Rowell, Mahoney, and Cloud, who rushed out next, pulling their shell-shocked lieutenant with them. McCormick tripped in the doorway, but Diedrich grabbed him by the back of his trousers and carried him out, followed by McGreevy and Kelley, who came out last. Rowell later testified that

> when everyone got out of the hootch, they were so shook up and scared they just ran in all different directions. It took me a while to get anybody at all together. . . . [T]he [unit] had been so lax . . . they made up their mind that it was over with, that the war was all in Laos and Cambodia now and they didn't have any problems. . . . Every day I tried to rack in their brains that this war is not over [and that] one of these days you are going to find out the hard way it's not over.

Outside, Private Kelley spotted a sapper behind the generator adjacent to their bunker and shot him with his M16. Sergeant Rowell had his own close encounter:

> I observed one of the enemy as he was trying to get to my [ammo] bunker. . . . He was slipping around throwing some charges in there when I shot about four rounds in him and he went down. . . . I tried to get up to [Section] 5's hootch [but] two NVA/VC, or whatever they were, with what looked like [.45-caliber] grease guns . . . threw a wall of fire at us. The only thing I could do was dive on over the hill to get away from it. We started again to go to the hootch, and they did the same thing again.

Coughtry and Pickering spotted Sergeant Shook crawling wounded from a burning hootch in the 81-mm section and dragged him back to a hole where they had found cover. Coughtry then crawled uphill toward Pfcs. Walter J. Driscoll and Charles E. Gordon, who were from his section and had been on phone watch in the gun pit. Heading for the sleeping bunker, they had run into a storm of grenades. Gordon had been wounded.

Private Coughtry pulled the shell-shocked Gordon down to their hole, then went back for Driscoll. "During the time that we were in the hole in the open, all we could do was try not to attract fire," stated Coughtry, the only one of the five with an M16. Shook spotted someone wearing a GI steel pot walking across the resupply pad below them. Coughtry was going to shoot, but Pickering, concerned about other sappers around them in the dark, told him to hold off. They didn't have any ammo to waste, he said. It could also be a GI. An explosion behind the figure silhouetted him clearly as he turned sideways with a rocket-propelled grenade launcher. Coughtry dropped the sapper on the pad—perhaps killing him, perhaps wounding him.

There was no one on guard at Bunker 11, which was heavily sandbagged and built right into the trench line. Private Schneider, a radioman, realized they were under attack when a mortar round landed right outside the door, blowing in the OD nylon curtain draped there—and blowing down his hammock, too. He crashed to the ground, fragments burning in his left knee.

Specialist Four Terry L. "Shorty" Rivero, a team leader in 1st Squad, Charlie Three, was also knocked out of his hammock by the blast, and the concussion blew out the candle they had made by twisting up the waxy cloth used to wrap mortar rounds. Privates First Class Bobby Joe Booth and John D. Saxty, and Sp4 Ralph S. Bowling, who had come over from 2d Squad, had been using the candle as they played poker in the cramped little bunker, sitting on the wooden-palleted floor.

Private Schneider sat up where he had fallen and whipped around to grab his M16, which was leaning against the wall. There was already a magazine in it, and he found two more amid their scattered gear. While pulling on his jungle boots, he screamed that they had to get outside because the enemy was be coming in right behind the mortars—an admonition he remembered from his infantry training. But his ears were ringing so fiercely he couldn't hear himself, and he had no idea if anybody else could either. He finally got to his feet and threw open the nylon curtain hanging over the doorway. There were four sappers right outside, crossing the trench between Bunkers 10 and 11 even as their own mortars continued to shriek in. They were heading straight for the artillery loaded down with satchel charges and grenades. Schneider stepped back in a panic, shut the curtain behind him, and—although he knew that he already had a round in the chamber—snapped back the charging handle three or four times to make sure, ejecting good rounds onto the bunker floor.

Calming down, Schneider stepped back out. The sappers he had originally seen were gone, but two more were in the trench itself—presumably left behind as security. They were watching the explosions up in the 155-mm area. Schneider quickly shouldered his M16, put his sights on the closer of the two—one sapper was about thirty meters away, the other fifty meters—and he ripped off an automatic burst, dropping the Vietnamese like a stone. The other sapper went down in the trench too, looking for cover. Schneider shouted excitedly to his companions that he had gotten one, but as he turned back he realized the second sapper had run up the trench toward him and flung a Coke-can grenade his way, shooting sparks like a firecracker. Schneider hit the dirt and started crawling away from where it looked like it was going to land. The grenade went off harmlessly, but when he looked up there was another one coming. The sapper threw four or five, and Schneider could do nothing but crawl quickly away from each. He saw the last one coming but didn't wait to determine where it was going to land before he took off—his mouth open to minimize the concussion as he had been trained, his eyes squeezed shut as he scuttled away as low and fast as he could.

The explosion flipped Schneider through the air and he landed on his back in the trench. As he blacked out he thought of his wife and how she would take the news of his death.

Shorty Rivero had just stepped outside behind Schneider when the grenades started coming, and though he scrambled back inside, one of them came through the door after him. Rivero was wounded, his M16 damaged. Bowling was hit, as was Booth—in his legs and in his face. His glasses were gone, and he couldn't see, so he told Rivero to take his

M16 as the team leader started back outside. Booth stayed by the door with the damaged M16, trying to rub the blur out of his eyes. Rivero joined Schneider, who had just sat back up, his M16 across his lap because he had hung onto it even as he blacked out. The knuckles of both his hands were shredded, and his left shoulder and arm were a bloody mess. Blood was running heavily down his throat, and he thought he had been hit in the jugular, but as he felt around in the dark he discovered instead a bad gash in front of his right ear. The fragment wounds burned hotly, but quickly dulled to a throbbing ache, which he tried to ignore as he concentrated on staying alive.

Shorty Rivero and Schneider were just getting organized when Saxty came out of the bunker, too. The grenade-throwing sapper stood up in the trench about thirty meters away, and in a case of mistaken identity Saxty rushed toward him, shouting, "Friendly!"

"Turn around, Saxty," Schneider screamed. "It's a dink!"

Saxty got within ten feet of the sapper before realizing his mistake. He threw his M16 to his shoulder and got only a click when he squeezed the trigger. He had forgotten to reload his magazines after rezeroing his weapon at the firing range that afternoon. Saxty spun around with the sapper giving chase down the trench line, grenade in hand. Saxty flashed past Rivero and Schneider and disappeared inside the bunker. The sapper, in hot pursuit, got about fifteen feet from Rivero and Schneider before he saw them, but he flung his grenade toward them before they could cut loose. They scrambled out of the way and the sapper escaped.

Still unable to hear, Rivero and Schneider used hand signals to communicate. They ended up at the prone, leg against leg, watching in opposite directions from the edge of the trench where it ran into Bunker 11. Rivero, facing the bunker, saw the grenade-throwing sapper trying to slip around the back of it and blew him away with his M16 on full automatic, emptying the magazine. The sapper was only eight feet away. Schneider couldn't hear anything, but when he felt Rivero's leg vibrating against his as he fired, he turned around to see the sapper lying right in front of Rivero in a blood-gushing heap. Rivero motioned to

Schneider to trade places—he didn't want to lie there, staring at the man he had just killed. They had no sooner gotten repositioned than Schneider felt Rivero's leg vibrating again as he fired on automatic. This time Rivero had shot a sapper leading a wounded comrade back toward the trench line from the burning 155-mm section. The other sapper, who had a bandage around his eyes, went down as Rivero and Schneider, who spun around then, fired at a range of ten feet. Pulling himself with his elbows, the sapper slipped out of sight over the edge of the trench, where he died.

Rivero was telling Schneider to get the case of grenades they kept on the right side of the bunker when Schneider saw two more sappers coming their way from the direction of Bunker 12. He could just make out the tops of their heads bobbing above the trench line as they moved in a crouched trot. The only ammo Schneider had left was the magazine in his M16, and he wasn't sure how much of that was left. Clicking the selector switch back and forth, he frantically tried to decide if he should aim and fire at the first one or put it on full auto and hope he got both in one burst before he ran out of ammo. Finally—all this took place in a matter of seconds—he squeezed off two rounds on semi at the lead VC. The sapper went down unscathed, seeking cover. Schneider started backing up in panic. A grenade came flipping over the bunker toward them, and Schneider popped up, spun around, and dove out of the way. He landed hard, right on top of his buddy, whose eyes bulged as the wind was knocked from him. Schneider took a fragment in the inner thigh of his left leg when the grenade exploded a second later.

Rivero motioned that they should make a run for the sandbagged emplacement behind them in the artillery area. Schneider nodded in agreement. Rivero took off, then dropped down after twenty feet to cover Schneider, who stepped on his loose boot laces as soon as he started running. He fell flat on his face, painfully scraping his knees. Rivero thought he had been hit, but he sprang back up, and together they flopped down behind the emplacement, scared and exhausted.

* * *

Rivero and Schneider covered the back of their bunker from their new position. The attack seemed to be ending and, in the fire- and flare-splashed darkness, Rivero could see three sappers pick up the body of the first one he had killed behind the bunker, then start back into the wire with it, heading downhill.

16

Fighting Back

Specialist Four David Tarnay saw the sapper who threw the grenade at the colonel's group when they originally ran to the battalion aid station from the burning, tear-gassed B-TOC. The sapper appeared like an apparition in front of them. Tarnay was unarmed, a radio in one hand, a fistful of antennas in the other. Before he could react, the sapper threw his grenade. Tarnay, flipped backward by the explosion, landed on his stomach, then rolled over, retrieved his radio, and rushed on into the aid station with the skin below his left knee split open. His hands were peppered with little fragments, as were his legs and his back up to his right shoulder.

Tarnay was wearing only his jungle boots and a pair of rolled-up trousers and was covered with soot. He left the aid station to find a weapon and in the dark tripped over the body of Pfc. Wilbert S. Dupree, a nineteen-year-old black wireman from HHC who had been in a one-man hootch behind the aid station when the attack started. Yeah, Tarnay recalls thinking as he looked at Dupree, that's it, we're all going to die here. He next stumbled over a dead sapper. Tarnay picked up his foe's AK-47 and the three ammo magazines in his belt. Moving on atop the berm between the silent, demolished bunkers, he spotted a sapper who was down on all fours in the wire, trying to withdraw from the burning hill.

"I made him do a dance," remembered Tarnay, who won a BSMv and Purple Heart for his actions that night. "It was payback."

Tarnay instinctively turned and ripped off a quick burst from the hip. The sapper jumped to his feet, trying to pull free of the wire. Tarnay shouldered the AK to pump off a more deliberate burst, and the sapper jerked like a spastic puppet, falling backward. "He sort of hung there in the concertina—and it felt good because they were cleaning our clock. I didn't know if we were going to make it through the next ten minutes. I was really, really pissed. I was going to make them pay."

Having crawled out of the Charlie Two CP, Lieutenant Sams—who was blind in one eye, bleeding from multiple wounds, and burned over most of his body—lay against the outside of the conex, pulling sandbags over himself to smother what he incorrectly thought were phosphorous burns. He had never found his M16. His platoon sergeant and radiomen were gone. He had no idea what was going on. Sams was still lying there under the sandbags when a diminutive, half-nude sapper with an AK-47 crept past on his way to the trench line. The sapper wasn't throwing any more grenades. He had done his job, and now he was getting out. This was the only enemy soldier Sams ever saw, and as soon as he disappeared over the berm, the lieutenant got up and headed for the company command post. His bare feet were as burned as the rest of him, but he felt no pain as he walked along.

Lieutenant Colonel Doyle and Captain Spilberg were still in position next to the blazing CP when Sams appeared, naked except for his undershirt, his body burned so red it practically glowed. Sams tried to sit down, but the colonel kept making him stand back up, concerned that he would go into shock if he stopped moving.

"What's your platoon area like?" Doyle asked, trying to keep the brand-new, shot-up lieutenant in focus.

"Hell, I don't know—I've just been trying to stay alive," replied Sams.

"Well, get a weapon, and go find out."

Lieutenant Sams found an M16 on the ground—he didn't even notice if there was a magazine in it—and headed off, half leaning on a wounded trooper who led the way since he could barely see. Doyle instructed Spilberg to move up the bunker line in the other direction to get the troops reorganized. The captain chanted his name in a loud whisper as he worked his way down the trench, hoping not to get blown away by accident.

Meanwhile, Tarnay and Pfc. John A. Bruno of Company A were using a hammock to drag casualties to the VIP helipad near the blazing B-TOC. At one point, Bruno ran into Sergeant Major Prosser, who had earlier gotten separated from Doyle—he didn't know if the colonel was dead or alive—and who had just secured an M16 from one of the wounded cooks in the demolished mess area. Bruno gave the sergeant major a few of his magazines as they grabbed a position between Bunker 6 and the burning quad .50. More ammo was brought up then by Sgt. Ricky D. Howerton, who ran the ammunition storage area, and two supply reps from Company B. After spending most of the fight in their hootch next to the mail room, they were now moving back and forth between the storage area and the trench line, firing hand flares and passing out grenades, magazines, and belts of machine-gun ammo. Few of the able-bodied men along this section of the line were grunts. There were almost none left. The fight was now in the hands of the support personnel.

Even the battalion mail clerk, Sp5 Eugene Cardillo, was in the trench between the burning bunkers, pitching frags.

In the light of the flares, Bruno and Prosser engaged and apparently eliminated a sapper who was trying to get away through the wire. With enemy fire snapping back at them, Bruno then tore the cover off the .50-caliber machine gun positioned on the berm and opened up into the wire while the sergeant major fed the ammo belt into it.

Bruno hit one more sapper, then the weapon jammed and he went to help with the wounded again. Sergeant Major Prosser cleared the malfunction and swung the .50-cal. back into action with Sfc. Lester A. Dalton, the senior mess steward, handling the ammo. It looked like Prosser chopped down three more sappers in the wire. Nearby, Sp6 Freddie L. Fillers, the head cook, had secured an M60 lying abandoned in the trench with spent brass all around it, and he added to the scythe of red tracers cutting through the wire—firing at movement, firing at nothing, just firing, firing, firing. . . .

At this point the quad .50 finally opened up. "Those quad .50s really go, and it felt good hearing them," recalled Spilberg, making the rounds on the other side of the base.

Sergeant Jack M. Clayburn, a squad leader from Battery G, 55th FA, ran the quad .50 attached to FSB Mary Ann. Hit by an RPG in the first moments of the attack, about ten thousand rounds in Clayburn's ammo bunker had previously been cooking off—hitting here, there, and everywhere, including right back into the gun crew's sleeping bunker. The bunker, which was filled with CS gas, also got hit with two satchel charges, blowing down a wall. When the ammo fire eventually died down, Clayburn got his people outside. His gunner, climbing aboard the smoking, semiroasted quad .50, started firing with all four barrels, walking bursts down the hill and into the valley—and straight across into the next hillside, where the sappers were probably withdrawing. He fired until the barrels burned out at about the same time the sun came up.

Fearing the worst, Captain Spilberg kept asking if anyone had seen Captain Knight. No one had. "Sometime that morning, I was informed by my RTO that I was the ranking man left in Charlie Company," testified Sergeant Head of Charlie One, who won a Silver Star for assuming command of the company. One of Head's troops, Sp4 Ed Newton, won an ARCOMv for hauling crates up from the ammunition storage area while Head himself, along with his platoon sergeant, got the ammo and hand flares distributed, repositioned the troops to cover gaps in the line, and maintained a heavy volume of fire on that side of the firebase as a precaution.

Sergeant Head's senior medic, Doc Vogelsang—who was a conscientious objector and winner of a Silver Star that night—rushed bareheaded and unarmed to the burning

Charlie Company CP, his medical gear in one hand and gas mask in the other. Vogelsang masked because of the smoke and CS, but the lenses fogged up and he ripped it off so he could treat the survivors grouped around the bunker.

Specialist Turner of Charlie One, packing an XM203, won the BSMv when he got down near the quad .50 at Spilberg's direction and lobbed grenades on a few last sappers way out in the wire.

In case some sappers were still lurking inside the perimeter, there was no shouting, only helmet-to-helmet whispering. Captain Spilberg grabbed four of Head's troops—Turner, Cahill, Sanders, and Papizzo—to reinforce Charlie Two. Spilberg also found Doc Carmichael treating Thompson, the supply sergeant who had lost both legs. "Captain Spilberg came by and gathered up four men and we carried the wounded soldier up to the area around the TOC," said Carmichael. The litter team included Sergeant Lopez, plus Captain Sampson and Lieutenant Clark, previously pinned down in the Echo Company headquarters. Moments before Spilberg arrived on the scene, Lopez had run in, shouting that he needed a tourniquet for Thompson. Lieutenant Good handed him some boot laces. Lopez took off, but returned shortly. "He said he needed some help," Sampson testified, "so Clark and I ran out and followed Lopez. While Lopez covered us with his M16, we picked Thompson up and we took him to the VIP pad. We were going to bring the medevacs in there. It was kind of slowing down at that time."

Lieutenant Good was still trapped in the headquarters building when Sergeant Farmer started getting the northern half of the firebase back under control with the recon platoon. Several of the recon troops had just transferred up from the Cav. "Well, welcome to Echo Recon and the First of the Forty-sixth, gentlemen," "Mad Jack" Farmer said to them as they hit the bunker line, cracking a grin under his red handlebar mustache as illume went up and fires blazed around them. The platoon sergeant, who was on his fourth tour, wore an ammo vest and carried an XM203.

Recon had no responsibility on the line except for Bunker 9, which it shared with Charlie Three. Farmer's troops, sacked out in a half-dozen hootches behind Charlie Three, had taken no action during the surprise attack other than to guard their windows and doors until Farmer finally got moving from hootch to hootch, putting everyone on line between Bunkers 8 and 10.

Farmer then went looking for Sergeant Powell, one of his squad leaders, shouting his name when he reached the door of the sniper hootch. "Yeah!" came an answer from inside.

"Powell, you still alive?" asked Farmer.

"Yeah!"

"Well, can you get out here?"

Holy shit, Powell remembers thinking. Here we go again. . . .

Sergeant Powell, a big, blond, sardonic NCO about to win his second Silver Star, had been drinking beer and smoking marijuana when the attack began. The battalion public information clerk, an ex-grunt, had been in the sniper hootch with him, and the conversation was good. Powell, happily stoned, found a big jar of peanut butter and another of jelly in the hootch, and he opened C-ration cracker tins until his fingers hurt—then the explosions began. Powell, wearing only jungle boots and cutoffs, ran outside to get his M16, which was hanging outside the hootch in a laundry bag to keep it clean. He had just grabbed the weapon—and his ammo vest, which was loaded with magazines—when a rocket-propelled grenade slammed into the next hootch, peppering him with fragments in his buttocks and his back and right shoulder.

Now, with the rest of the platoon laying down a wall of suppressive fire into the wire, Sergeant Farmer sent Powell up to Bunker 10 with Sp5 Ronald J. McCarthy, the platoon medic, and Pfcs. Allen D. Luck and Lindsey E. McKee. Specialist Patton called for help from inside the demolished bunker. McCarthy climbed in and picked up the beam stuck between the doorway and a pile of sandbags that had pinned Patton down. McCarthy bandaged his fellow medic in the beam of a flashlight held by another trooper, then two grunts loaded him on a stretcher and took off.

Sergeant Powell led the way toward Bunker 11 on his hands and knees so as not to make a silhouetted target. He eased up to a little bend in the trench and spotted two sappers six feet away on the other side. One was wounded and bandaged, and the other was helping him escape. Before they knew what was happening, Powell shot them both in the side of the head with his M16.

Sergeant Farmer, meanwhile, coordinated with Lieutenant Good, who was out of the headquarters building by then. They spread Echo Recon out to cover all the gaps in Charlie Two and Three. "I had my M60 man open up every five minutes with about a hundred-round burst," stated Farmer, who then grabbed Powell, Luck, and Brown, and headed into the burning artillery area. Brown was walloped and knocked down on his way up through the smoke and dust and CS, taking superficial fragment wounds in his arms and back. In the rush of the moment, he thought he had simply tripped. Two artillerymen heard Powell's shouts and answered from their demolished sleeping bunker. Knocking debris away to get in, Powell swung his flashlight beam across the bunker and saw one of the shell-shocked survivors sitting in the corner with a satchel charge on the floor less than four feet away. The sight of the dead in the bunker was devastating. "You couldn't even tell that they was people anymore," remembered Brown. They hauled the survivors out, then warned everyone to stay away from the bunker because of the unexploded ordnance inside. "We just kept going around the positions. If we found a wounded guy, two of us would help him up to the VIP pad. If the guy was dead, one of us would drag him down to the resupply pad. It was exhausting, and my cut-up arms were really burning from the sweat."

17

Picking Up
the Pieces

Captain Spilberg was back with Doyle at the south end of
the base when several sappers started uphill in their direction, throwing grenades. The enemy soldiers, invisible in
the smoke, were probably trying to recover casualties, but
the first gunship arrived at that moment and the enemy
broke off their attack.

Specialist Wise, severely wounded and crouched in the
back corner of his hootch, heard movement outside. He
raised his M16 toward the door and shouted, "You better be
American or you're going to be a dead motherfucker!"

"It's Sergeant Meyers!" came the return shout.

Sergeant Timothy J. Meyers, the senior battalion radioman, was wearing only shorts, but he had a flashlight and
his .45-caliber pistol. Meyers checked Private Detlef, the
other man in the hootch, then turned his flashlight on Wise.
"Oh my God," Meyers blurted when he saw what a bloody
mess his radioman was. "Hey, don't worry about it," Wise
said quickly, still numb with shock despite seven major
wounds. "I don't feel a thing!"

Wise asked what was going on. Meyers said that the
attack was over, that the gunships had just arrived and were
pushing the enemy back down the hill. Wise gave Meyers
his M16—"You're going to need this more than me!"—
then Meyers and Detlef toted Wise up to the aid station on a

stretcher. They laid him on the ground, and he rose up on his elbow, stunned at the destruction around him. One of the medics started to urgently remove Wise's bloody fatigues, but he stopped him. "Wait a minute," Wise said, "I don't feel anything—go help somebody that's hurt!"

Morale soared when the first gunship flashed in. Captain Norman W. Hayes, the aircraft commander, had been on standby at Hawk Hill when the 196th Brigade TOC duty officer rushed to Hayes's Huey to alert him that Mary Ann was getting hit. Hayes and his copilot, 1st Lt. Darrel E. Rexroat, were with Troop D, 1st Squadron, 1st Cavalry, which was under the operational control of the 123d Aviation Battalion, 23d Division. They had a Night Hawk helicopter equipped with a starlight scope, a Xenon infrared spotlight, and heavy-caliber weapons not normally mounted on a Huey. Night Hawk teams operated at night, as the name implies, hunting for targets of opportunity in preselected grid boxes and responding to nocturnal emergencies. To maximize response time, Hayes, Rexroat, and their four-man crew slept in the helicopter between missions; in this instance they were cranked and airborne within seven minutes. They were briefed by radio en route to Mary Ann, as was their chase ship, which had lifted off right behind them. Their race bogged down, however, when their straight-line approach to the embattled firebase took them right into fog-covered mountains. Hayes was forced to turn around. Climbing from three thousand to five thousand feet while banking east, he finally broke out of the white void, although he still had clouds above and below him. As Hayes flew in the firebase's general direction from an unfamiliar angle, he requested that illumination be fired at maximum altitude over the area to serve as a guide. He spotted the flares' glow some twenty klicks away reflecting against the base of the next layer of clouds, and headed toward it. The chase ship followed at a higher altitude, loaded with flares should any be needed.

Captain Hayes arrived over FSB Mary Ann at approximately 0325, forty-five minutes into the attack. "It seemed like it took forever," stated Sp5 Mario A. Cruz, crew chief and gunner of the 7.62-mm minigun mounted on the right side of the aircraft. Specialist Four Preston M. Epp, the starlight scope operator, was seated beside Cruz. Behind Hayes on the left side of the aircraft, Sp4 Samuel Echols manned a .50-caliber machine gun, and Sp4 James R. Carmean an M60. Hayes finally got the artillery lifted at this point—except for the illume rounds, which he flew under as they floated down. He had tried to get a check-fire on the way in to ensure the safety of his aircraft, but the fire direction officer at brigade had held off as long as possible, more concerned with the situation on the ground. In addition, the fire direction officer provided Hayes with the necessary gun data to avoid the trajectory of the artillery being fired from LZ Mildred.

Captain Hayes later testified:

> I was coordinating with [Lieutenant Colonel Doyle] . . . he wanted us to work on the southeast portion of the slope. . . . You could hear the enemy coming up the slope throwing grenades. . . . We put our lights on the perimeter and could actually see the VC/NVA in the wire. . . . It looked like they were trying to take people out of the wire. . . . We took a lot of tracer fire. . . . We engaged, and I know that anything we fired on ceased firing on us.

The firebase was a burning, smoke-shrouded mess. To stay out of the smoke, Hayes went in at three hundred feet, twice the altitude he usually assumed in a combat situation. Cruz opened up with his electrically powered minigun but had only gone through a fourth of his forty-five-hundred-round load when the ammunition chute separated from the weapon. The feeding mechanism had broken—an infuriating mishap. Echols, the .50-cal. gunner on the other side of the ship, was just as disappointed as Cruz. Echols had squeezed off a mere fifteen rounds when the weapon double-fed because of worn parts and a round exploded in the barrel.

Specialist Epp, the light man, fired his M14 rifle into the trash dump where he could see a half-dozen figures in the wire. Some were trying to hide, some were firing at the Huey—and one of them dropped as Epp's fire found its mark. Carmean was doing most of the firing at this point with his M60, getting one confirmed kill in the wire. The other crewmen dropped fragmentation grenades during two particularly low-level passes through the smoke.

Upon reaching the firebase, Captain Hayes had made an urgent request that all available medevacs and gunships be immediately dispatched to FSB Mary Ann. No other aircraft had arrived, however, before Hayes was forced to head for Chu Lai to refuel. While en route, he discovered that "there were no birds airborne. . . . I questioned them if they were inbound, and they said nothing."

The problem was that brigade and division were under the impression that FSB Mary Ann had simply been mortared. Specialist Carmean later described the frustration of the situation to investigators, saying that

the gunships weren't even scrambled until we had already arrived in Chu Lai . . . the .50 gunner [Echols] and I had gone to get ammo for the minigun and the M60. We were carrying a carton of ammo and passed two Cobra pilots walking out to their ships. . . . I asked them if they were going out to FSB Mary Ann, and they said yes. I told them they had better hurry up and get out there because the guys really needed you out there. They were just walking, and really made me pretty mad.

Carmean testified that the situation was so distressing before they departed to refuel and rearm that he and Echols had asked Hayes "to put us down on the ground, and maybe we could help them out. I was just so mad because I knew they needed people. They were hurt so bad and all their bunkers were on fire."

Captain Hayes zipped back to Mary Ann ahead of the Cobras, and Carmean got a second confirmed kill. Cruz, who had repaired his minigun, hosed down two sappers in the trash dump. Meanwhile, during Hayes's run to Chu Lai, the chase ship piloted by WO1 Loren E. Leonberger and WO1 Michael A. Silva from Company A, 123d Aviation Battalion, was the only helicopter over the battle. They had taken over, making grenade and machine-gun passes over the north end of the base while the artillery resumed firing below the south end. Leonberger had just enough fuel left to land on the VIP helipad and sit there for several long minutes while six or seven critical casualties were loaded aboard. It was the first medevac of the night.

Sergeant Meyers had taken over the radio from Lieutenant Colonel Doyle, and he stood on the helipad in his shorts to bring in the medevac. "I went out on that first Huey," recalled Sergeant Calhoun, who had five bullet holes in him. "Being from the country, we used to butcher hogs. You get a smell when you gut a hog—and I could smell it on the chopper from intestinal wounds. It was a sickening smell, and people were moaning and groaning and pleading. . . ."

More medevacs eventually landed in the light of the blazing B-TOC, usually after having to circle the base several times to find the LZ in all the smoke. Lieutenant Colonel Doyle hobbled bareheaded among the casualties, his flak jacket hanging open, his trouser leg split, and his leg bandaged. Doyle organized and encouraged, joking with the grunts about their million-dollar wounds. Captain Spilberg knelt beside little Pro—who had been mortally wounded—and held his hand as the light went out in his eyes. The 81-mm mortar section was pumping illume out, and Meyers controlled both the medevacs and the arty crashing onto the sapper escape routes below the trash dump. Smoke and embers swirled each time a chopper landed, and at one point they set fire to the switchboard conex. Thermite grenades were positioned to destroy the switchboard in case of emergency, and when they caught fire the whole place went up, melting radios, cables, and antennas to the floor. Grenade-launcher ammo inside also cooked off, puffing the metal walls out like a bullfrog. There was only one fire extinguisher left on the hill.

Sergeant Ledoux shouted at two friendlies he saw running by in the flarelight—it was Specialists Campbell and Davis, also from Charlie Two—and they got him to his feet and helped him to the helipad. The next Huey that landed was quickly loaded with litter cases, but a crewman shouted, "We've got room for one walking wounded!" Someone else looked at Ledoux, and asked, "Can he walk?" Ledoux jumped up despite his two AK-47 wounds. "Yeah, I can walk!" he shouted, so they strapped him inside the helicopter. Lieutenant Sams of Charlie Two reported back to Doyle at the VIP pad that everyone in his platoon was dead or wounded. "There was fire and smoke and all kinds of hell being raised by then," remembered Sams, who won the Silver Star for continuing to function despite massive burns. Illume was turning the night to day, and gunships were blazing away. The medics thumped Sams with a syrette of morphine, which calmed him, and he found a half-burnt poncho liner that he wrapped around himself as he sat on the pad. "The pain was tolerable. There were a lot of people that were really horribly wounded, and I encouraged the medics to take some others ahead of me as the medevacs landed."

The medics finally helped Sams into the gunner's seat on a helicopter. During the flight, the wind painfully buffeted his naked, burned body, and his poncho liner kept getting caught in the slipstream. "I was thinking, I'm going to fall out of this helicopter after all I've been through—I'm going to fall out of this damn thing and die! I hung on until we finally landed. The medics were waiting on the pad with their gurneys. I walked off the medevac and it was the last step I took for three months."

The Hueys landed on the floodlit pad at the 91st Evac Hospital. It was a madhouse, recalled Calhoun. Doctors hollered instructions as medics wheeled screaming casualties inside on gurneys. Calhoun asked for something for the pain—his left leg was so badly mangled it would eventually be amputated above the knee—but the medics told him they could not administer morphine because it would mask the seriousness of his injuries. Calhoun passed out and did not wake up until he was out of surgery. Three of the five bullets had gone through him, and the doctors taped the other two to his chest after removing them. The bullets were in perfect shape except for rifling marks, and he thanked God as he examined them that they hadn't expanded on impact. The damage they inflicted could have been so much worse.

* * *

The brigade command ship was flaring to land when the downdraft from its blades fueled the fires and sent flames roaring up twenty or thirty feet around it. The Huey pulled off, then made its approach from a better angle. Disembarking with Colonel Hathaway were the S3, Major O'Connor, and Lt. Col. Richard C. Martin, commander of the 3-82d FA. Doyle met them on the helipad. "Hathaway and O'Connor were dumbfounded and enraged as they looked around," said Spilberg. "They were in a state of shock—they had just walked into Auschwitz."

While Hathaway and Doyle spoke on the helipad, Major O'Connor wandered toward the aid station. He paused to light a cigarette. "Can we have some smokes?" Spilberg asked. The major threw the pack at him with an angry snap of the wrist.

Captain Spilberg passed the cigarettes out to the wounded, then sat down to light one himself, feeling an incredible rush of relief. "It was a full-scale disaster, but Doyle and Hathaway had tactical control at that point," he recalled. In addition, Hathaway had flown in with the brigade surgeon and an aid man from Company C, 23d Medical Battalion. "The doctors never left the rear, but this guy got on a helicopter and flew into the great unknown," added Spilberg.

The surgeon took over the triage at the VIP pad, and used Colonel Hathaway's Huey as a medevac ship. Spilberg held his shirt up and the surgeon slapped a field dressing on with instructions to get on the next chopper. "I'm not in any pain," Spilberg objected.

"We don't know how deep that shrapnel is," the surgeon said. "You might wind up with a colostomy."

Nevertheless, when Doyle told Spilberg to listen to the surgeon, Spilberg merely boarded a Huey on one side and hopped out on the other. The Huey lifted off, leaving him standing on the pad in full view of Hathaway and Doyle. "Sir," said Spilberg in an effort to explain himself, "I can't leave without my battalion commander—"

Doyle cut him off by turning to Hathaway. "Tell that captain to be on the next bird," Doyle requested.

"You be on that next bird," Hathaway told Spilberg.

That was that. Captain Spilberg, who was subsequently awarded a Silver Star, recommended that Doyle also be decorated. "I did not recommend it and didn't forward it considering the circumstances of the case," Hathaway testified later, adding that he was "tortured" by that decision. "I just felt that although he had conducted himself with a certain amount of valor, the situation had occurred because of shortcomings on his part."

The view of the attack from the company laagers many klicks away had been unreal. Lieutenant Bell of Alpha Company, urgently awakened by one of his RTOs, stared incredulously at the western skyline. They were in the middle of the jungle in the middle of the night—and the skyline was ablaze. There was a steady rumble in the distance. Bell, monitoring his radio, heard a gunship pilot report that he was ready to "expend his load," and get in reply, "Anything outside the wire's not ours—let 'em have it!"

"Do you need body bags?" asked a medevac pilot.

"That's affirmative."

"How many?" inquired the pilot.

"Bring all that you can get. . . ."

Lieutenant Bell and the battalion adjutant, who was preparing to assume command of Company B—because of Knight's death, the adjutant would get Company C instead—did a map recon by flashlight under a poncho, looking for logical enemy withdrawal routes. "We're ready to move," Bell finally informed battalion. "Don't pull us back to the firebase—let's go up into the hills and see if we can catch some of these guys."

Instead, Lieutenant Bell was instructed at sunup to march Alpha Company to LZ Mildred in case it became the next target. Meanwhile, Captain Kirkey of Company D was informed that he and his men would be lifted onto FSB Mary Ann to replace decimated Charlie Company. Most moves involved shuttling a few squads at a time aboard four Hueys, but when the fog cleared that morning fifteen slicks clattered into the pickup zone, taking aboard the entire company at once. The flock also included three gunships. It was not a good sign as far as the grunts were concerned.

* * *

Lieutenant Colonel Doyle checked his lines a last time with Hathaway, then the ruined commander of the Professionals was medevacked at first light. "I fear we had become lax in our security," wrote General Baldwin, the division commander.

Helicopter operations had been shut down because of heavy morning fog, but the general was able to get in around 0700 when the rising sun burned off the cloud cover. "The firebase was a shambles, with things burning all over the place, and with the people divided into two and only two categories. There were many who were sitting around with a rather dazed look on their faces and commiserating with each other. There was another group which was actively and energetically trying to pick up the pieces."

Before leaving, Doyle had placed Lieutenant Good of Echo Recon in temporary command of Company C. "As usual in cases like this, one man stood out above the crowd as a calm and resourceful leader," Baldwin wrote, referring to Good. "He had the defense of the firebase pretty well organized, and was even getting patrols out to try to find the enemy force."

The sappers were, of course, long gone. Colonel Hathaway and Major O'Connor took command of the base after Doyle was evacuated and used salvaged radios to set up new TOC in the artillery mess hall. The last of the wounded were medevacked after first light—there were thirty dead and eighty-two wounded—and a steady stream of Hueys brought in badly needed ammunition, medical supplies, and new bunker material. Scout ships buzzed around the firebase, looking for the enemy's escape routes, and artillery blindly pounded the surrounding mountains, seeking revenge.

Fifteen dead sappers were found on the base and in the wire. More had been killed and dragged off, as evidenced by blood trails, but the official body count was fifteen—exactly and embarrassingly half the number of U.S. KIAs on FSB Mary Ann. The American dead—some burned to charcoal—were zipped up in body bags and lined up in rows to one side of the resupply pad. Other body bags were lumpy with dismembered body parts. Flies buzzed all over the rectangular, OD body bags, which were sticky in spots with blood.

Major Donald C. Potter, the battalion executive officer, was picked up by the 196th command chopper at the 1-46th rear in Chu Lai, and made it out to FSB Mary Ann by 0900. With Potter on the ground as acting battalion commander, Hathaway and General Baldwin helicoptered out. Captain Kirkey and Company D began landing at about 1100 with their escorting gunships in a protective orbit around the firebase, which was still dotted with a few fires and hazy with lingering smoke. The shell-shocked survivors of Company C went out on Delta's Hueys, climbing aboard after taking one last look at the KIAs on the pad. The body bags were being sprayed with insect repellent, which seemed horribly ignoble.

Before himself leaving, Major O'Connor told Kirkey to "get locked in—get the place cleaned up."

Meanwhile, Major Potter, per instructions from Hathaway, ordered Lieutenant Good to bury the enemy bodies before they became a health hazard. Potter told Good to place the bodies in an eroded, scooped-out area below the resupply pad on the side facing the water point. Potter planned to blow the side of the pit with a C-4 charge, and thus simply and efficiently bury the bodies. The dead sappers were loaded in the back of the base utility truck, but for reasons never explained, five of the bodies ended up in the trash dump at the north end of the firebase.

It was noon by then, and hot. The bodies were getting ripe. Major Potter didn't want to put the troops through the "unpleasant ordeal" of reloading the bodies, and unloading them again at the helipad, so he told Kirkey to "go on and burn them down there in the trash dump." Kirkey suggested that they use C-4. "Fine, go ahead and use that and gasoline," Potter answered. Kirkey detailed the task to one of his new platoon leaders. The bodies were repeatedly doused with gasoline and torched over the next several days. There was no apparent venality involved, and it did not occur to Potter and Kirkey, who had more pressing matters at hand, that whatever the reason, burning enemy bodies was a war crime. This incident would come back to haunt everyone involved.

* * *

Chief Warrant Officer Kane shut down his LOH at Hawk Hill after following blood trails that led off into green oblivion and walked into the 196th Brigade TOC. "If Doyle were here right now, Colonel Hathaway would fire him!" shouted Major O'Connor. Kane reported to Hathaway. "It wouldn't have happened to Watson," Kane said, referring to a battalion commander with a reputation for being hard-nosed about everything—even security precautions, the great failing of most units. "Watson would have routed the enemy before they got past the wire."

"Exactly," snapped Colonel Hathaway.

The mood was equally somber at the 23d Division TOC. When S.Sgt. Bruce Buehrig of the G2 section reported in for duty, he routinely asked the NCO he was replacing, "How's it going this morning?" He asked the same question every morning. This time, though, the other sergeant just shook his head and pointed to the casualty column affixed to the map board behind the intelligence desk. "Jesus Christ, what happened?" Buehrig asked incredulously.

The staff officers in the D-TOC were convinced that General Baldwin would be immediately relieved of command. When Baldwin returned from FSB Mary Ann, he tried to encourage his gloomy staff. "We'll get this thing back on track. Hold your head up. These things happen in war."

Baldwin remained poker-faced behind his glasses, but he was obviously distressed. "At the five o'clock briefing, General Baldwin, the two assistant division commanders, and the key staff officers were not in any positive frame of mind," recalled Sergeant Buehrig. "It was a very dour, straightforward, let's-get-this-over-with briefing. There was none of the customary interplay with the briefing officer. The general sat there, and he was not animated as he normally was, he wasn't following things as closely. I think he was very depressed."

It was obvious that the bunker guards had been asleep, which meant that they had been relatively unsupervised. "A lot of junior officers didn't want to be too hard on their guys," CW2 Kane reflected. "It's thoroughly amazing what officers will neglect to do in the interest of goodwill and of being a buddy—or to just get some cooperation out of draftee troops. Doyle was always aggressive on everything else, but he wasn't a hard-ass about making sure his junior officers kept their guards alert. I don't think there's any way around that fact. I hate to say it, because Doyle did not get a fair shake in the investigation, but he had a certain amount of contempt for the enemy, and for all his experience he didn't take the proper precautions."

Shortly after General Baldwin returned to his headquarters, he gave the new division personnel officer, Lt. Col. Clyde J. Tate, command of the 1-46th Infantry. Before heading off, Tate had his jeep driver stop at the 91st Evac Hospital so that he could speak with Doyle, who he knew by his hard-charging reputation, and who he had met once during a previous visit to FSB Mary Ann. Doyle was in one of the wards, one leg and both arms wrapped in bandages.

Tate pulled up a chair. "I'm going out to the battalion," he said. "What can you tell me about it?"

"Have I been relieved?" asked Doyle.

"Bill, I do not know. All I know is that I've been told to go out to the firebase and take the battalion," replied Tate.

Doyle had hoped to rejoin the Professionals when his wounds healed. Disappointed, he nonetheless told Tate, who was an up-from-the-ranks paratrooper on his second combat tour, "I'm glad it's you rather than some of the candy asses we got around here."

Following a briefing at brigade, Lieutenant Colonel Tate flew into FSB Mary Ann at approximately 1630 on March 28, 1971. "We can't land, I think they're still under fire," the helicopter pilot told Tate over the intercom as they approached. Some thirty minutes earlier Mary Ann had, in fact, taken 12.7-mm machine-gun fire from the ridgeline to the north, wounding one GI. Gunships had been requested, but the enemy, having made their defiant gesture, chose not to engage. They were presumably still watching, however, and Tate's Huey hovered over the helipad just long enough for the new battalion commander to jump from the skid.

Major Potter met Tate on the pad. "If this is my hill, I got to find out what's going on," said Tate, and with that he dropped his ruck and went from bunker to bunker with the exec. One of the grunts lit a cigarette while Tate was at his position. "Son, give me one of those," Tate said, slinging his M16 so he could light up. Tate had stopped smoking eight years earlier, but he puffed on that cigarette as though he had never stopped. He smoked his way through the remainder of the battalion's time atop FSB Mary Ann. "There was a lot of tension," Tate remembered. "I had to plan like they were coming back. The kids were jumpy, especially that first night, and everybody was hitting hand flares off their knees. They must have had twenty-five flares apiece, and they kept going up all night long. Even if I could have gotten control of it, you had to let them do it because they were scared and flares made them feel more comfortable. Every little noise they heard, they thought the sappers were coming back."

Lieutenant Colonel Tate was under much unspoken pressure to tighten things up, and he came on strong. Lieutenant Schmitz wrote home that the new CO was "formal—in control of details—even the very hairs of your head are numbered." On Tate's second day at FSB Mary Ann he entered the B-TOC and spotted a fifth of bourbon sitting on one of the radios. "I had no idea who it belonged to—and nobody spoke up because I busted that damn bottle over the radio," recalled Tate. "I was pissed off, and I said that there would be no more alcohol on that hill. There were a lot of bottles on that hill in addition to the normal beer ration, and it was a thing that was accepted. I gave everybody twelve hours to get all the alcohol assembled in one place, and then it was packed up and taken to the rear."

Meanwhile, the enemy continued to make his presence known. On March 29 the ARVN artillery was pulled out and replaced by Battery B, 1-14th FA, from LZ Mildred. Two tubes had already been choppered back to FSB Mary Ann, and a Chinook was hovering over the parapets with the third slingloaded beneath it when ten rocket-propelled grenades were launched farther up the ridgeline to the north. The RPGs fell short, impacting just below the bunker line. In response, the crews of the howitzers already in position fired straight into the ridge with beehive rounds, shattering trees and silencing the enemy fire.

On March 31 a squad-sized sweep from Captain Kirkey's Delta Company had not gone fifty meters beyond the bunker line when an enemy mortar started thumping. The men scrambled back to their bunker as six rounds exploded where they had been. That night Echo Recon, positioned on the line facing the water point, heard what sounded like concertina wire being snapped in two near the big boulder on the slope. Two sappers were spotted in the wire when the flares went up. Echo Recon showered the area with grenades, and in the morning found a dead sapper with an AK-47 lying naked atop his satchel charges and Chicoms. The platoon went in for stand-down that afternoon.

Lieutenant Colonel Tate was on a recon flight five klicks northwest of FSB Mary Ann on the afternoon of April 1 when he spotted activity on a jungled mountainside. The LOH dropped down and the activity came into focus as bivouacked enemy soldiers. The LOH banked away under fire, and Tate, having fixed the location on his map, called for arty and air strikes. Company D went to a 100 percent alert on the line that night when the recently returned radar team picked up the movement of approximately three individuals below the water point. The radar team followed the enemy in and, when they were within a hundred meters, the mortars started coughing and the grunts opened up with grenade launchers. Another enemy body was found the next morning.

Captain Edward L. Oliver, the battalion adjutant, had been lifted out of Company A's position aboard an LOH the morning of the sapper attack to take command of Charlie Company in Chu Lai. After bringing the unit back to strength with replacements and in-country transfers, Oliver took the new company back to FSB Mary Ann on April 3, 1971. There was a memorial service that afternoon on the resupply pad. "I have neither the language nor the wisdom to honor these men enough," Capt. Neal Davidson, the battalion chaplain, said as he stood bareheaded before loosely assembled Charlie Company. One reporter wrote that the grunts were "expressionless." Davidson had a great reputation. He flew out to the firebase immediately after the attack, for example, so he could be on the bunker line that uptight, postbattle night. The shock and bitterness and guilt ran too deep, however, to respond even to a chaplain that devoted. There was really nothing to say as Davidson stood in front of a single helmet-topped rifle and an empty pair of jungle boots, intoning the name of each man who had been killed that night:

- Capt. Richard V. Knight, Company C, 1-46th Infantry
- 1st Lt. John L. Hogan, Battery B, 1-14th FA, attached to 1-46th Infantry
- 1st Lt. C. Barry McGee, Company C, 1-46th Infantry
- S.Sgt. Terry H. Price, Company C, 1-46th Infantry
- Sgt. Ronald J. Becksted, Company C, 1-46th Infantry
- Sgt. Michael L. Crossley, Company C, 1-46th Infantry
- Sgt. Warren P. Ritsema, Company C, 1-46th Infantry
- Sp4 Victor R. Bennett, Company C, 1-46th Infantry
- Sp4 Richard J. Boehm, Company C, 1-46th Infantry
- Sp4 Richard R. Carson, Company C, 1-46th Infantry
- Sp4 James E. Edgemon, Company C, 1-46th Infantry
- Sp4 Myron B. Johnson, Company C, 1-46th Infantry
- Sp4 Robert J. Schumacher, Company C, 1-46th Infantry
- Sp4 Donald M. Stotts, Company C, 1-46th Infantry
- Pfc. Druey L. Hatfield, Company C, 1-46th Infantry
- Pfc. Michael S. Holloway, Company C, 1-46th Infantry
- Pfc. Laymon Palmer, Company C, 1-46th Infantry
- Pfc. Dallas D. Robinson, Company C, 1-46th Infantry
- Pfc. Paul A. Sheer, Company C, 1-46th Infantry
- Pvt. Steven D. Plath, Company C, 1-46th Infantry
- Pvt. Clark V. Shawnee, Company C, 1-46th Infantry
- Sp5 Kyle S. Hamilton, HHC, 1-46th Infantry
- Pfc. Wilbert S. Dupree, HHC, 1-46th Infantry
- Sgt. Michael J. Bayne, Company A, 1-46th Infantry
- Sp4 Larry W. McKee, Company A, 1-46th Infantry
- Sp4 Larry D. Austin, Battery C, 3-16th FA
- Sp4 Clifford W. Corr, Battery C, 3-16th FA
- Sp4 Roger D. Whirlow, Battery C, 3-16th FA
- Pfc. Donald C. Bennett, Battery C, 3-16th FA
- Pfc. William W. Kirkpatrick, Battery C, 3-16th FA

Lieutenant Colonel Tate gestured toward the American flag flying above that end of the resupply pad. "The other night, thirty of your buddies gave their lives to keep that flag on that pole," the battalion commander said. "We may have been hit. We may have been hit hard, but we're not down and we're not out—and that flag's going to stay there. The only thing that can take the First of the Forty-sixth off this hill is an order telling us to hand it over to the ARVN—and I know you men feel the same way." Lieutenant Colonel Tate's speech "went down like lead," noted a reporter at the ceremony. The division inspector general, a lieutenant colonel, was also on the firebase that day, taping interviews with the survivors of the sapper attack. Company C was ordered the next day to finally bury the five sappers burned in the trash dump, plus one still entangled in the tactical wire. "He was stinking up the whole side of the hill," wrote Private Ziems, whose squad handled the task. "The sapper had been hit by the quad .50, and the five-foot dink was now about seven feet long and looked like mincemeat. We could smell the decomposing body right through our gas masks. We didn't take long digging the grave, just getting it deep enough to cover him and hide the smell. When I tried sliding him into the hole, his head fell off onto my shovel, so I threw it down between his legs."

During Delta Company's stand-down, Sergeant Olints visited Sp4 Don Rice in the 91st Evac Hospital. Rice had been in Olints's squad before joining the mortars on the hill— only to take a mortar round through his bunker roof two weeks before his scheduled departure for home. Rice had pads taped over both eyes, his shattered arm and leg were encased in plaster, and he had so many small wounds that he looked like a mummy with all the bandages.

"Snowflake?" Olints said tentatively.

"Who is it?" Rice answered in his blindness.

It broke Olints's heart to see the humorous, good-looking Rice in such a helpless state. Rice grabbed Olints's hand with great emotion and told him how wonderful the nurses were and how the doctors thought they were going to be able to save his remaining eye. He kept talking until he faded off into sleep.

Olints walked outside. "I sat down and tears were coming down my face. Some nurses came by and I turned away from them. I didn't want them to see an infantryman crying."

Sergeant Olints went into another ward to see Sgt. Dave Thompson, who had been a point man in his squad before getting a supply job on the hill. Olints had no idea what he was going to say to a guy with no feet, but Thompson made it easy. Thompson sat up grinning when Olints walked in and, throwing the covers aside to show his stumps, exclaimed, "They call me 'Shorty' now!" Thompson was just glad to be alive, and he talked like his old self with Olints, revealing no bitterness. Olints, meanwhile, kept glancing at a black trooper he recognized from the firebase who was paralyzed and strapped into some type of rotating bed. "The look in his eyes. . . . To this day, I have such a guilty conscience that I wasn't man enough to walk over to that guy and ask him how he was doing. The hospitals were almost as tough as combat."

LZ Mildred was shut down on April 2. Captain Oliver and the rebuilt but still demoralized Charlie Company conducted a combat assault off FSB Mary Ann on April 4. "Ed, you've got to go back out there, and you've got to get a kill very quickly," Colonel Hathaway said as he walked the new company commander down to the helipad. "If you don't get a kill, you've lost the unit. They need to get their heads back up, and they need to be pulled together as a team."

Company C was laagered on a hillock southeast of Mary Ann during the night of April 5-6, when a GI with a starlight scope spotted an NVA about fifty meters to the north. Oliver automatically took off his helmet as he got on the radio, and he was standing up with a handset to each ear so he could communicate with battalion and his platoons simultaneously when he gave the order to commence firing into the pitch-black jungle.

Captain Oliver was knocked out when the fireworks began. The command group thought he had been killed, but he sat up moments later, cursing. It turned out that he had a small fragment wound in the back of his head from a claymore or grenade launcher. The wound was not caused by the enemy, because the enemy did not return fire. After getting back on the radio, Oliver was informed that one

NVA had appeared to fall in the initial shockwave of fire, and another was seen rushing away. Illume burst overhead, but forty-five minutes later the firing began anew when four NVA were spotted. Oliver called for arty support and everything settled down again until the starlight scope operator picked up three more enemy soldiers trying to drag off what looked like a dead comrade. Still later, there was more movement, which a grenadier fired on. After surveying the scene with a starlight scope, the company claimed a second confirmed kill, although no bodies or blood trails were found at daylight.

On April 9, Charlie Company walked into a camouflaged bunker complex, complete with bamboo piping to provide running water to an underground kitchen. Oliver ordered mechanical ambushes set up on all the trails leading into the area, and within a matter of hours one of them was detonated. Oliver and a squad-sized patrol found an NVA lying on the trail with both legs blown off, his AK-47 beside him. Another AK had been dropped nearby where a second enemy soldier, probably assisted by a third, had limped off through the brush, losing a lot of blood along the way. The scene was great for morale, just as the brigade commander had predicted.

On April 18, however, a squad from Charlie Three, moving down a trail to police up its mechanicals, was ambushed. Two casualties were medevacked to Mary Ann, one tagged routine, the other urgent. Tate stood in the doorway of the battalion aid station as the Medical Platoon leader tried to revive the latter casualty; he finally stopped, muttering, "I can't do anymore."

"Did you lose him?" Tate asked.

"Yeah," the medical officer said simply and sadly.

The ARVN decided that they did not want FSB Mary Ann, and the Professionals, who had been planning to move off all along, closed the position down on April 24, 1971. Tate and the new battalion sergeant major hauled the flag down after everything else had been lifted off in phases, then they joined Lieutenant Schmitz's thirteen-man security team aboard the last Chinook. Gunships flew cover around the deserted hill as Schmitz, the last man out, hooked up the conex packed with TOC radios and supplies to the bottom of the Chinook, then climbed aboard through the hatch in the belly.

"We stripped the hill," said Tate. "When we left it was just a dirt hill with holes in it, and a lot of hard memories."

18

Repercussions

General Baldwin, an undemonstrative, even-tempered officer who rarely raised his deep voice in anger, was not provoked to clean house after the sapper attack on FSB Mary Ann. "I believe that almost all military units have at one time or another suffered a setback at the hands of a skillful, resourceful enemy," the division commander wrote, adding that "a single failure is not proof that an organization and its leaders are all bad." In a report dated May 12, 1971, the 23d Division's Inspector General (IG) laid out the specifics of what had gone wrong at FSB Mary Ann, and Baldwin, reviewing the section on the inadequacy of the perimeter defenses, placed the blame squarely on the battalion and company commander involved. He also noted that "our troops were asleep," and that "after the attack began, too many hid in their bunkers, rather than getting out to drive off the enemy." Despite "an understandable reluctance to ascribe blame to soldiers and junior NCOs," they were ultimately "victims of their own failure to do what they were told to do." Baldwin did not judge these grunts too harshly, especially when considering the "patience," "skill," and "excellent preparation and reconnaissance" exhibited by enemy sappers. "There is also an understandable reluctance to acknowledge that in any given circumstance the VC/NVA might just do a better job than we do," Baldwin concluded about the whole mess, ". . . it was obvious that the enemy soldiers who participated in this attack were highly motivated. Although we have some difficulty appreciating it, the fact is that most VC/NVA soldiers appear to believe in what they are doing and they believe in the rightness of their cause. On the other hand, for a variety of reasons, the same could not be said of the average American infantry soldier in Vietnam in the Spring of 1971."

Baldwin did not believe that much could be done beyond acting on the 23d IG's recommendation that "Strong command emphasis be placed on upgrading fire base security procedures and improving defensive measures against sapper attacks."

The general wrote to his wife on May 23, 1971:

> I hope to have written "finis" on the Mary Ann incident. Certain members of my staff felt I needed to blame someone in order to satisfy higher headquarters. As a matter of fact, [the division IG] carefully wrote a paper which absolved the brigade commander, but found the dead company commander and the wounded battalion commander culpable of negligence and dereliction of duty. I thought on this one a long while and finally decided to make my decision on the basis of whether or not I would have relieved these two men had they come out of the attack unscathed. My answer was "no"—therefore I recommended that the case be closed without further action. We'll see . . .

General Baldwin and Colonel Hathaway cut Doyle on his efficiency report in such a way that he still had a career. "Undeniably he was careless," Baldwin later wrote. "This carelessness was costly. Had he not been wounded, I would have severely reprimanded him verbally, but . . . I believe his qualities of leadership to be of such value that I would have left him in command of the 1st Battalion, 46th Infantry."

Shortly after Baldwin submitted the 23d IG's report on FSB Mary Ann to General Abrams, the deputy MACV IG and his staff began their own investigation of the incident. The MACV report duplicated most of the specific findings of the 23d IG, but held that culpability for the disaster extended all the way up the chain of command to Baldwin himself.

General Abrams thus ended Baldwin's career. Abrams had apparently wanted Baldwin to make an example of Hathaway and Doyle by relieving them of command. When he did not, Abrams concluded that Baldwin lacked the judgment needed to command in combat. "I suspect that's just exactly what happened," said Maj. Gen. A. E. Milloy, a former 23d Division commander. Given the political climate and the public's impatience with continuing casualties in a war that was supposed to be all but over, the FSB Mary Ann incident had been a tremendous embarrassment to the command. In addition, Abrams—a legendary, highly decorated, table-pounding commander of unyielding standards—was furious at what had become an epidemic of unnecessary casualties as the war wound down and standards of alertness and performance lapsed. If Abrams wanted to give his unit commanders a wake-up call there was no more effective, ruthless, and straightforward way to get their attention than to publicly extinguish the careers of Doyle, Hathaway, and Baldwin. "The investigation was just a head-hunting expedition," said one battalion commander. "What happened to Hathaway and Baldwin was a shame. They were fine commanders, and did not deserve what the powers that be did to them. The one person responsible for what went on on that hill was the battalion commander on that hill, but it was a time in the war when three casualties was too many."

General Baldwin was interviewed by the deputy MACV IG, a full colonel, on June 12, 1971. Baldwin was being defensive when he later described the IG as a "bitter man who was totally out of touch with the reality of conditions." The rich if one-sided detail in the IG's final report to Abrams, as well as the transcript of Baldwin's conversation with the IG, does not reveal the incompetent colonel of Baldwin's description. In fact, it appears that Baldwin misspoke during his interview with the IG. When the IG asked if Baldwin was aware that the acting battalion commander of FSB Mary Ann had ordered that the bodies of several sappers be burned, Baldwin answered, "I am aware of that and I directed that those bodies be buried." When the IG then asked if the burning was a war crime, Baldwin allowed that it was. The IG asked if the war crime had been reported to higher headquarters, as required by MACV Directive 20-4. "It was not," Baldwin answered. This line of questioning was leading to an obvious, career-ending conclusion, and Baldwin then went on record with another version of events. "I was informed that some of the enemy dead were in the trash dump," he said. "I got ahold of the brigade S3 and instructed him in no uncertain terms that those bodies were to be removed from the trash dump and were to be buried. Now this is the extent of my knowledge of it. I answered your question incorrectly when I said that I knew that somebody had ordered they be burned. I did not know that."

In 1969, Col. George S. Patton reportedly displayed a Vietnamese skull at his change-of-command ceremony upon leaving the 11th Armored Cavalry Regiment. The MACV commander had always ignored such "war crimes" as technicalities. Colonel Hathaway, an infantryman in two wars, was thus galled when the MACV IG began making an issue of bodies that had been burned simply as a sanitation expedient. Hathaway was, in fact, "a little baffled" by the entire postbattle chain of events. "I fully expected to be relieved on the spot, and had this happened I would have been hurt but I would have understood," Hathaway wrote. He received no criticism from Baldwin, however. "Things went on almost as usual," Hathaway continued. "The brigade was relocated to another area. I was notified of my selection for promotion to brigadier general, and was routinely told that I was to be assigned to MACV as J1 [personnel officer]. I even went to MACV Headquarters for a brief orientation visit. The night before the change of command, I received a phone call to turn over my command as planned, but to remain in the division as there was to be an IG investigation from MACV."

Almost three months after the attack, the inspector general wanted to know what had happened to the dead sappers. "They were buried," Hathaway answered. The IG then showed Hathaway a photo taken by Capt. George F. Bennett, the 196th Brigade Public Information Officer (PIO), which showed the charred remains of the sappers and carried a caption indicating that the bodies had been "carried to the dump to be burned." Bennett had previously prepared numerous photos and an informal report about the attack for Hathaway. The IG asked Hathaway if he was aware that the acting battalion commander on FSB Mary Ann had ordered that the bodies be burned. "I absolutely was not," Hathaway replied. The IG asked if the burning of the enemy bodies had come to his attention "before my bringing it up here today?" Hathaway said that it had not, adding that he could not account for the photo and its damning caption. "When I read through the report I did not pick that up . . . my specific instructions, and I was very specific about this, were that the enemy dead were to be carried outside the perimeter and be buried."

Unfortunately for Hathaway, the deputy MACV IG interviewed Major Potter, the acting battalion commander in question, who stated that "when the brigade commander was back out, he asked me what happened to the bodies. So I told him they were burned." The IG also spoke with Captain Bennett, who testified that he had not only personally shown Hathaway photos of the burned sappers, but had discussed with him the negative impact it would have on the unit's reputation if a civilian correspondent happened upon the scene in the trash dump. Baldwin and Hathaway helped hang themselves with their apparently slippery testimony regarding the burned bodies, however unfairly persecuted they must have felt. Both knew that no real war crime had been committed.

The IG reinterrogated Hathaway and wrote that "when confronted with the evidence" from Potter and Bennett, "Hathaway admitted having had knowledge of the burned bodies." Hathaway would always contend later that he had not intentionally misled the IG. "The disposition of the VC bodies was not of great concern to me," he wrote, noting that he had only a "vague" memory of the entire incident.

THE MASSACRE AT FIREBASE MARY ANN

"If I were going to lie to an investigating officer why would I pick a subject which was so easily checked and which had no real effect on me?"

The deputy MACV IG's fifty-eight page report on FSB Mary Ann was presented to General Abrams in July, 1971. According to the investigation:

- Maj. Gen. James L. Baldwin (CG, 23d Infantry Division) was "unaware of the actual defensive posture as it existed on FSB Mary Ann" because "directives requiring written reports on brigade and division inspections of fire support bases were not being enforced. . . . There appeared to be a degree of laxity and acceptance of permissiveness within the division staff." Furthermore, Baldwin "knew that bodies had been burned, but failed to have an appropriate report submitted to MACV and failed to take any action with respect to the individuals who committed the offense."
- Brig. Gen. Bertram K. Gorwitz (assistant division commander, 23d Infantry Division) made "no written reports" of his firebase inspections. "The conditions that existed at FSB Mary Ann . . . should have been detected if meaningful visits had been made and inspection reports properly rendered and analyzed."
- Col. Alphus R. Clark (chief of staff, 23d Infantry Division) "denied under oath . . . that he had knowledge that the bodies had been burned when he in fact had seen the report and photographs provided him by COL Hathaway."
- Col. William S. Hathaway (CO, 196th Infantry Brigade, 23d Infantry Division) "was not aware of the actual defensive posture that existed" at FSB Mary Ann, and despite "frequent" inspections of the base, "failed to detect the deficiencies and take corrective action." Hathaway was also "evasive with respect to the matter of the burned enemy dead and in his initial interview . . . knowingly provided false and misleading testimony under oath as to his knowledge in this matter."

- Lt. Col. William P. Doyle (CO, 1-46th Infantry, 196th Infantry Brigade) "was derelict in the performance of his duties" in that he was "not aware of the actual defense and alert condition of the FSB." The enemy's attack was successful because the "FSB was not prepared for an attack nor alert."

- Maj. Donald C. Potter (XO, 1-46th Infantry) "ordered the burning" of the dead sappers, despite having been previously "advised on the proper procedures for handling enemy dead."

- Maj. Stanley J. Wisniewski (S3, 1-46th Infantry) "was negligent in checking the defenses of FSB Mary Ann."

- Capt. Richard V. Knight (CO, Company C, 1-46th Infantry) was guilty of a "definite dereliction of duty" in that he did not fulfill "his responsibility for the security of the FSB."

- Capt. Charles D. Kirkey (CO, Company D, 1-46th Infantry) "assigned the detail" that burned the enemy bodies, although he had previously "been briefed on the proper handling of enemy dead."

- Capt. Donald M. Sampson (CO, Company E, 1-46th Infantry), 1st Lt. Rafael C. Rivera (Support Platoon leader, HHC, 1-46th Infantry), and Sgt. Maj. Carl M. Prosser (HHC, 1-46th Infantry) were all "ineffective."

- Capt. Virtus A. Savage (artillery liaison officer, 1-46th Infantry) and Capt. Edwin W. Conatser (CO, Battery B, 1-14th FA) "failed to effectively plan for defensive and counter-mortar targets" around FSB Mary Ann. Furthermore, "at the time of the attack, 11 days after their move to [LZ] Mildred, CPT Conatser still had not computed the firing data for the counter-mortar program. No one in his chain of command had discovered this deficiency."

- Col. John R. Sadler (artillery commander, 23d Infantry Division), Lt. Col. Richard C. Martin (CO, 3-82d FA), and Maj. Edward A. Godwin (S3, 3-82d FA) "all had various checks and inspections designed for command subjects and gunnery subjects but none of them made specific checks designed to determine the adequacy of the fire planning system within the division artillery,

checks that would ensure that LNOs were planning
needed fire support rather than just planning what was
asked for by the supported Infantry Commander."
Martin and Godwin "both claimed that the LNO with
the infantry units had full responsibility for the fire
support planning, and that the fire plan was approved
by the infantry battalion commander. [They thus]
failed to recognize and accept their responsibilities for
defensive fire support planning. . . . If the ony fire support needed by the infantry commander was that which
he asked for or wanted, then the infantry commander
would not need an Arty LNO. . . . The DS artillery
commander should insure that the infantry commander gets the artillery support he needs, whether he wants
it or not. . . ."

General Baldwin was convinced that the MACVIG "was
not attempting to make an impartial, objective investigation," but was instead "attempting to prove a conclusion
which he had already reached" so as to justify disciplinary
actions already decided upon by General Abrams. Abrams
had, in fact, never wanted Baldwin in his command given
his relative inexperience with maneuver units; and according to Lt. Gen. William J. McCaffrey, deputy commanding
general, U.S. Army, Vietnam (USARV), "It soon became
apparent that General Baldwin was ill at ease as a division
commander." McCaffrey scored Baldwin in his efficiency
report as a "brilliant officer of high character," but a
"consistent pessimist" who was "more suited to staff work
than to command assignments."

Baldwin returned home for a thirty-day leave on June 13,
after eleven months in Vietnam. He had six months left, but
Gen. William Westmoreland, then army chief of staff,
contacted Baldwin during his leave and informed him that
Abrams had relieved him. Baldwin's replacement, Maj.
Gen. Frederick J. Kroesen, a charismatic, three-war infan-
tryman, assumed command on July 9. "In a very few days,
Kroesen had the Americal running like a Swiss watch,"
McCaffrey recalled. Baldwin was relieved in deed, but not
in name. Technically, he was simply "reassigned." His

career was over, nonetheless. Lieutenant General James W. Sutherland, the XXIV Corps commander who had operational control of the 23d Division, wrote in Baldwin's efficiency report that "General Baldwin has had to make some hard decisions concerning replacement of ineffective commanders, drug abuse problems and morale and discipline. In the majority of cases General Baldwin's decisions and actions were sound and effective. In some instances by his statements and actions he raised doubts in the minds of his superiors as to his judgment and decisiveness in making the most difficult decisions."

Baldwin was surprised by his relief. He should not have been. "At that time in the war, with national politics and the anti-war sentiment the way it was, if Dwight Eisenhower had been commanding the Americal he would have been relieved," General McCaffrey later wrote. In August, 1971, General Abrams approved McCaffrey's recommendations that

- General Baldwin be reduced to brigadier general and receive a written reprimand.
- Colonel Hathaway be removed from the list of brigadier general selectees and receive a written reprimand.
- Lieutenant Colonel Doyle and Major Wisniewski be eliminated from the service.
- Colonel Clark, Major Potter, Captain Kirkey, and Captain Sampson receive written reprimands.
- General Gorwitz, Colonel Sadler, Lieutenant Colonel Martin, Captain Conatser, Captain Savage, and Lieutenant Rivera receive written admonitions.

Most of the disciplinary action was handled at the USARV level, but the cases against Baldwin, Clark, Hathaway, Doyle, and Wisniewski were bucked upstairs. In October, 1971, General Westmoreland concurred that Baldwin should be reduced to brigadier general and reprimanded, but recommended that Colonel Hathaway not only be reprimanded and removed from the brigadier general's list, but reduced to lieutenant colonel. Westmoreland also recommended that Clark be reduced to lieutenant colonel.

Westmoreland thought that Doyle and Wisniewski should be reprimanded, not that they be eliminated from the service. Doyle, he recommended, should merely be reduced to major, and Wisniewski to captain.

General Westmoreland's recommendations were forwarded to Secretary of the Army Robert F. Froehlke, who agreed with most. "However, I do not concur in that portion of your recommendation to reduce MG James L. Baldwin to the rank of brigadier general," Froehlke wrote to Westmoreland. "I believe that a division commander in his circumstances is too remote from the day-to-day events at a fire support base like Mary Ann to be held accountable to this degree for the deaths and injuries which occur."

In early November, 1971, the five officers were formally notified of the pending administrative action and given thirty days to present rebuttal information before the army secretary took action. Colonel Clark, an old soldier of sterling reputation who was deeply embittered at having his name dragged through the mud, was exonerated at that time of the charge that he had lied under oath when he denied knowledge of the burned enemy bodies on FSB Mary Ann. Clark's military lawyer claimed that Clark had given the Bennett report and photos only a perfunctory review before rotating home six days after the sapper attack. Most of Bennett's photos were of the physical destruction of the base. Only a few showed the burned bodies in question, and close examination was required to detect the charred remains amid the debris in the trash dump. Even if Clark had spotted the bodies, which he insisted he had not, only a careful read of the photo captions, which were not on the photos, but were included in the written report, would have revealed that the bodies had not been burned during the combat on the base. Baldwin and others stepped forward and declared that the deliberate burning of the bodies had never been discussed with Clark before he departed.

Major General Baldwin's notification of pending administrative action included a fact sheet which stated that while "primary responsibility falls at the battalion level," the former 23d Division commander was guilty of a "degree of culpability" because his command group "was unaware of the true defensive stance of Fire Support Base Mary Ann and did not utilize the staff available to make itself aware. Thus, various division policies were unheeded at the operational level."

Baldwin was also charged with having "knowingly violated MACV Directive 20-4 by failing to report a known incident of the mishandling of enemy bodies."

Baldwin wrote in rebuttal that he accepted "responsibility for failing to make an issue of the improper disposition of enemy bodies." Regarding the other charges, however, Baldwin reminded his superiors that the 23d Division "had absolutely no information from any source which would have indicated any intent on the part of the enemy to attack Mary Ann." The real problem was that "the troops and their junior leaders did not consider themselves sufficiently threatened to demand their alertness." Believing the division had done its part and the rest was up to those at the company level, Baldwin wrote:

> The wire obstacles were . . . built to a standard which exceeded that prescribed by higher headquarters. . . . In order to gain access to the base the sappers were required to cut their way through the wire. . . . I do not believe that anyone expects a barbed wire obstacle to do more than to delay an attacker and to facilitate his detection by the defender. . . . [T]he obstacles achieved their basic purpose of delay. The fact that the enemy went undetected was not, in my judgment, a product of an inadequacy of the obstacles. Instead, it was a product of a lack of alertness on the part of the defenders.

Baldwin emphasized that Hathaway and Doyle were superb commanders, writing that if the troops showed a "lack of defensive awareness," it was because the division had "abandoned such practices as periodic firing of 'mad minutes' and indiscriminate firing of flares . . . in order to respond to the considerable pressure on us to reduce ammunition expenditures."

Baldwin spent an hour with Secretary of the Army

Froehlke. "I came away impressed that he was an officer with an outstanding record and a man of integrity," Froehlke later wrote, adding that Baldwin was "very persuasive in pleading his case. Nevertheless, I did concur that the letter-of-reprimand should be issued. I think I can best describe the situation as one that may not have been fair to Baldwin but was right for the Army."

In the end, Froehlke administered a letter of admonition, which is less severe than a formal reprimand. The letter, dated April 20, 1972—when Baldwin was the Deputy Chief of Staff for Logistics at the Pentagon—read in part:

> You are hereby admonished for your performance of duty in connection with defensive preparations for an enemy attack on Fire Support Base Mary Ann. . . . The ineffective defense plans of Fire Support Base Mary Ann were to an extent caused by the failure of command within the 23d [Division]. . . . An investigation revealed that you were unaware of the ineffective defensive posture of Fire Support Base Mary Ann and that you did not effectively use your staff or your chain of command to obtain information on the degree of alertness and on compliance with directives at fire support bases, as evidenced by the lack of preparedness at Fire Support Base Mary Ann on 28 March 1971.

The admonition avoided the "war crime" issue, either to avoid scandal in the press or because someone in the power structure had "realized that the matter had been blown out of proportion," as Hathaway wrote.

General Baldwin retired in 1972 and died of a bone cancer–related heart attack in 1979 at age fifty-eight, leaving a widow and four adult children. "Later in life, he became very closed-mouth about it all," wrote one of Baldwin's sons. "His name was spread across the front pages of the national papers as an incompetent. His 'friends' avoided him in the halls of the Pentagon."

Captain Strand later reflected that unlike Baldwin of the Americal, the 101st Airborne Division commander went on to promotion and greater glory after the unimaginative, uncoordinated frontal assaults up Hamburger Hill in May, 1969, and the sapper attack on nearby FSB Airborne—which was almost as bad as FSB Mary Ann in terms of casualties, and worse in terms of inadequate security. FSB Airborne was in the hotly contested A Shau Valley, and there was every reason to believe it might be attacked. "Some of the things that happened in the 101st Airborne were much more tragic and stupid than whatever happened on Mary Ann, but you don't see the 101st take the kind of knocks we did from the army hierarchy because of its history and its traditions," said Strand, who is convinced that Baldwin would never have been relieved if he had been in any other division except the one associated with My Lai. The Americal's reputation had already been shattered in the public eye. "It was a political thing," Strand said. "Scapegoats were needed to calm the press and Congress, which was receiving angry inquiries from families that had lost sons on Mary Ann. The Americal was a good target for the army to show everybody that when mistakes were made they took action. What happened to Baldwin was wrong, but it's not hard for me to understand given how big organizations work. There have to be those who take the blame to show the humanness of this big monolithic organization."

Like Baldwin, Colonel Hathaway, slapped with a reprimand, remained taciturn about the incident after retirement. He died from bone cancer in 1994. The army decided not to demote Lieutenant Colonel Doyle and Major Wisniewski, but froze their careers in place with letters of reprimand. "You failed to increase the alert status of Fire Support Base Mary Ann commensurate with the low illumination condition and predicted enemy offensive," Doyle was informed in his official notification of charges. He was also accused of failing "to conduct frequent practice alerts and adequate inspections," of failing "to utilize listening posts or local patrols or to designate a reaction force," of failing "to insure that anti-intrusion devices were employed," of failing to "require adherence to the fire base security and standing operation procedures," of failing to "plan or ascertain the adequacy of artillery support," and of failing to "integrate available South Vietnamese artillery resources at Fire Support Base Mary Ann." The fact sheet accompanying the charges indicated that Doyle "appeared overly preoccupied with offensive operations, and he emphasized those to the practical exclusion of the defense. . . . [H]e neglected to instill concern for the base's safety in his subordinates or to order even the most elemental defensive safeguards employed."

The fact sheet added that Doyle "ran the unit more by force of his personality than through any regularized procedures," and that "he 'detailed' responsibility to his subordinates and did not adequately insure that those instructions . . . were carried out."

Captain Strand said that the charges against Doyle were preposterous and added that "the army refused to accept that shit happens in war, even to good units. There wasn't a trend of poor leadership that led up to the sapper attack, as one would expect." Colonel Hathaway felt the same way. Doyle might have run the unit by force of personality, as charged, but it was the personality of a commander who "had the rare ability to pass his enthusiasm down to the lowest member of his battalion," Hathaway wrote in Doyle's defense. "In this day of dissension and resistance to authority, he fostered a seldom found aggressive spirit . . . he had charisma. The usual problems associated in the Army today were almost totally absent in his unit, he inspired his men to do better, and he did so by force of his personality."

Strand also prepared a letter in Doyle's behalf, writing:

Had not LTC Doyle insured that his instructions were carried out, that staff procedures were regulated, that defense was as important as offense, then I propose that LTC Doyle would have been a failure and relieved from command far before the time of the sapper attack on Mary Ann. Were LTC Doyle as poor a commander as the report implies, the Battalion would not have been one of the most successful of the battalions in the 23rd Infantry Division as it, in fact, was. . . . It may be claimed that the battalion was "lucky," but to be "lucky" so consistently is uncanny.

Neither Strand nor Doyle put any criticism of Captain Knight or his sleeping troops into the record. In his spirited rebuttal, Doyle instead attacked the charge that he had not correctly utilized the ARVN artillery on FSB Mary Ann ("they were not there to support me and I had no responsibility or command authority"), and tore into the allegation that he should have upgraded the alert status on the firebase given the low illumination that night and the predicted enemy offensive. Doyle contended that

> the investigation proves that the area threatened did not include Mary Ann. This fact is brought out again and again in the statements of the Brigade S-2, Division G-2 and a search of the XXIV Corps, USARV, and MACV intelligence reports. The statement of the Brigade Commander to the MACV Inspector General supports my contention that the alert status is not tied directly to low illumination, and the fact that other battalions were instructed to increase security while the 1/46th was not, indicates the lack of any known threat to LZ Mary Ann. Therefore, I submit that there was no "predicted enemy offensive" at that time, and at that place.

Whatever Doyle wrote, however, about his emphasis on security paled when compared to the sight of his gutted B-TOC and the thirty American body bags lined up on the resupply pad at FSB Mary Ann.

Froehlke wrote to Doyle on April 20, 1972:

> You are hereby reprimanded for your substandard performance of duty in connection with defensive preparations for an enemy attack against Fire Support Base Mary Ann on 28 March 1971, while you were serving as Commanding Officer, 1st Battalion, 46th Infantry, 23d Infantry Division (Americal). An investigation revealed that you did not supervise properly the defense of Fire Support Base Mary Ann. Specifically, there was no increase in the alert status on the night of 27–28 March 1971 commensurate with the low level of visibility and the predicted enemy offensive in some parts of the

brigade area. There was inadequate adherence to the fire base security and standing operating procedures. There was inadequate artillery support planning. Your deficiencies in planning and supervision resulted in a defensive posture in which the troops on the fire support base were not alert and were not prepared to conduct the defense of the base in a professional manner.

Lieutenant Colonel Doyle continued to wear the uniform after his career was snuffed out. According to Strand:

Bill Doyle was a realist. He had a favorite saying out on the firebase, and he got us all to say it, especially when we got back to Chu Lai and drank a few beers: "This army's all right. Hard but fair." I can remember him looking me in the eye when I saw him after he was back in the States, and he said, "This army's all right. Hard but fair—and I'm going to make the best of what I've got." He had such a great reputation that people took care of him. He got assignments that weren't embarrassing, and he worked for people he knew. He was still able to contribute until the time he retired. He didn't lay back—he worked his butt off until the time he quit.

Beneath the surface, however, Doyle had what his second wife called a "festering wound." Doyle remarried in April, 1972, just two weeks before being reprimanded, and his honeymoon was cut short so he could make a personal and unsuccessful appeal to General Westmoreland. "What happened on Mary Ann really tormented Bill Doyle until he died," said a contemporary. "He ended up hitting the bottle very heavily. He died from a heart attack. He had a very hard life because of Mary Ann."

Doyle was living with his second wife on his father-in-law's dairy farm in Raphine, Virginia, when he died at the age of fifty-two in March, 1984. Spilberg called him "the last casualty of Firebase Mary Ann." Doyle was buried at Arlington Cemetery on a beautiful spring day, and those marching behind his caisson included two general officers from his successful combat tour with the 4th Division, plus

Colonel Hathaway and three of his former captains—Strand, Spilberg, and Oliver.

Strand observed that

> Doyle was a two-fisted drinker . . . but I don't think that's what killed him. It was that he isolated himself. You go from a job where your adrenaline is pumped up all the time, and then you move out to a dairy farm where you don't have anyone to talk with. You just kind of slowly go into a hole, and I think that's what happened to Doyle. He just slowly died internally.
>
> I remember stopping by to see him, and I had my kids with me. We took my son out and Doyle gave him a BB gun and told him to go shoot some target practice. My son asked, "Well, aren't you going to stay here with me?" Doyle said, "What for, I told you what to do"—and he started coming out of his shell. He started being the old Bill Doyle. I could see this old man metamorphosing into the old Bill Doyle, and it was neat to see. It was still there, but it had gotten so buried that he finally died.

Captain Strand (S3 and commander of Company A, 1-46th Infantry) retired as a lieutenant colonel with three BSMv's, four MSMs, three ARCOMs, and the Purple Heart. The father of four is now a phone company executive and lives with his wife in Fort Leavenworth, Kansas.

Captain Spilberg (commander of Company A) got out with the Silver Star, two BSMv's, one BSM, and three Purple Hearts. The father of two, he was divorced after the war and currently receives disability compensation for Post-Traumatic Stress Disorder (PTSD). He owns a small bathroom refinishing business and lives with his second wife in Chicago. Lieutenant Bell is now an unemployment supervisor living with his wife and son in Searcy, Arkansas. Lieutenant Noonan won two BSMv's, two ARCOMs, and the Purple Heart. An insurance executive, the divorced father of two lives in Mechanicsburg, Pennsylvania.

Sergeant Concepcion was medically retired and lives with his wife and four sons in Moreno Valley, California. Specialist Cleek made sergeant; the divorced father of three now works for a cable television company in Sevierville,

Tennessee. Specialist Riley was promoted to Specialist Five, and discharged with the BSMv and two ARCOMs. He works for a moving company and lives with his family in Newport, Kentucky. Specialist Tarnay is a Hughes Aircraft engineer living with his wife and four children in Los Angeles. Private Voros got the BSMv and Purple Heart when he lost his legs; he now lives with his second wife in Akron, New York. Private Gittens, plagued by PTSD for which he received a 100 percent disability rating, lives with his family in Brownsville, Minnesota.

Captain Gallagher (commander of Company B) won a BSM, Air Medal (AM), and ARCOM. Now a stockbroker, he lives with his family in Los Gatos, California. Sergeant Shook got the ARCOMv and Purple Heart. A chemical company employee and part-time farmer, he lives with his wife and two sons in Spencerville, Ohio. Specialist Arias was discharged a sergeant. An insurance adjuster, he lives with his family in Rialto, California. Specialist Noller made sergeant and won a BSM and two ARCOMs. Divorced with one daughter, he is now an asphalt company operations manager living in Albuquerque, New Mexico.

Lieutenant Doyle (Company C) is presently a psychologist with the Massachusetts Department of Mental Health, and lives with his wife and three children in Randolph, Massachusetts. Lieutenant Mack made captain and got out with the BSMv, BSM, ARCOMv, and Purple Heart. Married and the father of three, he owns two veterinary laboratories and lives in Elmhurst, Illinois. Lieutenant Sams was awarded the Silver Star, BSM, ARCOM, and Purple Heart, plus a 100 percent disability rating for the burns he received on FSB Mary Ann. He is now associate vice president for continuing education at Greenville Technical College and lives with his wife and son in Taylors, South Carolina.

Sergeant Calhoun received a BSM, ARCOM, and two Purple Hearts, plus a 100 percent disability rating for the leg he lost. The father of four lives with his wife in Ware Shoals, South Carolina. Sergeant Eades won two BSMv's, one BSM, and the Purple Heart. Now the manager of a steel construction company, he lives with his wife and two children in Newton, North Carolina. Sergeant Ledoux received the BSM and Purple Heart. Married before the war, he has two children and is a warehouseman with Mobile Oil in Orange, Texas. Sergeant Neill is now a printer with Hallmark Cards, and lives with his family in Lecompton, Kansas. Sergeant Salmen won the BSMv, BSM, ARCOM, and Purple Heart. Now a salesman with Sears, he lives with his wife and three children in Sioux City, Iowa.

Specialist Murphy, medically discharged as a sergeant, is now director of Admissions and Records at Montgomery County Community College, and lives with his wife and three children in Wayne, Pennsylvania. Specialist Wise got out as a sergeant after seven years (his wife didn't want to make a life in the military), having been awarded the ARCOMv and Purple Heart. Formerly a Coca-Cola delivery man, he now has an associate degree in computer drafting and lives with his wife and two children in Angleton, Texas. Private Cahill was promoted to Specialist Four; a film maker for the Eastman Kodak Company, he lives with his wife and three children in Hilton, New York. Private Creaven, who received a 100 percent disability rating for his wounded arm, is married, and president of the Veterans for Peace chapter in Gainesville, Florida. Private Grooms was discharged as a Specialist Five with the Silver Star, BSM, and Purple Heart, plus a 60 percent disability rating because of the limited motion of his bullet-shattered arm. He was divorced thirteen years after the war, the father of three. Now a paramedic, he is attending medical school and lives with his second wife and fourth child in Kirksville, Missouri. Private Massich got out as a Specialist Four with the ARCOMv, ARCOM, and Purple Heart. Never married, he is a warehouseman for a taconite mine in Hibbing, Minnesota. Private Schneider was discharged as a Specialist Four with a BSM, ARCOM, and Purple Heart. He is a machinist/mechanic on the Burlington Northern Railroad, and he and his wife, having raised three children, live in Alliance, Nebraska. Private Ziems, who got out as a sergeant, is a farmer and lives with his wife and two children in Ewing, Nebraska.

Captain Kirkey (commander of Company D) won a BSM, AM, and ARCOMv, but was passed over for major and released from the Army in 1980. Presently a U.S. Army

Reserve lieutenant colonel, he is a Department of the Army education specialist at Fort Gordon, Georgia. Married before the war but divorced during grad school (he has one daughter), he lives with his second wife and step-daughter in Martinez, Georgia. Lieutenant Harrell won two BSMv's, four ARCOMv's, and two Purple Hearts. Now a senior real estate appraiser for the Florida Department of Revenue, the divorced father of two lives in Tallahassee, Florida. Lieutenant Schmidt got out with the Silver Star, two BSMv's, and two Purple Hearts. A construction company executive, he lives with his wife and daughter in Lakewood, Colorado. Lieutenant Schmitz received two BSMv's, one BSM, and an AM, but dropped the idea of a military career and went on to graduate from law school. Following an intense rethinking of his political and religious beliefs, he resigned his reserve captaincy in 1979 as a conscientious objector. He subsequently returned his medals in protest of President Reagan's policies regarding Nicaragua, where he went as part of a Witness for Peace delegation in 1987. Married before the war, but divorced afterward with two children, he is now director of Human Services for the Salvation Army in upstate New York, and lives in Syracuse.

Sergeant Olints, having won the Silver Star, BSMv, BSM, AM, ARCOM, and Purple Heart, returned to his job as a tool and die maker. He lives with his wife in South Windsor, Connecticut. Specialist Meek got out as a sergeant with the BSMv and two Purple Hearts. The divorced father of one put twenty years in on a Ford assembly line, then won the state lottery. Remarried and retired, he lives in Monroe, Michigan. Specialist Parks made sergeant and won two BSMv's and two Purple Hearts. He is now a manager at an asphalt manufacturing company. Married and divorced with one child after the war, he is remarried with two more children, and lives in Akron, Ohio. Specialist Rice was medically discharged with a 100 percent disability rating after receiving a BSMv, BSM, ARCOM, and two Purple Hearts. A part-time wood craftsman, he lives with his wife in Cincinnati, Ohio. Private Stainton got out as a Specialist Four with the BSMv and two Purple Hearts. Now a county payloader operator, he lives with his family in Pulaski, New York. Private Vann receives a 100 percent medical disability pension, and lives with his wife and two children in Erwin, North Carolina.

Lieutenant Hewitt (Echo Recon) won the Silver Star, BSM, and AM. While working out his PTSD, he traveled the world for five years, then was a logger in Idaho. Now settled down with a wife and three children, he is a unit operator at a power plant and lives in Waverly, Tennessee. Sergeant Norris earned the Silver Star, two BSM's, three ARCOMs, and two Purple Hearts. Receiving a disability pension because of a stroke, he lives in Louisville, Kentucky. Sergeant Powell came home with his two Silver Stars, one BSM, the Purple Heart, and a serious case of PTSD. His wife divorced him, but they remarried when he got himself back together. Now an inspector with a plate-glass company, he lives with his wife and two daughters in New Washington, Ohio. Specialist Downey, a thrice-married pipeline construction worker, lives in Fontana, California. Private Brown, who is completing his engineering degree, builds drilling rigs for an oil company and lives with his wife and five children in Casper, Wyoming.

Sources

Aside from contemporary newspaper accounts, the sapper attack on FSB Mary Ann has gone unremarked except for an obligatory paragraph or two in general histories of the Vietnam War. Documents stored at the National Archives's Suitland, Maryland, Branch are, however, an excellent launching pad for researching the debacle. The 23d Infantry Division Inspector General's report is especially valuable because it contains transcripts of interviews conducted with most of the survivors. The interviews are of such detail that the location of every soldier on the base at the time of the attack can be reconstructed. The efforts of supporting aviation units are also covered in detail.

Thorough as they are, the official reports are of the dry-as-dust variety. Even the interviews have a certain reserved quality, as one might expect from grunts sitting before a division IG. To flesh out the human drama of the story, I relied heavily on my own interviews with surviving veterans. "We've been waiting twenty years for someone to tell our story," one ex-captain remarked to me. The cooperation extended to me by the vets I was able to track down bore this remark out. Those who still had journals or old letters broke them out, and various firefights were described in painful detail, down to the dialogue of the moment. With occasional editing for clarity, the dialogue recounted here is word-for-word as it was remembered by the men who were there.

I was also fortunate to have made contact with Tim Baldwin, son of the late Maj. Gen. James L. Baldwin. Tim shared his father's papers with me and, having done considerable research himself into a subject that has been the cause of much family pain, allowed me access to his thick file of documents and correspondence regarding the tragedy and its aftermath. Tim's interest in the subject is such that on February 18, 1993, during a trip to Vietnam, he and a group of indigenous guides hiked up to the now-deserted site of FSB Mary Ann. The locals had stripped the firebase of virtually every scrap of wood and metal, so all that remained were rusting artillery casings and overgrown depressions where bunkers had been. Tim mounted a commemorative plaque on a tree at the base of the hill and was assured by the Vietnamese present that an incense burner would be mounted underneath so that the dead of both sides would be properly honored by local custom.

Interviews with Author by Telephone

Acosta, Jaime P. June 10, 1992. San Leandro, California.

Arias, David P. May 6, 1992. Rialto, California.

Bell, R. Scott. April 16, June, August 17, November, and December 8, 1992, and November, 1993. Searcy, Arkansas.

Bell, Zeddie T. November, 1993. Jacksonville, Illinois.

Brown, Brad L. May 13 and 31, 1992. Casper, Wyoming.

Buehrig, Bruce. July 9, 1992, and November, 1993. St. Louis, Missouri.

Cahill, William G. June 19, 1992. Hilton, New York.

Calhoun, John C. October 27, 1992. Ware Shoals, South Carolina.

Carvell, Col. Richard F., Ret. September 19, 1992. Charleston, West Virginia.

Cleek, Carl E. November 28, 1992. Sevierville, Tennessee.

Conatser, Lt. Col. Ed W., Ret. July 6, 1992. Falls Church, Virginia.

Concepcion, Francisco. September 22, 1992. Moreno Valley, California.

Creaven, James P. June 29 and July 10, 1992, and October 10, 1993. Gainesville, Florida.

Downey, Robert J. December 26, 1992. Fontana, California.

Doyle, Peter K. July 8, 1992, and September 19, 1993. Randolph, Massachusetts.

Eades, W. Allen. July 26, 1992. Newton, North Carolina.

Froehlke, Robert F. November, 1993. Minneapolis, Minnesota.

Gallagher, Peter J. June 2, 1992. Los Gatos, California.

Gesse, Larry J. August 13, 1992. Franklin, Indiana.

Gittens, Edward C. June 14 and 26, 1992. Brownsville, Minnesota.

Golden, Charles. July 1, 1992. Opelika, Alabama.

Grooms, Paul G. November 30, 1992. Kirksville, Missouri.

Harrell, Hugh W. June 17, 1992. Tallahassee, Florida.

Hewitt, Carl D. October 4, 1992. Waverly, Tennessee.

Kane, Joseph. May 11 and July 12, 1992. Smithtown, New York.

Kirkey, Charles D. July 28 and August 14, 1992. Martinez, Georgia.

Kroesen, Gen. Frederick J., Ret. November, 1993. Falls Church, Virginia.

Lange, Mrs. Pat Doyle. May 3, 1994. Scottsdale, Arizona.

Ledoux, Jerry. June 7, 1992. Orange, Texas.

Leventhal, Steve. May 25, 1992. East Windsor, New Jersey.

Mack, Daniel J. November, 1993. Elmhurst, Illinois.

Massich, David G. August 13 and 17, 1992. Hibbing, Minnesota.

Meek, William B. May 12, 1992. Monroe, Michigan.

Milloy, Maj. Gen. A. E., Ret. September 18, 1992. Scottsdale, Arizona.

Murphy, Dennis J. September 23, 1992. Wayne, Pennsylvania.

Mylan, Thomas H. May 26, 1992. Minneapolis, Minnesota.

Neill, Craig A. September 27, 1992. Lecompton, Kansas.

Noller, Gary L. May 31, 1992. Long Beach, California.

Noonan, Robert J. December 3, 1992. Mechanicsburg, Pennsylvania.

Norris, Michael. December 20, 1992. Louisville, Kentucky.

Olints, Andrew H. May 26 and June 8, 1992. South Windsor, Connecticut.

Oliver, Lt. Col. Edward L., Ret. March 29, 1993. Summerville, South Carolina.

Parks, Jeffery E. June 15 and 28, 1992. Akron, Ohio.

Powell, Ervin E. August 15, 1992. Plymouth, Ohio.

Rice, Donald L. April 17, 1992. Cincinnati, Ohio.

Riley, Michael P. November 28, 1992. Newport, Kentucky.

Rowell, Easton M. 1992. Macon, Georgia.

Saint, Gen. Crosbie E., Ret. October, 1993. Alexandria, Virginia.

Salmen, James L. July 23, 1992. Sioux City, Iowa.

Sams, Jerry W. 1992. Taylors, South Carolina.

Savage, Virtus A. February 6, 1993. Spokane, Washington.

Schmidt, Arthur D. June 25, 1992. Lakewood, Colorado.

Schmitz, Thomas F. May 27, 1992, and October 7, 1993. Syracuse, New York.

Schneider, Thomas R. July 1, 1992. Alliance, Nebraska.

Shields, Dennis. July, 1992. Shelbyville, Illinois.

Spilberg, Paul S. April 13, 14, 17, 29, and 30, and July 21, 1992; November 1992; and November 1993. Chicago, Illinois.

Stainton, Robert H. May 11, 1992. Pulaski, New York.

Strand, Lt. Col. John A., Ret. May 26 and June 7, 1992. Fort Leavenworth, Kansas.

Tarnay, David J. January 31, 1993. Los Angeles, California.

Tate, Col. Clyde J., Ret. January 27, 1993. Olympia, Washington.

Tetu, Col. Robert G. June 6, 1992. Alexandria, Virginia.

Vann, Sexton M. July 23, 1992. Erwin, North Carolina.

Voros, Edward W. June 25, 1992. Akron, New York.

Wise, Harold D. July 12, 1992. Angleton, Texas.

SOURCES
Correspondence

23d Infantry Division Personnel to Family and Friends

Baldwin, Maj. Gen. James L., to wife. November, 1970–May, 1971.
Brown, Brad L., to wife. December, 1970–March, 1971.
Cahill, William G., to parents. October, 1970–April, 1971.
Gilliland, Charles L., to Dennis Murphy. April 8, 1971.
Gittens, Edward C., to parents. October, 1970–April, 1971.
Noonan, Robert J., to Paul Spilberg. February 24, 1971.
Pfau, Ted, to Robert Noonan. February 5, 1971.
Shook, Ronald L., to parents. November, 1970–May, 1971.
Spilberg, Paul S., to wife. September, 1970–August, 1971.

23d Infantry Division Personnel and Others to Author

Arias, David P., 1993.
Baldwin, Tim, 1992–93.
Bell, Zeddie T., 1993.
Brown, Brad L., 1992–93.
Buehrig, Bruce, 1993.
Cahill, William G., 1992–93.
Carvell, Col. Richard F., Ret, 1992–93.
Clark, Col. Alphus R., Ret., 1993.
Conatser, Lt. Col. Ed W., Ret., 1992–93.
Concepcion, Francisco, 1993.
Downey, F. Gerald, 1983–86.
Doyle, Mrs. William P., 1993.
Doyle, Peter K., 1992–93.
Eades, W. Allen, 1992–93.
Foss, Col. Peter J., Ret., 1992–93.
Grooms, Paul G., 1993.
Hathaway, Col. William S., Ret., 1993.
Hewitt, Carl D., 1992–93.
Mack, Daniel J., 1993.
Massich, David G., 1992–93.
McCaffrey, Lt. Gen. William J., Ret., 1993.

Murphy, Dennis J., 1992.
Neill, Craig A., 1993.
Noller, Gary L., 1992–93.
Noonan, Robert J., 1993.
O'Connor, Col. Hugh T., Ret., 1993.
Olints, Andrew H., 1992–93.
Powell, Ervin E., 1993.
Rhodes, James R., 1992.
Riley, Michael P., 1992.
Salmen, James L., 1993.
Sams, Jerry W., 1993.
Schmitz, Thomas F., 1992–93.
Schneider, Thomas R., 1992–93.
Shook, Ronald L., 1992–93.
Stainton, Robert H., 1993.
Tate, Col. Clyde J., Ret., 1992–93.
Voros, Edward W., 1992–93.
Ziems, Dennis A., 1992–93.

Other Correspondence

Clark, Col. Alphus R., Ret., to Tim Baldwin. July, 1991.
Doyle, Mrs. William P., to Tim Baldwin. June–July, 1991.
Froehlke, Robert F., to Tim Baldwin. June, 1991.
Hathaway, Col. William S., Ret., to Tim Baldwin. August, 1991.
Kroesen, Gen. Frederick J., Ret., to Tim Baldwin. August–September, 1991.
Schmitz, Thomas F., to Tim Baldwin. January, 1992.

Unpublished Written Material

Personal Journals

Carvell, Lt. Col. Richard F., 1970.
Doyle, 1st Lt. Peter K., 1971.

SOURCES

Documents

Bennett, Capt. George F. "Informal Investigation—LZ Mary Ann." 1 April 1971.

"Daily Staff Journal or Duty Officer's Log, 1st Battalion, 46th Infantry, 196th Infantry Brigade, 23d Infantry Division." October, 1970–April, 1971.

Robinson, Lt. Col. Thomas J., Inspector General, 23d Infantry Division. "Report of Investigation Concerning Attack of Fire Support Base Mary Ann, Quang Tin Province, Republic of Vietnam, 28 March 1971." 12 May 1971.

Sikes, Col. Arthur E., chief, Investigations Division, Headquarters, U.S. Military Assistance Command, Vietnam. "Report of Investigation to Access the Effectiveness of the Functioning of Command Within the 23d Infantry Division as it Pertains to the Attack Against FSB Mary Ann." 5 July 1971.

U.S. Army Officer Efficiency Reports

Baldwin, Maj. Gen. James L. Deputy Commanding General, XXIV Corps. July–November, 1970.

———. Commanding General, 23d Infantry Division. November, 1970–June, 1971.

Doyle, Maj. William P. Operations Officer, 3d Brigade, 4th Infantry Division. December, 1967–July, 1968.

Doyle, Lt. Col. William P. Commanding Officer, 1–46th Infantry, 196th Infantry Brigade, 23d Infantry Division. October, 1970–March, 1971.

Spilberg, Capt. Paul S. Commanding Officer, Company A, 1-46th Infantry, October, 1970–March, 1971.

Statements Regarding Administrative Action Against Maj. Gen. Baldwin, Col. Clark, Col. Hathaway, Lt. Col. Doyle, and Maj. Wisniewski

Bailey, Maj. Robert D., to Clark (statement of support). December 21, 1971.

Baldwin, to Clark (statement of support). December 14, 1971.

———, to Doyle (statement of support). n.d.

———, to Froehlke (rebuttal of pending administrative action). December 10, 1971.

Bennett, Capt. George F., to Clark (statement of support). December 22, 1971.

Bowers, Maj. Gen. Verne L., Adjutant General, U.S. Army, to Baldwin (notification of pending administrative action). November 8, 1971.

———, to Clark (dismissal of pending administrative action). n.d.

———, to Clark (notification of pending administrative action). November 8, 1971.

———, to Doyle (notification of pending administrative action). November 8, 1971.

———, to Hathaway (notification of pending administrative action). November 8, 1971.

———, to Wisniewski (notification of pending administrative action). November 8, 1971.

Clark, to Froehlke (rebuttal of pending administrative action). January 4, 1972.

Doyle, to Froehlke (rebuttal of pending administrative action). December 28, 1971.

Ferraris, Capt. Victor A., to Doyle (statement of support). n.d.

Froehlke, to Baldwin (letter of admonition). April 20, 1972.

———, to Doyle (letter of reprimand). April 20, 1972.

———, to Hathaway (letter of reprimand). April 20, 1972.

———, to Westmoreland (recommendation of administrative action to be taken). October 14, 1971.

———, to Wisniewski (letter of reprimand). April 20, 1972.

Hathaway, to Doyle (statement of support). December 20, 1971.

Kirkey, Capt. Charles D., to Doyle (statement of support). n.d.

Milloy, Maj. Gen. A. E., to Clark (statement of support). December 29, 1971.

Schmitz, Capt. Thomas F., to Doyle (statement of support). December 1, 1971.

SOURCES

Strand, Capt. John A., to Doyle (statement of support). December 16, 1971.

Westmoreland to Froehlke (recommendation of administrative action to be taken). October 12, 1971.

Whitley, Capt. Thomas H., to Doyle (statement of support). December 22, 1971.

Magazine and Newspaper Articles

Americal (Quarterly magazine of the Americal Division, Vietnam). 1970–71.

Evans, Sp5 Dan. "Death and Destruction Crept in With the Fog." *Pacific Stars & Stripes,* April 1, 1971, p. 6.

Larsen, Jonathan. "The Massacre at Fire Base Mary Ann." *Time,* April 12, 1971, p. 26.

Peterson, John. "Massacre at Maryann." *The Overseas Weekly* (Pacific Edition), May 1, 1971, p. 10.

Proffitt, Nicholas C. "The Hell at Mary Ann." *Newsweek,* April 12, 1971, p. 45.

Southern Cross (Newspaper of the 23d Infantry Division). 1970–71.

Books

Browne, Corinne. *Body Shop: Recuperating from Vietnam.* Briarcliff Manor, N.Y.: Stein and Day Publishers, 1973.

Chanoff, David, and Doan Van Toai. *Portrait of the Enemy.* New York: Random House, 1986.

Cosmas, Graham A., and Lt. Col. Terrence P. Murray. *U.S. Marines in Vietnam: Vietnamization and Redeployment, 1970–71.* Washington, D.C.: History and Museums Division, Headquarters, U.S. Marine Corps, 1986.

Fulghum, David, Terrence Maitland, et al. *The Vietnam Experience: South Vietnam on Trial, Mid–1970 to 1972.* Boston: Boston Publishing Company, 1984.

Nolan, Keith William. *Into Laos: The Story of Dewey*

SOURCES

Canyon II/Lam Son 719; Vietnam 1971. Novato, Calif.: Presidio Press, 1986.

Perret, Geoffrey. A Country Made by War: From the Revolution to Vietnam—the Story of America's Rise to Power. New York: Random House, 1989.

Stanton, Shelby L. The Rise and Fall of an American Army: U.S. Ground Forces in Vietnam, 1965–1973. Novato, Calif.: Presidio Press, 1985.

Westmoreland, William C. A Soldier Reports. Garden City, N.Y.: Doubleday and Company, 1976.

Zaffiri, Samuel. Hamburger Hill: May 11–20, 1969. Novato, Calif.: Presidio Press, 1988.

Index

Sit Down, Rambo! —

Hollywood can't equal the real-life adventures these books recount...